STRATEGY IN
THE MISSILE AGE

"In these windings [of special interest] the logical conclusion is caught fast, and man, who in great things as well as in small usually acts more on particular prevailing ideas and emotions than according to strictly logical conclusions, is hardly conscious of his confusion, one-sidedness, and inconsistency."—KARL VON CLAUSEWITZ, *On War*

"And is anything more important than that the work of the soldier should be well done?"— PLATO, *The Republic*

STRATEGY IN
THE MISSILE AGE

BY BERNARD BRODIE

THE *RAND* CORPORATION

PRINCETON, NEW JERSEY
PRINCETON UNIVERSITY PRESS

First PRINCETON PAPERBACK Edition 1965

Second printing 1967

Third printing 1969

Fourth printing 1970

Fifth Printing 1971

Printed in the United States of America
by Princeton University Press, Princeton, New Jersey

The occasion of putting this book into a new, paperback edition reminds one that some time has elapsed since the original publication, and that in the field of modern strategy time tends to deal severely with concepts as well as facts. On the whole this book has fared very well, but five years nevertheless warrant a statement about what one would do differently if one were writing the book today. I am indeed pleased that in the present instance such a statement need be neither long nor involved.

The fact that five years have elapsed is less important than that the date of publication preceded the coming to power of the Kennedy and subsequently the Johnson administrations, which have pursued an ideology in defense matters markedly different from that which infused the previous administration. Actually, speaking in a descriptive rather than a causative sense, this book as originally published in 1959 turned out to be a projection of the intellectual structure within which the defense doctrines and distinctive military postures of the Kennedy administration were to take shape. I might also say that though that structure, as represented in the book, was not by any means solely my own creation, I had nevertheless made some contributions to it, chiefly in the area of thought about limited war.

I mention this mainly to put into some perspective my later criticisms of certain administration defense policies that seemed superficially to be entirely in line with ideas advocated in the original volume. For example, my article "What Price Conventional Capabilities in Europe?" published in the May 23, 1963 issue of *The Reporter* systematically criticized what I held to be excessive devotion to the idea of resisting possible Soviet aggression in Europe mostly by conventional means—though I had apparently advocated comparable ideas in my Chapter 9.

One relevant fact and partial explanation is that when the book was written (some parts of it were first composed long before 1959), those sections that deal with limited war, and especially with conventional capabilities for fighting a limited war, had to be advanced against much intellectual opposition. Actually, my own writings, then classified, urging that more study and resources be devoted to limited-war capabilities date from the beginning of 1952 (when I first heard of the thermonuclear weapon to be tested in the following November), and at that time the views I was expressing met in some quarters not only opposition but amazed disbelief. It is difficult to recall now that at that time it was a completely accepted axiom—despite the on-going Korean experience, which was regarded as entirely aberrational—that all modern war must be total war. This idea had been by no means completely dissipated at the time of the publication of the book in 1959.

In that respect the situation today is vastly different. The present frame of mind on relevant issues within the defense community of the United States would make unnecessary today the tone of advocacy sometimes manifested in the book. On the contrary, if it were being written today it would be more appropriate to point out (as I tried to do in the above-mentioned article and in other papers) the limitations and drawbacks attending possible over-emphasis of what is basically a good and necessary idea.

What other changes in circumstance are worth noting for this new edition? So far as concerns changes in the world of things rather than ideas, far the most important in the five years since publication has been the revolution in the degree of security built into the strategic retaliatory forces of the two major nuclear powers, especially those of the United States. I did indeed stress in the book the importance of such a change which was already beginning, but the degree to which it has in fact taken place has considerably outrun my expectations. Our Secretary of Defense, Mr. Robert S. McNamara, and other members of the Kennedy-Johnson regime, were quick to recognize the importance of this vulnerability problem and to push programs designed to cope with it. Among the most important of these have been the Navy's Polaris submarine and the Air Force's Minuteman missile programs. The former puts under water and the latter under ground in hardened silos the inter-mediate and the long range missiles of which the major part of our retaliatory capability is already or soon will be composed. Thus, in time of crisis, which may in fact include actual hostilities with our major opponent, the pressure for "going first" with our strategic forces is not only reduced but well-nigh eliminated. This change introduces immeasurably more stability into any crisis situation—a fact somewhat intriguingly reflected in the term "crisis management" that has lately made its way into the fashionable jargon of the times. Or, to use another term that has come into wide use of late, "escalation" to general war is far less to be feared from any commitment to limited war than was formerly the case—even, I would hold, if nuclear weapons should be used.

An interesting concomitant of the change I have just described has been the development of an obvious dilemma with respect to targeting for general war—a dilemma that was also anticipated in the book, on pages 289-94. Where both sides have large retaliatory forces of relatively low vulnerability, attack upon enemy cities looks more than ever unattractive. On the other hand, the likely accomplishments of a "counterforce strategy" become also relatively unpromising. This dilemma contributes to diminishing the incentives for going first in a strategic exchange. One is both less worried about the vulnerability of one's retaliatory forces and also less eager to get on with a not-too-promising target list. This new, or developing, situation is not without its special problems; certainly the utility of the "massive retaliation" threat against local aggression has diminished even further (if it is not already at zero), but the situation is nevertheless, in the net, far more salubrious and comforting than was the case in 1959.

One should not omit mention also of the revelations attendant upon the great Cuban crisis of October 1962 and its most successful resolution for the United States. What looked in the beginning like an extraordinarily bold and venturesome act on the part of the Soviet leaders turned out in its conclusion and its aftermath to underline the degree to which those leaders were determined to avoid hostilities with the United States—perhaps due in part to the fact that they were less given than our own leaders to distinguishing between local and general war and less ready to think of the possibility of keeping the former from graduating into the latter. At any rate, the conduct of the Soviet Union since that time concerning such trouble spots as Berlin has reflected a so much better perception of us and what we will tolerate or not tolerate that we have some reason for expecting that their relatively conciliatory policies will survive the replacement of Mr. Khrushchev by others in October 1964. Certainly the consequences thus far of this historic confrontation seem to have been from our point of view entirely salutary.

Against the above described changes, those involving developments in active anti-missile defenses are of quite modest importance. Though everyone agrees that producing a highly effective anti-missile missile defense would be of the first order of strategic importance, no sophisticated worker in the field has any expectation of such a thing occurring in the foreseeable future. There is indeed a considerable consensus that technological development in this area should be pursued and that significant though strictly relative gains are to be expected from doing so. But nobody expects anything like an impenetrable umbrella of anti-missile defenses to be erected over our cities or our own missile emplacements—certainly not within any meaningful time span—and no one expects the opponent to do significantly better. It is the old story of ingenuity in defense having to reckon with ingenuity in offense, with the latter having a large margin of the advantages.

The principle of civil defense has indeed made almost no progress since the publication of the book. Any reasoned exposition of the advantages of putting very modest proportions of our entire defense resources on developing such capabilities is likely to engender in this country impassioned outbursts of opposition. The reason seems mainly to be that while offensive missiles and devices for their protection promise to *deter* war, fallout shelters and the like appear to have minimum utility for deterrence and are urged mostly for the sake of saving lives if general war does in fact occur. It is not really surprising that many people derive an additional sense of security from attacking what could be of use only if the unthinkable happens.

I suppose also that the considerable orientation of the book towards developing the historical origins of contemporary situations has had as much to do as my lucky guesses concerning the future in explaining the relatively small degree of obsolescence imposed by five years of time, during which events seemed to be moving so rapidly. At any rate, it is possible for me to envisage with great pleasure and minimal misgivings the reissue of this volume in a paperback edition. I should like also to express at this time my gratitude for the extremely favorable reception accorded the original edition and its several reprintings both in the United States and abroad.

BERNARD BRODIE

Santa Monica, Calif.
November 5, 1964

⤙ PREFACE ⤚

WHILE writing this book I tried to keep my prospective audiences distinctly in mind in order that I might better communicate with them. I kept first in my thoughts the officers of the American armed forces, especially those who are students in the several war colleges of the United States. However, I also hoped it would be useful to the rapidly increasing number of civilians, whether scholars, political leaders, or simply citizens, who are becoming seriously interested in national security problems. For their sakes I took added care to avoid the use of military jargon and to explain the few esoteric terms I did use.

The division of this book into two parts of quite different character may indicate a certain want of cohesion, but readers who lack the time or inclination to take that guided tour of the past which comprises most of Part I can plunge directly into Part II. My own view is that Part I traces the development of certain characteristics of modern military thinking which have had and continue to have great influence on national security policies in the United States and elsewhere, and which begin to look somewhat strange the moment one stops taking them for granted.

Some readers may regard it a blemish of the book that I nowhere hesitated to express a particular point of view, where I had one, rather than strain after a detachment which would mask my convictions. I tried to be objective, but not impartial. By that I mean that I tried honestly and earnestly to consider the various sides of a controversial issue before coming to my own conclusions, and I know I avoided any bias for or against the service mainly affected by the book's contents. Inherited axioms had almost no effect upon my thinking; I say "almost" because it is possible they had an inverse influence, due to my deep-seated impulse to shy at axioms. My military readers will no doubt make some correction for this defect when they notice it. I permitted myself to act the advocate especially where I was conscious of moving against a strong tide of opinion currently influencing national policy.

I was able to do this because the writing of the book, though carried out as a RAND Corporation project, was a one-man enterprise in which I was accorded full freedom to develop my thesis as I saw fit. Most of my RAND colleagues, I am sure, agree with most of what I say, and many agree essentially with the whole of it; but I am aware too that some whose opinions I respect differ from me on some of my conclusions. The RAND Corporation as such must therefore be exonerated from responsibility for my views.

Nevertheless, this book would have been a poorer one had I written it elsewhere. I am speaking partly of a general environment of thought within the organization, but I am aware also of obligations to specific persons in the RAND community. Those to whom I am especially indebted include J. F. Digby, M. W. Hoag, V. M. Hunt, H. Kahn, W. W. Kaufmann, A. W. Marshall, H. S. Rowen, T. C. Schelling, H. Speier, and A. J. Wohlstetter. Others who read the manuscript in whole or in part and contributed valuable criticisms and suggestions are A. W. Boldyreff, H. A. DeWeerd, A. L. George, H. Goldhamer, A. M. Halpern, O. Hoeffding, F. C. Iklé, P. Kecskemeti, B. H. Klein, M. M. Lavin, J. E. Loftus, R. N. McKean, and my wife, Fawn M. Brodie.

For style editing I must thank especially I. C. C. Graham, and also E. G. Mesthene and B. W. Haydon. Typing and similar work was nobly done by Janet V. Hamilton and

Joanne R. Bobo, and Joan Charvat prepared the index.

This study was undertaken by The RAND Corporation as a part of its research program for the United States Air Force. The officer whom I wish especially to thank for his interest and encouragement is Lieut. Gen. John A. Samford, U.S.A.F.

BERNARD BRODIE

Santa Monica, Calif.
March 20, 1959

⤙ CONTENTS ⤚

⤙ PART I ⤚

ORIGINS OF AIR STRATEGY

⊰ 1 ⊱

INTRODUCTION

In book VI of Milton's *Paradise Lost*, the Angel Raphael is recounting to Adam the story of the war in Heaven which resulted in the fall of Satan and his followers. After the first day of fighting, Raphael relates, the issue was still in doubt, although the rebellious angels had received the more horrid injury.

Gathered round their campfire that night, their leaders consider how they may overcome their disadvantage. Satan is persuaded that their inferiority is one of weapons alone, and he suggests:

> perhaps more valid Armes,
> Weapons more violent, when next we meet,
> May serve to better us, and worse our foes,
> Or equal what between us made the odds,
> In Nature none: . . .

At this point his lieutenant, Nisroc, rises to exclaim enthusiastic agreement, finishing his speech with a promise:

> He who therefore can invent
> With what more forcible we may offend
> Our yet unwounded Enemies, or arme
> Ourselves with like defence, to mee deserves
> No less then for deliverance what we owe.

All this proves to be mere window dressing, for Satan now announces that he has already invented the instrument which will shift the balance. The instrument, several of which are constructed at his direction during the celestial

3

night, turns out to be a field gun—which, as Raphael assures Adam, is likely to be reinvented by the latter's own progeny "in future days, if malice should abound."

The following day the rebel seraphs, exploiting to the utmost the advantages of tactical surprise, and skillfully applying techniques of psychological warfare, secretly bring up their field pieces and commit them at a critical moment to action. At first the infernal engines wreak dreadful execution. But the loyal angels, not to be surpassed in the application of science to war, in the fury of the moment seize upon the "absolute weapon." Tearing the seated hills of Heaven from their roots, they lift them by their shaggy tops and hurl them upon the rebel hosts. Those among the latter who are not immediately overwhelmed do likewise. In a moment the battle has become an exchange of hurtling hills, creating in their flight a dismal shade and infernal noise. "War," observes Raphael, "seemed a civil game to this uproar." Heaven is threatened with imminent ruin, and the situation is resolved in the only way left open—the direct intervention of God, who sends His only begotten Son to end the conflict. The Son of God succeeds without difficulty in casting the bad angels into outer darkness.

The war in Heaven dramatizes the chief dilemma which confronts modern man, especially since the coming of the atomic bomb, the dilemma of ever-widening disparity in accomplishment between man's military inventions and his social adaptation to them. Milton's angels were able to devise new weapons and apply them with a celerity which man has not yet attained. But even in an environment most favorable to peace, with an omniscient and all-powerful God as a directly interested party, these nearly perfect celestial beings suffered the outbreak among themselves of a civil war that was saved from being suicidal only by the fact that angels cannot die. Their superlative intelligence was reflected in the application of new techniques of warfare, but the origin of the war itself was marked by the absence or lapse of wisdom. Although Milton was conscious of the paradox, his experience with mankind, more limited in wisdom as well as capable of dying, persuaded him that it was not absurd.

Until recently the deadliest weapon known to man represented only a modest refinement of the field gun which Milton describes in his poem. Now, however, we can come much closer to matching, in kinetic-energy equivalents, the hills hurtling through space; we have thermonuclear weapons and the planes and ballistic missiles to carry them. Moreover, in the weapons field we are in the early stages of a swift technological evolution that seems to be still accelerating.

Within half a century we have had also two world conflicts that revealed something basically new in the nature of war. Before 1914 the wars to which civilized governments resorted were somehow, with a few exceptions, limited in their potentialities for evil. War had always been violent, but only rarely had the violence been uncontrolled and purposeless. War or the threat of war had a well-recognized function in diplomacy, one might almost say a regulatory function. Its institutionalized quality, reflected in an overlay of antique customs, traditions, and observances, tended to limit further a destructiveness already bounded by a primitive military technology. Poets and moralists agreed with politicians that while war always embraced the tragic and sometimes the senseless, the resort to it was often enjoined by honor as well as interest. Resort to war was not in itself wrong. There were, according to a time-honored distinction, just wars and unjust wars. Whatever its character, every war offered opportunities for personal and group conduct that might earn the highest praise. The wise as well as the foolish cherished the noble emotions associated with terms like "valor," "gallantry," and "glory."

The first World War proved, and the second one confirmed, that the twentieth century not only had put into the hands of each great nation a war machine of far greater power than any known before, but also had seen a near-collapse of the factors previously serving to limit war, including that of common prudence. In the course of World War I, the original cause of the outbreak and the initial purpose with which each belligerent had entered the quarrel were forgotten. The war created its own objectives and stimulated commitments among the allies that made it practically impossible to end the conflict short of the collapse of either side.

Each side turned out, however, to have enormous reservoirs of strength. Over a century earlier Adam Smith had calmed a young friend's fear that England would suffer ruin in her wars against Napoleon with the comment: "Sir, there is a great deal of ruin in a nation." The twentieth century was to bring him undreamed-of confirmation. Military theories, which tend always to assume that the opponent's strength is brittle, collapsed in the face of the enemy's refusal to collapse. Each side revealed under test a previously unimagined capacity to endure losses in life and treasure.

Until our own century, the methods of fighting on land or sea were so limited, technologically and otherwise, that the damage caused could generally be contained by means of unhurried political decisions, usually made by others than the generals who did the fighting. If the war threatened to incur excessive costs or political risks, the politicians could usually halt it. The generals could busy themselves exclusively with the military operations, without bothering themselves about the complex and, to them, questionable motives of their governments. Social and political usage permitted the soldiers to indulge their contempt for the politicians or "frocks," whose interference in military matters they hardly tolerated.

So recent a conflict as World War I was characterized on both sides by such an attitude on the part of the soldiers, who in the main succeeded in having their way against the despairing and mostly helpless political leaders. The shambles left by World War I, however, reduced the independence as well as the prestige of the military. In the second World War the politicians were, except in Japan, much more the masters of events than in the first; but in the main they exercised their control through selective approval of military theories developed, as of old, in a fairly undefiled universe of "strictly military considerations."

Today, however, with truly cosmic forces harnessed to the machines of war, we have a situation for the first time in history where the opening event by which a great nation enters a war—an event which must reflect the preparations it has made or failed to make beforehand—can decide irretrievably whether or not it will continue to exist. Obviously, therefore, we cannot go on blithely letting one group of specialists decide how to wage war and another decide when and to what purpose, with only the most casual and spasmodic communication between them.

The Intellectual No-Man's Land

There exists in America no tradition of intellectual concern with that border area where military problems and political ones meet. Although ideally the military approach to strategic problems needs to be extended and leavened by the relevant insights of the statesman, such insights are usually undeveloped among those civilian officials or politicians with whom the American military actually have to deal. The civilian official in the State Department will rarely know much about current military problems and will therefore have no feeling for their relevance to the issues in his own jurisdiction. The National Security Council is for that and other reasons mostly a monument to an aspiration. The aspiration is undeniably sound, but whether any real enrichment of strategic thinking has proceeded from it is another question.

The secretaries of Defense and of the three services usually tend toward a narrow view of their administrative function, and incline to avoid if they can intervention in what they call "strictly military decisions," though they are not always permitted to. Since they are normally selected for talents in fields other than the military and rarely tarry long in their high public posts, their modesty is probably for the best. To the extent that their curiosity about professional mysteries gets the better of their non-interventionist convictions, the service secretaries tend to become simply the chief civilian spokesmen for the special views of their respective services.

Administrative officers in other departments are bound to be more remote from military affairs and absorbed in a vast variety of other matters. So too are members of Congress. Yet the latter cannot escape intervention in military affairs through the machinery of appropriations and through investigations of alleged wrongdoing or errors of judgment. The consequences of such intervention can be far-reaching. Reasonably enough, the Congressman is quick to admonish himself and his colleagues not to be "armchair strategists." His obligation to vote on military bills forces him to come to some conclusions on military matters and he usually does so by deferring to whatever military spokesman he happens to like and respect, or to one who for some reason or other currently commands the most confidence. In a word, the politician tends to attach himself to the service faction that is most congenial to him or whose point of view is at the moment being given the most eloquent utterance.

Any real expansion of strategic thought to embrace the wholly new circumstances which nuclear weapons have produced will therefore have to be developed largely within the military guild itself. There are some institutional inhibitions to such expansion, and stimulus from outside the profession will no doubt assist the process of adjustment. But the professional military officer is dedicated to a career that requires him to brood on the problems of war, in which activity he finds himself with very little civilian company. He does not have to be persuaded of his need for seasoned political guidance; the problem is rather one of making such guidance available to him on appropriate occasions and at appropriate levels.

However, high level policy guidance is not all that matters. Now that we confront a situation where all-out war can destroy the national community, the soldier's plans for the defense of the country must take full account of this possibility and its implications. They must do so not merely in terms of some final adjustment at the National Security Council level, but intimately, at every stage in the evolution and development of those plans.

The basic fact is that the soldier has been handed a problem that extends far beyond the *expertise* of his own profession. He has learned to collaborate well enough with the physical scientist, to the mutual profit of both and to the advantage of their nation, but when it comes to military questions involving political environment, national objectives, and the vast array of value-oriented propositions that might be made about national defense, his liaison with people who are relatively expert in these fields leaves much to be desired. In this area the military are bound to be much less conscious of their need for assistance than they are in the field of technology. At the same time, specialists in the social sciences are usually insensitive to the existence of special military needs and also to their own deficiencies for meeting those needs.

One of the chief reasons for this failure of communications is the barrier of secrecy, in the main unavoidable but also disturbingly costly to the progress of understanding. This barrier conceals far more, relatively, than it ever has before. That is not primarily because the people who control security are more jittery than they were twenty years ago; it is mostly because the things protected are by their nature vastly more significant to all of us. An intercontinental ballistic missile carrying a thermonuclear warhead is something that can affect us much closer to home and much more immediately and entirely than, say, the radar mounted on warships, our most jealously guarded secret device when we entered World War II. The ship-borne radar was something remote from our homes and strictly tactical; the ICBM is, in the most compelling meaning of the word, strategic. Similarly, questions like whether or not our strategic bombers are carrying thermonuclear weapons in their practice flights, or any of a number of other questions that could be asked about missiles and weapons progress, are obviously more vital than any that could have been raised concerning the posture and disposition of our military forces prior to World War II. In short, it is not that our officials are more secretive, but rather that the things which must be kept secret are very much more important.

Yet we must not put too much blame on the security barrier for the general ignorance of defense problems. The amount of information available to the public on military and strategic affairs is very much greater than the casual observer would guess. To gather it systematically requires interest and effort. The security barrier unquestionably tends to depress such interest. Its effects, however, would not be critical if civilian scholars, especially those in the behavioral sciences, understood the stakes involved and also the opportunities available to them to contribute their special insights and skills to a great common problem. This book is in part intended to help them make that contribution.

The Traditional Military Depreciation of Strategy

Nevertheless, it is the military audience primarily that the analyst has to meet and communicate with on strategic problems, for they must remain the prime movers of change in this field. One of the barriers he encounters in trying to reach them is the general conviction, implicit throughout the whole working structure and training program of the military system, that strategy poses no great problems which cannot be handled by the application of some well-known rules or "principles," and that compared with the complexity of tactical problems and the skills needed to deal with them, the whole field of strategy is relatively unimportant.

This view is not often expressed in so many words, and it is therefore interesting to find a good statement of it by the late Field-Marshal Earl Wavell, one of the most scholarly and urbane of modern generals. Captain B. H. Liddell Hart had commented somewhere that because of certain recent developments strategy was gaining in importance at the expense of tactics. "I cannot agree," said Lord Wavell:

I hold that tactics, the art of handling troops on the battlefield, is and always will be a more difficult and more important part of the general's task than strategy, the art of bringing forces to the battlefield in a favorable position. A homely analogy can be made from contract bridge. The calling is strategy, the play of the hand tactics. I imagine that all experienced card-players will agree that the latter is the more difficult part of the game, and gives more scope for the skill of the good player. Calling is to a certain degree mechanical and subject to conventions: so is strategy, the main principles of which are simple and easy to grasp. . . . But in the end it is the result of the manner in which the cards are played or the battle is fought that is put down on the score sheets or in the pages of history. Therefore, I rate the skilful tactician above the skilful strategist, especially him who plays the bad cards well.[1]

Many generals, from Napoleon to Eisenhower, have asserted in one form or another the idea that the main principles of war "are simple and easy to grasp," but it is remarkable that even the reflective Lord Wavell, a man not easily ruled by traditional axioms, should have joined the chorus. The one fatal mistake of his own military career involved an error in strategic judgment, and in one place he candidly admits as much. In the early part of 1941—only one year before he wrote the passage quoted above—he gave his military approval to the British expedition to Greece and committed a considerable portion of his forces to it, without having first disposed of Rommel in the desert. In his mem-

---

[1] *Soldiers and Soldiering*, Jonathan Cape, London, 1953, p. 47.

oirs he excuses himself on the ground that the Greek expedition would have been justified had he faced an ordinary commander in the Western Desert, but he "had not reckoned on a Rommel."[2] And he has nothing to say about the fate of the expedition in Greece.

In Wavell's reply to Liddell Hart, one notices the traditionally narrow conception of strategy as "the art of bringing forces to the battlefield in a favorable position," a conception which excludes consideration of the ultimate objectives of the campaign and even more of the war itself. With a broader view of strategy, Wavell might have sought to excuse the intervention in Greece. The idea that strategy, like bidding in bridge, "is to a certain degree mechanical and subject to conventions" betrays the almost universal assumption that the ends or objectives of the military effort are always given or obvious. As the Korean War indicates, however, the question of ultimate goals may be quite confounding the moment it is admitted to be a real question. For wars of the future it may well be the greatest single question facing us.

Even if one accepts for the moment Wavell's limited definition of strategy, one cannot help marvelling at the cavalier way in which he dismisses strategic decisions as not only less difficult but also less *important* than tactical ones. Less difficult, within the limits he applies, they certainly are. The "main principles" of war of which he speaks represent for the most part, as we shall later see, modest refinements upon common sense. In contrast to tactical problems, which make heavy demands on technical skill and which in war are always multiple and often presented under great stress, the strategic decision is as a rule simple and gross in its content, is usually made in relative freedom from the heat

[2] *Ibid.*, p. 78.

and vicissitudes of battle, and may be of a kind which is made but once in a campaign or even in the entire war. In the latter event, especially, how crucial that it be correct!

Even within Wavell's narrow definition of strategy, we find plenty of examples of costly mistakes. When Admiral William F. Halsey in the supreme test of his art at Leyte Gulf threw his entire vast Third Fleet against the wrong force, he effectively nullified both his own sterling qualities as a leader and fighter and the American advantage in possessing the far superior fleet. The American landing forces whose protection was his first responsibility did not suffer the disaster his action invited, but he did lose the opportunity the Japanese had placed in his hands to destroy their main fleet.

One thinks also of the arresting sentence with which Sir Winston Churchill qualified an otherwise harsh criticism of Sir John Jellicoe's conduct at Jutland: "Jellicoe was the only man on either side who could lose the war in an afternoon." What a world of meaning lies in that admission! No wonder Jellicoe was cautious! Perhaps he was too cautious, but his reasons for being so were good ones.

To use an example closer to the heart of our subject, let us remember that the Allied strategic bombing campaign in World War II is rarely criticized on tactical grounds. Early opinions that escort fighters were unnecessary even for daytime sorties proved wrong, and the lack of long-range fighters was remedied as soon as possible. There were a few other mistakes, but there is no serious dissent from the general consensus that, for a new type of operation, the whole job was magnificently handled. All the important and voluminous criticisms of the effort center upon questions that are essentially strategic. Were the basic military resources absorbed by strategic bombing too great in view of the returns? Could not these resources have been better used, even in the form of air power, for other military purposes? Were not the wrong target systems selected? And so forth. Whatever views one may have about the answers to these questions, or the spirit behind the questioning, the questions themselves are neither irrelevant nor unimportant.

Finally, as an example of sound strategy at the highest level of decision, after the United States entry into World War II the Allies elected to concentrate on defeating Germany and Italy first rather than Japan. What could have been more simple and more obviously correct? Yet we know this commitment was painful to certain high military authorities in the United States and, perhaps unconsciously, resisted by them. We also know how fortunate it is that the basic resolve behind that decision never faltered.

It is hard to escape the conclusion that Lord Wavell's view reflects a peculiarly professional bias. It is a commonplace that all professions, owing their very existence to the intensive specialization of their members, are characterized by particular group attitudes which often strike persons outside the group as being unduly narrow and limiting. Economists, for example, are often disdainful of the political or sociological considerations that qualify the application of their otherwise correct and valuable theories, and social reformers are often just as disdainful of economic reasoning. Physicians and lawyers, too, have their characteristic ways of looking at human problems. The military guild has its own brand of professionalism, to some facets of which we shall have occasion to refer in subsequent pages.

There is no doubt that tactics and administration are the areas in which the soldier is most completely professional.

The handling of battles by land, sea, or air, the maneuvering of large forces, the leadership of men in the face of horror and death, and the development and administration of the organizations that effect these purposes are clearly not jobs for amateurs. In these tasks there is no substitute for the hard training and the experience which the services alone provide.

During war the tests of command become far more exacting than in peacetime, and some officers turn out to be more talented than others—more imaginative in their adaptation to new tactical conditions, more inspiring as leaders, and sturdier in the face of adversity or unpleasant surprises. But unless the officer attains some independent and important command, he may never in his career have to make a decision that tests his insight as a strategist. Small wonder, then, that the services on the whole have paid relatively scant attention to the development of strategic theory. As a corps commander in the German Imperial Army once said to a young staff officer who sought to develop his own strategic ideas: "His Majesty only keeps one strategist [Schlieffen], and neither you nor I is that man."[3]

The professional officer, stimulated always by the immediate needs of the service to which he devotes his life, becomes naturally absorbed with advancing its technical efficiency and smooth operation. This task has become ever more exacting with the increasing complexity and rapidity of change in military technology. Nelson, whose flagship at Trafalgar was forty years old but equal in fighting capacity to the majority of the ships engaged, could spend his life learning and perfecting the art of the admiral without fearing that

[3] Walter Goerlitz, *History of the German General Staff, 1657-1945,* Praeger, New York, 1953, p. 134.

its foundations would shift under his feet. Today the basic conditions of war seem to change almost from month to month. It is therefore hard for the professional soldier to avoid being preoccupied with means rather than ends. Also, his usefulness to his superior hangs upon his skill and devotion in the performance of his assigned duties, rather than upon any broader outlook, and if there is one thing that distinguishes the military profession from any other it is that the soldier always has a direct superior.

Some conception of ends there has to be, but its formulation is not the stuff of day-to-day work. Presumably it is the province of a few in exalted rank, who have been prepared for their high responsibilities by passing slowly through the tactics-oriented lower ranks and whose advancement has been based primarily on their success in posts of command, that is to say on their qualities of leadership. The inevitable tendency is to accept as given the ends handed down by traditional doctrine, usually in the form of maxims or slogans. It is perhaps not surprising, therefore, that in modern wars the big blunders have usually been strategic rather than tactical. The Japanese attack at Pearl Harbor, for example, was for its time a beautiful piece of tactical innovation, and within narrowly defined limits it even made good sense strategically; but beyond those limits, what a colossally stupid thing to do!

Instances of grave tactical blunders are certainly not lacking in the history of war, but it is characteristic of tactical errors that they tend to be self-exposing, if not in relation to some theoretical ideal then at least in relation to the best the enemy can do. In the past, it has usually been possible for strong nations to recover from them, even if at heavy cost in blood and possibly strategic position. Strategic errors may or may not expose themselves in some obvious fashion during the course of a war, or even afterwards, and they are therefore much less likely to damage the reputations of those responsible for them.

The French general staff's complete underestimation of the machine gun prior to World War I was a grievous tactical error for which the French nation paid bitterly in blood in the opening Battles of the Frontiers in 1914. But still more dangerous was the error of conception which had produced those battles where they occurred, which had sent the hastily mobilized French armies charging off to the east while the Germans wheeled down on their flank and rear. Moreover, the fact that the French and the British high commands continued throughout the war to mount offensive after useless offensive in the teeth of the same terrible and confounding weapon that had caused the initial French disasters is traceable less to gross tactical incompetence than to a narrow strategic doctrine which knew no horizons beyond the immediate needs of the battle. That doctrine left them no alternative to the "Big Push," whatever its cost. Because they recognized no other viable strategy they could not for three long years accept the fact that they had devised no tactical answer to the machine gun. Necessity, which frequently exists only in the mind, is less often the mother of invention than of obstinacy, and the obstinacy of those three years exacted from France a penalty which continued to exert its effects over the years, contributing to the collapse of 1940, and which cannot be fully summed up even now.

Today we are talking not about machine guns and barbed wire but about a weapon that may in a single unit destroy all of Manhattan Island and leave some of it a water-filled crater. We may as well admit that the strictly tactical problem of destroying Manhattan is already absurdly easy, and time promises to make it no less easy. That is only to say that its protection, if it can be protected, is henceforward a strategic and political problem rather than a tactical one.

Why Look Back?

It is characteristic of our convictions, in strategy as in all affairs of life, that we tend to regard them as natural and inevitable. However, if we examine the history of the ideas contained in those convictions, we usually find that they have evolved in a definitely traceable way, often as the result of the contributions of gifted persons who addressed themselves to the needs of their own times on the basis of the experience available to them. Our own needs and our experience being different, we are enabled by our study to glimpse the arbitrariness of views which we previously regarded as laws of nature, and our freedom to alter our thinking is thereby expanded. Where new circumstances require fundamental adjustments in our thinking, such aids to adjustment may be very useful.

In the age of missiles, thermonuclear warheads, atomic-powered submarines capable of strategic bombing, and other comparably fantastic systems, it may seem atavistic to look back to strategic views which antedate World War I. However, while air power, in which we must now include long-range missiles as well as aircraft, is of recent origin, ideas about war and how to fight it are not. The original theories about the use of air power had to make some adjustment to pre-existing strategic ideas, and it is in that adjusted form that we have inherited them. Inasmuch as these theories evolved and developed in a pre-nuclear age, they may themselves be of dubious relevance to our times.

In any case, we should not deceive ourselves that we have the ability to start from scratch with completely fresh ideas and, guided merely by logic, to fashion a strategy according to the needs of the time. This is too much to expect of human beings. For better or for worse we shall be applying our intellects, as presently furnished, to new and baffling problems, and whether the results will be good or bad depends to some extent on the character of the furnishings—whether they are mere habits of thought which we have not reconsidered for a long time, or on the contrary, ideas which are old only because they have deserved a long life. In practical terms, therefore, we shall in the following pages attempt to scan the earlier development of strategic theory, particularly with respect to its influence on the development of air power doctrine, and then consider some of the strategic policy choices confronting us today.

A word is necessary about the definition of "air power." For the purposes of this study it will be convenient to accept a view that has always prevailed among airpower theorists—that *strategically* the term air power applies to that force of aircraft and missiles which is operated more or less independently of ground and naval forces for generally independent purposes. This does *not* imply or prejudge any position on the so-called "tactical use" of aircraft, either as to its importance or the methods of pursuing it. The use of air power in support of ground or naval operations simply forms a different subject, which we shall be concerned with only fleetingly in what follows. For that matter the tactics even of strategic bombardment operations will for the most part fall outside our purview. It is a subject mostly for specialists, and is in addition much more hedged about with security considerations than the broader issues we shall be considering.

⤙2⤚

PROLOGUE TO AIR STRATEGY

MILITARY STRATEGY, while one of the most ancient of the human sciences, is at the same time one of the least developed. One could hardly expect it to be otherwise. Military leaders must be men of decision and action rather than of theory. Victory is the payoff, and therefore the confirmation of correct decision. There is no other science where judgments are tested in blood and answered in the servitude of the defeated, where the acknowledged authority is the leader who has won or who instills confidence that he will win.

Some modicum of theory there always had to be. But like much other military equipment, it had to be light in weight and easily packaged to be carried into the field. Thus, the ideas about strategy which have evolved from time to time no sooner gained acceptance than they were stripped to their barest essentials and converted into maxims or, as they have latterly come to be called, "principles." The baggage that was stripped normally contained the justifications, the qualifications, and the instances of historical application or misapplication.

The Principles of War

The so-called "principles of war" derive from the work of a handful of theorists, most of them long since dead. Their specific contributions to living doctrine are not widely known, because their works are seldom read. The richness of their ideas is but poorly reflected in the axioms which have stemmed from those ideas. Nevertheless, those theorists have enjoyed, in what is supposed to be the most pragmatic and practical of professions, a profound and awful authority.

Air power is too young to have among the theorists of its strategy more than one distinguished name, and he has carried all before him. Douhet's indebtedness to his precursors in the general area of military strategy was objectively small enough, and in his eyes even smaller. He refused to justify his ideas according to whether they did or did not accord with some inherited gospel, being much more interested in whether they accorded with the facts of life as he saw them. He was too proud of his intellectual independence to appeal to the authority of the old principles, even where they happened to support his own views. Indeed, his essential, correct, and enduring contribution lay in his turning upside down the old, trite military axiom, derived from Jomini, that "methods change but principles are unchanging." He insisted instead that a change in method so drastic as that forced by the airplane must revolutionize the whole strategy of war.

But Douhet's most devoted followers do not feel comparably compelled to emphasize the violent break with the past which their doctrine represents. Like military officers of other services, they are eager to acknowledge allegiance to the traditional principles of war, even when they have but scant familiarity with those principles.

Thus, the controversy over the proper role of air power has often, on its more intellectual fringes, revolved around the question whether the Douhet thesis (loosely, the supreme emphasis on strategic bombing) does or does not conform to the tried-and-true, "enduring" principles of war. On occasion the argument has taken the form of exegesis of venerated authorities like Clausewitz, who after all has been dead for a century and a quarter.[1] Douhet is himself too controversial and for Americans too "foreign" to carry much weight in his own name. He is therefore rarely cited in support of a point of view, but a proposal for the use of air power that runs counter to his doctrines may well be crushed under the ponderous assertion that it "violates all the principles of war."

What are the ancient teachings to which appeals are so frequently made? More important, how do they derive such commanding authority? We are not here interested in the history of strategic thought for its own sake. On the contrary, we are concerned with a body of ideas or axioms to which *in our own time* millions of lives have been sacrificed, and on the basis of which great battles have been organized and fought. More to the point, we are concerned with a heritage of thought which even today dominates the great decisions of our national defense.

The so-called "principles of war" are usually presented in lists of some seven to eleven numbered maxims. They are supposed to be unchanging despite the fantastic changes that have occurred and continue to occur in almost all the factors with which they deal. In the world of ideas such durability is usually characteristic either of divine revelation or of a level of generality too broad to be operationally interesting.

[1] See, for example, Capt. Robert H. McDonnell, "Clausewitz and Strategic Bombing," *Air University Quarterly Review*, vi (Spring 1953), 43-54. This article is a reply to the book by Admiral Sir Gerald Dickens, *Bombing and Strategy: The Fallacy of Total War*, where Admiral Dickens argues that strategic bombing offends against the Clausewitzian doctrine "that the subjugation of an enemy is best accomplished by defeating its armed forces in battle." Replying to this and like objections, Capt. McDonnell asserts that what is needed is a "closer examination of Clausewitz's principles." For a more general effort to equate Air Force doctrine with the traditional principles of war, see Col. Dale O. Smith and Maj. John D. Barker, "Air Power Indivisible," *Air University Quarterly Review*, iii (Fall 1950).

In fact the hallowed "principles" are essentially common sense propositions which are generally but by no means exclusively pertinent to the waging of war.

The propositions usually stress the desirability of: avoiding undue dispersion of strength in order to maximize the chances for superiority at the decisive point (principle of mass or concentration); choosing firmly one's course of action and adhering to it despite distracting pressures (principle of the objective); pressing vigorously any advantage gained, especially after a victory in battle (principle of pursuit); seizing the initiative at the appropriate time and exploiting it to force a favorable decision (principle of the offensive); guarding one's forces and communications against surprise attack, even when on the offensive (principle of security); making good use of stealth and deception (principle of surprise); putting to the fullest effective use all the forces available (principle of economy of force); and so on.

There are occasional additions to or subtractions from this list, depending on the whim or bias of the individual compiler. Incidentally, the listing of principles of war is a modern habit or vice, and probably reflects a more general contemporary tendency to condense and encapsulate knowledge. Although older writers often referred to "principles of war," they did not attempt to define or specify what they meant. The first listing of principles in United States Army training manuals occurred in *Training Regulations 10-5*, of 1921, which simply named the principles without explanation.

Let us not deny the utility of these generalizations. We know, for example, that war as a whole, and individual battles, are always marked by a multiplicity of demands upon the leader's forces and that he is fortified in his resolution to ignore some of them by awareness of such a rule as that called the "principle of concentration." It has had much confirmation in experience. Strategic writers often cite various historic violations of the rule which had unfortunate or disastrous consequences, as when the younger Moltke fatally compromised the Schlieffen plan in 1914 by successive reductions in the concentration on his right wing, first to strengthen his left and then to send reinforcements to threatened East Prussia.

It would be equally useful, and much more novel, to cite also instances where unreasoning devotion to a "principle" or slogan has proved unfortunate, as when Admiral Halsey declined on the basis of that same principle of concentration to divide his tremendous force at Leyte Gulf, electing instead to throw the whole of the great Third Fleet against a puny decoy force under Admiral Ozawa. Halsey could have divided his fleet in order to meet both enemy naval forces operating in his area, as some of his close associates expected him to do, and still have remained overwhelmingly superior to each. To achieve superiority is after all the whole reason for concentration, but he had been brought up on a slogan which historically has had a special appeal to the United States Navy: "Don't divide the fleet."[2] Thus the supreme embodiment of American naval might was deployed at a critical moment in simple obedience to an antique slogan. At Chancellorsville, Lee divided his force in the face of a greatly superior enemy, in order to carry out a maneuver

[2] See my review article, "The Battle for Leyte Gulf," *Virginia Quarterly Review*, XXIII (Summer 1947), 455-460. In U.S. naval history, the slogan "Don't divide the fleet" has been applied especially to a division of the main naval forces between the Atlantic and Pacific Oceans. In the days before the U.S. had a "two-ocean navy," it was axiomatic that she could be a first-rate naval power in one ocean but not in both simultaneously. However, this slogan served to refortify the more general and ancient idea that it is bad to divide one's forces in the presence of the enemy.

which won the battle for him. But one can hardly make a principle out of a brilliant gamble.

Because the classic principles are mere common sense propositions, most of them apply equally to other pursuits in life, including some which at first glance seem to be pretty far removed from war. If, for instance, a man wishes to win a maid, and especially if he is not too well endowed with looks or money, it is necessary for him to clarify in his mind exactly what he wants of the girl—the principle of the objective—and then to practice rigorously the principles of concentration of force, of the offensive, of economy of force, and certainly of deception.

It is not necessarily damning to the principles of war that they are applicable also to other pursuits but it does indicate that such principles are too abstract and too general to be very useful as guides in war. Their essential barrenness is perhaps suggested by the fact that recent interpreters have often confused the classic meaning of some of the phrases they employ. The term "economy of force," for example, derives from an interpretation governed by the nineteenth century connotation of the word "economy," meaning judicious management but not necessarily limited use. Thus, the violation of the indicated principle is suggested most flagrantly by a *failure to use* to good military purpose forces that are available—for example McClellan's failure at Antietam and Hooker's at Chancellorsville to bring their reserves into action. Of late, however, the term has often been interpreted as though it demanded "economizing" of forces, that is, a withholding of use.[3]

[3] For a more extended discussion of the relevance and irrelevance of strategic principles, see my "Strategy as a Science," *World Politics*, 1 (July 1949), 467-488; for an historical account of the listing of principles, see

Sir Winston Churchill has said in one sentence perhaps all that needs to be said on this subject. "The truths of war," he concedes, "are absolute, but the principles governing their application have to be deduced on each occasion from the circumstances, which are always different; and in consequence no rules are any guide to action."[4]

If we wish to avail ourselves of whatever light the wisdom of the past can throw upon our present problems, we must go beyond the maxims which are its present abbreviated expression. The maxim may be the final distillate of profound thought; but it is likely to be such only at its first use, when it is still an apt expression and not yet a slogan. When it becomes common currency it is likely already to be counterfeit.

The Creators of Modern Strategic Thought

There is not much use in attempting here to summarize all strategic thinking before Douhet, since much of it is presently irrelevant, but it is useful to consider the way in which certain ideas of great current importance have been derived. Two are especially relevant to the present and future: first, the theory of the offensive (about the general validity of which there is no dispute but which has in the past taken some extreme and particularized forms); and second, the somewhat dimly lit idea that war should express and project national policy. The latter thought, embodied in Clausewitz's much-quoted but little-understood assertion that "war is a continuation of policy by other means," happens never to be

---

also the article by Lt. Col. M. L. Fallwell, "The Principles of War and the Solution of Military Problems," *Military Review*, xxxv (May 1955), 48-62.

[4] *The World Crisis*, Scribner's, New York, 1931, p. 576.

included in lists of "basic principles"—an omission that is both curious and significant.

As one goes in quest of the wisdom of the past on the subject of war, one notices first of all how small is the number of general treatises on strategy even over the span of centuries. There have been many great soldiers in the past, and military historians have favored us with thousands of volumes recounting the exploits of outstanding military leaders, as well as of many others not so outstanding. But this richness of writings in military history does not prepare us for the poverty in theoretical writings on the strategy of war. Indeed the few theorists have enjoyed an exceptional scarcity value.

Karl von Clausewitz is the first great creative figure in modern strategy, just as Adam Smith is the first great figure in modern economics, a science that is in many respects remarkably analogous. Unlike Smith, however, whose *Wealth of Nations* proved to be only the headwaters of a large and still expanding river of thought to which many great talents have contributed, Clausewitz stands almost alone in his eminence. His is "the first study of war that truly grapples with the fundamentals of its subject, and the first to evolve a pattern of thought adaptable to every stage of military history and practice."[5] In these respects his work has never been equalled. Others may be worthy of honor, especially his contemporary, Antoine Henri Jomini, but they do not challenge his preeminence. Indeed it was difficult to be original in this field after Clausewitz. Not until two-thirds of a century later does anyone appear of anything like comparable stature, and Alfred T. Mahan, by confining himself to the operations of naval war, put his work into a more limited

[5] H. Rothfels, "Clausewitz," ch. 5 in *Makers of Modern Strategy*, ed. by E. M. Earle, Princeton University Press, Princeton, 1943, p. 93.

context than did Clausewitz. After Mahan we come to Douhet, a name unique in a new and separate field of strategy. The special case of Douhet we shall reserve for another chapter.

Let us acknowledge that we are skipping over the names of some distinguished theorists, who would have to be discussed or at least mentioned in any history of modern strategic thought. Some made original and incisive contributions; others are important more because of their influence on their times. One of the former is Ardant du Picq, and one of the latter is Ferdinand Foch, both of whom we shall discuss presently. The fact remains that only a small number of men have left written judgments and precepts that influenced the thinking of soldiers in their own and subsequent generations, and the scope of those judgments has been on the whole fairly static and limited.

There were thinkers and writers on strategy before Clausewitz, just as there were thinkers and writers on economics before Adam Smith, but their approach was generally fragmentary and they dealt with long-since-vanished conditions. The talented military leader managed usually to know what he was about and why. This priceless insight made up for a lack of comprehensive, coherent theory. Today theories are comprehensive enough, and sufficiently verbalized, and all the more rigid for being so. It is not for nothing that all the great theorists of war, including Clausewitz and Jomini and even Douhet, have fervently reiterated that there is no substitute for talent in the commander.

Admittedly we have little to learn from the purely military strategy of pre-Napoleonic wars, but we may have something to learn from the eighteenth century concerning the use of war in the pursuit of political purposes. In this broader approach to strategy the age was perhaps more rational than ours, or at any rate less confused. Unfortunately, a number of myths about the warfare of the eighteenth century have made too many modern students of war turn away from it as uninteresting. We must, for example, dismiss the notion that the military maneuvers of the eighteenth century were marked by a disdain for combat. One thumb-nail formulation has it that the eighteenth century did not understand the utility of the decisive battle, which is supposed to have been discovered by Napoleon. Yet when since the eighteenth century has an admiral been tried and shot for failing to press an opportunity for a decisive action, as poor John Byng was in 1756? And what more decisive battle could one want than Marlborough's victory at Blenheim?

Another common view is that eighteenth century battles were rarely or never bloody. This view is simply fantastic, casualty rates having been in fact extremely high in battles both on land and at sea. It would perhaps be more correct to say that eighteenth century commanders abhorred the bloody battle which was also indecisive, and that some of the greatest of them learned from hard experience to be skeptical of the outcome of pitched battles between fairly evenly matched armies. Such was certainly the experience and the conclusion of Frederick the Great, who was cured of his itch for battles by his Pyrrhic victory at Torgau, and whose military writings over a period of forty years became steadily and markedly less given to offensive ardor.

Since it would hardly do for the modern military writer to be contemptuous of Frederick, the authority usually quoted (by Foch, for example) to show the stereotype of eighteenth-century military thinking is Marshal de Saxe: "I do not favor pitched battles, especially at the beginning of a war, and I am convinced that a skillful general could make war all his life without being forced into one." However, anyone who reads in de Saxe's *Reveries* the few paragraphs immediately following the statement just quoted, where he insists upon the necessity for impetuous pursuit after victory in battle, will realize that he was not nearly so cautious as Foch and others made him out to be.[6]

The Napoleonic Pattern

The era of modern war on land, however, did begin with Napoleon, whose genius lay less in novel tactical and strategic combinations than in his ability to see basic changes in strategic conditions going on before his eyes and to exploit them. With national armies raised by conscription and supported by the whole people, one could do what was not possible with mercenary forces maintained by the prince for strictly dynastic purposes. They could be more ruthlessly expended in campaigning, because new levies would bring forward ample replacements. Moreover, in Napoleon's hand they were guided by a will that knew no governance apart from an utterly ruthless personal ambition.

Under him there evolved a pattern which—despite its failure in Iberia, in Russia, and finally at Waterloo—was to captivate subsequent generations of soldiers down to our own time. It was the pattern of the impetuous campaign

[6] The complete *Reveries* of de Saxe are contained in *Roots of Strategy,* ed. by Maj. Thomas R. Phillips, Military Service Publishing Co., Harrisburg, Pa., 1940, pp. 177-300; the passage quoted is on p. 298. The same volume contains Frederick's *Instructions to His Generals, 1747* (pp. 311-400), but unfortunately none of his later writings. For an excellent commentary on Frederick and his other writings, see ch. 3 by R. R. Palmer in *Makers of Modern Strategy*, pp. 49-62. The latter volume, oddly enough, contains nothing on de Saxe, but it is nevertheless valuable.

capped by the decisive battle. The strategic object was to bring superior forces to bear on successive portions of the opposing forces before the latter had a chance to unite. Tactically, the system depended on the attack of a dense mass of troops, without regard to losses. The purpose of so attacking was to register a conclusive victory before going on to the next item of business.

Napoleon understood as well as any soldier of his time the importance of pursuit after victory in order to destroy the forces of an opponent, which might otherwise go on fighting. He was, however, also astute enough to capitalize on the medieval outlook, still surviving in the eighteenth century, which tended to acknowledge the "honor of the battlefield," that is, mere possession of the ground on which the fighting had taken place, as a sufficient token of victory. Thus, many of his victories could hardly be called "decisive" in the modern sense, but so long as they built up his reputation and brought his enemies to sue for terms, they served his purpose.

Some of his famous campaigns, that of Wagram for instance, were a good deal less crushing to the defeated than has sometimes been made out. However, monarchs reared on the old traditions of limited commitments in war had no stomach for the heavy outlays required to redress defeats when the enterprise seemed to promise so little profit. They were solidly enough established and sufficiently undisturbed by nationalist fervor to be able to cede a little territory here and there without fear of losing their thrones. As late as 1859 a European monarch could still say, as the young Emperor Francis Joseph did in terminating the brief Franco-Austrian War with the cession of Lombardy: "I have lost a battle; I pay with a province." The same emperor did not have the freedom to act as urbanely in the last years of his long reign, which ended in 1916. Such attitudes Napoleon accommodated by practicing moderation towards his more powerful opponents, while gobbling up the weaker ones. When he lost his moderation he brought against himself a determination and a power that effected his doom.

Napoleon's attitude towards the intellectual basis of his art is reflected in a number of his famous maxims, of which the following is representative: "Read over and over again the campaigns of Alexander, Hannibal, Gustavus, Turenne, Eugene, and Frederick. Make them your models. This is the only way to become a great general and to master the secrets of war." What he was urging was a creative reading of history, not a sterile review of rules and principles, which then scarcely existed in any systematic form. Such also must have been the prescription of his great predecessors. Frederick wrote his own treatises on strategy, but in his active years in the field there had been little of the sort for him to read. The Marshal de Saxe began his *Reveries*, written as a pastime while he was sick, with an eloquent denial that there was any such thing as a science of strategy. Similarly, at sea there were great admirals before Nelson—Blake, de Ruyter, and Suffren among others—but they neither left nor inspired textbooks. Nelson's own formidable talent had to wait nearly a hundred years to be fully interpreted by Mahan, an American naval officer turned scholar.

Clausewitz and Jomini

Napoleon's startling innovations and even more startling achievements inspired the work of Clausewitz and Jomini. Of the two, Clausewitz was clearly the greater but Jomini was much the more influential, at least outside Germany. The mere fact that all of Clausewitz's major work was published posthumously while Jomini enjoyed a remarkably full literary career through a very long life was a large factor of advantage for the latter. Also, Jomini wrote in French, a much more international language than the German of Clausewitz.[7] Above all Jomini was easier to comprehend than Clausewitz, more concrete and "practical," and more determined to provide guidance for action and to arrive at "fundamental principles."

Clausewitz's appeal is limited, for he is much more given than Jomini to "undogmatic elasticity" in his opinions, and he is more metaphysical in his approach. Although an active professional soldier, he wrote with competence on philosophical problems pertaining to the theory of knowledge, and in his military writings he sometimes used the technical idiom of the professional philosopher of his time. Besides, his insights, like those of all great thinkers, can be fully appreciated only by readers who have already reflected independently on the same problems.

Jomini, a Swiss career officer who served first Napoleon and then Alexander I in high staff positions, is supposed to have been read avidly by the leading generals of both sides in the American Civil War. Mahan later acknowledged him to be "my best military friend." Today the name of Jomini is less frequently heard than that of Clausewitz, but neither of them is much read.

The influence of Clausewitz within Germany was assisted

[7] Such differences are not likely to be nullified by translations. Many of Clausewitz's military writings, and all of his non-military ones, have not yet been translated into English. Prior to the excellent translation of *Vom Kriege* (*On War*) by O. J. Matthijs Jolles, Modern Library, Random House, New York, 1943, the standard translation was the inaccurate and awkward one of Col. J. J. Graham (1st ed., London, 1873; 3rd ed., revised by Col. F. N. Maude, London, 1918).

by the fact that one of the most intelligent and devoted of his disciples was the elder Moltke, who spent sixty years on the Prussian General Staff, including over thirty years as its chief, and who combined to a quite remarkable degree the qualities of scholar and of military leader. This strong influence persisted through the regime of Schlieffen, who was the next-but-one of Moltke's successors as Chief of the General Staff.

By the time of Schlieffen's replacement by the younger Moltke (nephew of the elder), Clausewitz had become a shade rather than a living spirit, quoted abundantly but not studied in any comprehending fashion. Perhaps the significance of the gradual attenuation of Clausewitz's influence is best illustrated by the difference between Schlieffen and his successors concerning what was to be done if the Schlieffen War Plan failed in the test. Schlieffen, while not politically oriented, was still strongly imbued with the idea that strategy was but an arm of national policy. He was therefore convinced that if the initial onslaught upon France failed to win a decision, Germany should immediately take steps to achieve a negotiated peace.[8] To the enormous subsequent cost not only of Germany but of the whole world, such a thought never entered the heads of those who finally executed the plan and saw it fail.

In both Clausewitz and Jomini one finds discussed at length most of the basic ideas which were later to be exalted to the status of "principles." These ideas had been conceived and applied to war long before. One finds some of them being pretty clearly formulated and applied in Xenophon's

[8] See *The Causes of the German Collapse in 1918*, ed. by R. H. Lutz from the officially authorized report of the German Reichstag, Stanford University Press, Stanford, 1934, p. 201.

account of the Persian expedition in the fourth century B.C. If all Clausewitz and Jomini had done was to develop these ideas as generalizations, their names would have been by now largely forgotten.

What makes large portions of their work come alive today, especially that of Clausewitz, is not the elucidation of principles but rather the wisdom which they brought to their discussion of them. In the case of Clausewitz this wisdom is reflected in a breadth of comprehension which makes him dwell as tellingly on the qualifications and exceptions to the basic ideas he is expounding as he does on those ideas themselves. For example, in a chapter extolling the virtues of what we would now call the principle of pursuit, he argues, against certain critics of his time, that Napoleon acted rightly in not following this principle at the bloody Battle of Borodino, where he abandoned the battlefield to a Russian army which he had beaten. For to have completed his victory would have cost him more troops than he could afford in view of the losses already sustained and the over-riding necessity of bringing an army of impressive size to Moscow, access to which had already been assured by his success. "Certainly the sparing of one's own instrument of victory is a vital question if this is the only one we possess, and we foresee that soon a moment may arrive when it will not be sufficient in any case for all that has to be done. . . ."[9] Nor does Clausewitz offer this example in a spirit of the exception which proves the rule. On the contrary, he presents it to show the limitations of even the worthiest rule (the principle of pursuit had for Clausewitz a quite special value) and to underline again the tyranny of circumstance and the importance of keeping one's mind clear about the objective. We shall meet another

[9] *On War* (Modern Library ed.), pp. 216f.

reference to this same battle when we discuss Foch, and we shall see how the relevant thoughts have become cheapened.

The wisdom of Clausewitz is revealed also in a contribution not merely distinctive but very nearly unique. No other theorizer on military strategy has penetrated so incisively to the nature of the relationship between war strategy and national policy. We shall look further into his views on this issue later on, but for the moment it is enough to say that in his mind policy had to control operations rather than the reverse. His insistence on the dominance of the aim over the action pervades his entire work. It is not with him, as with so many others, a matter of paying lip service to an ideal which is then ignored.[10]

Later writers like Foch and Douhet lost the point entirely. No doubt the immense tragedy of World War I, in a real sense a war without a purpose, is to be explained on grounds other than mere forgetfulness of Clausewitz's admonitions about relating means to ends; but it is nevertheless remarkable that no military leader on either side of the conflict— and for that matter few besides the historian Hans Delbrück among noteworthy civilians—seemed to be aware of and to protest against the ongoing obliteration of this all-important idea.

Clausewitz is often misinterpreted on this score because the fruits of his brooding thought are transmitted by capsular quotations taken out of context. It is ironical that some of the very quotations which are often cited to prove that he was the prophet of total or "absolute" war are wrenched from a chapter (Ch. 1, Bk. 1) in which he specifically insists

[10] Clausewitz's discussion of this theme in *On War* occupies particularly chs. 1 and 11 of bk. 1; ch. xxii of bk. 7, and all nine chapters of bk. 8.

that "war is never an isolated act" and that military method must always defer to the political object.

He is especially subject to such misinterpretation because of his subservience to the dialectic method of the contemporary German philosopher Hegel, whom he studied with great reverence. For example, after vigorously building up a case, as though he meant it, for war being *in theory* subject to no limitations of violence, he goes on to develop with equal vigor the point that *in practice* there must be many qualifications to the theoretical absolute. In this procedure we recognize the Hegelian thesis and antithesis, leading to a synthesis.[11] His method, plus the natural inclination of a searching mind to work all around a subject, makes Clausewitz quotable on whichever side of an issue one desires, and he has been amply abused in this fashion. Moreover, he is of all the noteworthy writers on strategy the one least susceptible to condensation. The efforts in that direction have almost invariably condensed out the wisdom and left the clichés, or rather what have since become clichés.

The Decline of Strategic Theory

Now we must consider what developed from the groundwork which Clausewitz and Jomini so brilliantly laid down at the beginning of the century preceding the first World War. The military profession is not a scholarly calling, as its members would be the first to insist. It requires in its leaders, and therefore emphasizes in the training of its officers, character traits such as loyalty, physical courage, boldness, decisiveness, and above all leadership. There are also important technical skills to be absorbed. These are not incompatible

[11] *Ibid.*, bk. 1, ch. 1. Hegel, ten years older than Clausewitz, died in the same cholera epidemic (1831) that took off the latter.

with scholarly values, but they do not permit much accent upon the latter, nor will the pursuit of normal duties leave much time for them. Lord Kitchener, Britain's first soldier in World War I until his death in 1916, once said that until laid up with a broken leg he had had no time to read and only his own experience to go on. Except for the physical injury and its consequence, his experience was certainly not exceptional.

The military profession is, however, an esoteric calling, requiring familiarity with specific tools, skills, and organizational peculiarities that are likely to be utterly bewildering to the scholar outside the profession. Therefore the study of strategy, which is in part historical but in larger part also analytical and speculative, has tended in the past to fall between two stools, being neglected by the professions of arms and of scholarship alike.

Until the coming of atomic weapons, which produced such a wrench from the past, writings in strategy were usually built upon critical study of the military history available to their authors. Military history provided vicarious experience, broader in scope and cheaper to acquire than that available to one individual in his lifetime. To be useful the history had to be accurate and preferably recent, it had to be read, and it had to be interpreted with insight and imagination.

Where it was not so read and so interpreted, the officers responsible for the formulation of service doctrine tended to rely exclusively on that inevitably incomplete military experience which was intensely personal to them or their immediate colleagues. As a result we have seen deep and persistent military controversies where each side has implemented its arguments with historical "facts" wrested out of context and otherwise distorted.

Foch and His School: Romanticists in Strategy

It is instructive to consider how the classics fared in the period leading up to World War I. Ferdinand Foch, whose fame as the Allied generalissimo towards the end of the war has tended to obscure his earlier renown as a theorist, avowed himself an admirer of Clausewitz, though it is hard to find the evidence of it in his writings. Where Clausewitz was the philosopher, wrestling with conflicting insights into apparent contradictions, Foch was the instructor, intent on indoctrination. His aim was not to explore but to persuade, which meant inevitably to oversimplify and exaggerate. As the intellectual leader of the "Young Turks" on the French General Staff prior to the war, Foch was influential enough in his time; but he is interesting to us also because he represents far better than the classic and complex Clausewitz the current of military thinking in our own time. We shall later find Douhet in the same current, even though he seems to be swimming against it.

Foch was a forceful lecturer and writer and an equally effective soldier. On the battlefields of World War I he sensed more quickly than most of his colleagues the weakness or irrelevance of some of the notions which, as a writer and as a professor at the *École supérieure de guerre*, he had been so instrumental in promulgating. It took real magnanimity as well as insight for him to say, as he is reported to have said to his staff following the disastrous French offensives at the frontiers in the opening weeks of the war: "Gentlemen, it remains for you to forget what you have learnt, and for me to do the contrary to what I have taught you." Unfortunately, it was another two years before this sentiment, if he ever actually expressed it, was to signify for him much more than a momentary mood.

Foch frequently inveighed against all dogmas—except his own, which were couched in admirably terse and epigrammatic language. His talent for expression no doubt enhanced his influence. The historical knowledge he possessed was always at the command of his convictions, and it was also colored by the literary romanticism of the century in which he was reared.

The romantic in Foch is revealed partly by the role he gave to the supreme commander, and especially to the quality of *will* in that exalted figure. Let us be clear that he was not creating a complete myth. No one will deny the importance of spirit as well as competence in a supreme commander. It is no doubt true also that the tightness of control exercised by the French High Command, in contrast to the looseness of the German, had a good deal to do with the outcome of the first Battle of the Marne. But that is not the same as saying that Joffre was a genius, or that his will became the dominant force in the battle. The question is one of emphasis, and when one reiterates, as Foch did, that the courage or fortitude of the least soldier is simply a reflection of that of the supreme commander, the emphasis is getting pretty extreme.

One of the consequences of the emphasis on the role of the commander was an insistence on *unity of doctrine*, in order to assure a perfect coordination of effort on the part of all subordinate commanders towards the objective in the mind of the supreme commander. Now unity of doctrine is no doubt a good thing for exactly the reason mentioned, but to inculcate it also means, unavoidably, to intensify that ancient disease of the profession, *rigidity* of doctrine. Rigidity of doctrine we have always with us, and it is hardly necessary to devote a powerful intellectual effort to advancing it.

Another consequence of the emphasis on the commander's will was the exaltation of the moral, or what we now call morale. In an era when war material was changing so rapidly and threatening to put the general under the dominance of the scientist and engineer, how comforting it was to be reminded of Napoleon's dictum that "the moral is to the material as three is to one." Clausewitz, to be sure, had gone out of his way to point out that armies, even when commanded by Napoleon, had rarely defeated opposing armies of as much as twice their size—thus indicating a certain boundary on the influence not only of morale but also of skill in generalship. And when greatly superior forces were defeated by lesser ones, Clausewitz hinted, it was usually as much owing to gross incompetence on the one side as to exceptional competence on the other. Let us acknowledge the genius of blunder as well as the genius of correct action! The former has appeared at least as often as the latter and has had at least as much influence on history. But this unromantic view would not have appealed to Foch.

The Exaltation of the Offensive

Related to his emphasis on the commander's will, and also romantic in its orientation, was Foch's exaltation of the offensive. We shall see later how Douhet responded to this theme, rejecting it in relation to ground warfare—on the basis of World War I experience—but embracing it in unqualified form for aerial war. There are other reasons, however, for paying special attention to Foch's doctrines on the offensive.

Military doctrine is universally, and has been since the time of Napoleon, imbued with the "spirit of the offensive." There are some very good reasons for this, which we shall review elsewhere. As with many other ideas which have a sound basis in reason, constant and fervent reiteration has created distortions, like the attitude, for example, which regards a healthy respect for enemy capabilities as defense-minded and hence ignoble. In war-planning studies, the fact that the other fellow is also indoctrinated with the spirit of the offensive may be grudgingly admitted on the first page or two where postulates or "hypotheses" are set down, but rarely does it become a real operational consideration in the body of the study. In the usually long interludes between wars, it is both easier and pleasanter to dwell on what we shall do to the enemy on D-day than on what he will seek to do to us. Our plans are much more easily developed and pushed to a properly offensive conclusion if we can imagine the enemy as inert or at least passive.

We shall return to this theme at a more appropriate place; but perhaps these preliminary remarks will serve to justify what would otherwise seem a disproportionate amount of space and attention to Foch's theories of the offensive. These are presented here as a case study in military aberration, and of a kind of aberration which in one form or another is always reappearing. If our considerations bring us to dwell on events of World War I, which is too fast receding from the memories of present-day officers, we have no apologies. For that war, the greatest catastrophe in modern times, may have more lessons for the future than World War II, which was in fact its offspring.

Clausewitz had reasoned that the defensive was the "stronger form of war," since it was normally and appropriately adapted by the weaker side. The abiding reason for this was that the defender could always exploit "the advantage of the ground." Clausewitz was careful to distinguish between a defensive attitude and passivity. A properly active defense could also exploit the advantages of initiative and surprise, which were by no means reserved exclusively to the attacker. "The defender," he said, "is in a condition to surprise incessantly, throughout the course of the engagement." To be sure, an army on the attack derives from the act of attacking a feeling of superiority which stimulates its courage, "but the feeling very soon merges into the more general and more powerful one which is imparted to an army by victory or defeat, by the talent or incapacity of its general."

If the defense is properly conceived and ordered, "attack will no longer seem so easy and infallible as it does to the vague imagination of those who can only see in the offensive courage, strength of will and movement; in the defensive, helplessness and apathy." All this being acknowledged, it is of course hardly necessary to add that the winning of a favorable decision requires that the defender ultimately go over to the offensive and be successful in it. Indeed, "a swift and vigorous transition to attack—the flashing sword of vengeance—is the most brilliant point of the defensive."

The aggressor attacks *because* he has or thinks he has a significant superiority, momentary or otherwise. "Whoever is ready first, if the advantage of surprise is sufficiently great, goes to work offensively for *this* reason, and he who is ready last can only in some measure, by the advantages of the defensive, make up for the disadvantage which threatens him."[12]

Jomini, too, acknowledged that "in tactical operations the

[12] *Ibid.*, pp. 320-332. For an interesting comparison with contemporary Soviet doctrine, see R. L. Garthoff, *Soviet Military Doctrine*, Free Press, Glencoe, Ill., 1953, ch. IV.

advantages resulting from taking the initiative are balanced by the disadvantages." Waterloo was hard to forget. But there is significantly greater fervor when he expresses the view, already accepted by Clausewitz, that "the best thing for an army on the defensive is to know *how* to take the offensive at a proper time and *to take it*." Moreover, he insists, *in strategy* "the army taking the initiative has the great advantage of bringing up its troops and striking a blow where it chooses, while the army which awaits an attack is anticipated in every direction, is often taken unawares, and is obliged to regulate its movements by those of the enemy."[13] Even more than Clausewitz he had a reverence for boldness in a commander. "I would make [war] brisk, bold, impetuous, perhaps sometimes even audacious."

Jomini, as we have seen, was in any case more influential, certainly in France, than Clausewitz, but it happened also that in the period between Jomini and Foch there had appeared in France the brilliant and scholarly work of Colonel Ardant du Picq. Du Picq had become intrigued with the fact that in the famous battles of antiquity the victor always came off with far fewer casualties than the defeated. At Pharsalus, for example, Caesar lost but two hundred soldiers, while of Pompey's army 15,000 perished and more than 24,000 fled only to surrender the following day. The account is Caesar's, but du Picq found it entirely credible, especially since there were many other battles with like results.

Du Picq decided that the losing side must have been the first to give way to fears present on both sides. In running away, the defeated soldiers presented their defenseless backs

---

[13] A. H. Jomini, *Summary of the Art of War*, condensed version ed. by Lt. Col. J. D. Hittle, Military Service Publishing Co., Harrisburg, Pa., 1947, p. 103.

to the pursuers, allowing themselves to be mowed down with impunity. Pompey's original mistake at Pharsalus, he concluded, was in remaining immobile while Caesar's soldiers charged. The stimulus of action and the ardor of attack were felt only among Caesar's men.

Du Picq became entirely absorbed in the psychology of the soldier in combat. His insights were, however, realistic rather than romantic. Discipline, he said, was important because it made men fight despite themselves. Fear was an omnipresent factor in battle, and the general who knew best how to control it would be the successful one. "Absolute bravery," du Picq held, "is infinitely rare, because in the face of danger the animal sense of self-preservation always gains the upper hand." And again: "Are there so few really brave men among so many soldiers? Alas, yes."

Another and related point made by du Picq was to have a heavy influence on subsequent thinking. He insisted that war does not become deadlier with the improvement of weapons. Fighting simply takes place at greater ranges, and men take greater precautions against being hit. "Man is capable of standing before a certain amount of terror; beyond that he flees from battle." However, he was far from dismissing the importance of the tactical changes wrought by modern weapons (by which he understood the weapons of the 1860s, including those of the American Civil War). The nature of ancient arms, he said, required close order, in which it was easier to maintain discipline. "Modern arms require open order and are at the same time of such terrible power that against them too often discipline is broken." He pointed out also that in modern armies losses could be as great for the victor as for the vanquished, whereas ancient battles were massacres in which the victor often had negligible

46

losses. The fact that the modern soldier is often a replacement fighting among strangers further burdens morale.

Du Picq's entire published writings were, after his death, gathered within the covers of one small book.[14] His literary style was unusually lucid and forceful. These facts undoubtedly increased his influence on the generation which followed him. Easy as it was to master his work, however, one has the feeling that detached quotations from it had more far-reaching effects than the work itself. His book, like so many others, was ransacked for rules of thumb. One of the most frequently uttered mottoes of the French Army prior to 1914 was a quotation from du Picq: "He will win who has the resolution to advance." His incisive and important remarks about the influence of modern arms on battle tactics were slighted in favor of the grosser recollection that he had generally discounted their impact on casualties.

The school of which Foch was leader sloganized du Picq and romanticized his "lessons." Its members exalted the offensive in all its forms, tactical as well as strategic, and refused to be confined by any considerations of circumstance. A conspicuous coiner of maxims among France's "Young Turks" was Colonel de Grandmaison, among whose often-quoted sayings we find the following: "In the offensive, imprudence is the best safeguard. The least caution destroys all its efficacy." Grandmaison, who became chief of the operations branch of the General Staff, was the favored pupil

[14] The standard American translation into English, by Col. J. N. Greely and Maj. R. C. Cotton, was published under the title *Battle Studies*, Military Service Publishing Co., Harrisburg, Pa., 1920, 1947. Purporting to contain all du Picq's extant writings, the book totals only 273 pages, including some 36 pages of introduction by other writers. Du Picq died of wounds received near Metz in August 1870, while leading his regiment into its initial engagement of the Franco-Prussian War.

and protégé of Foch. Theirs was the religion of *l'offensive brutale et à outrance*.

Did no one admonish them with a soft "Gentlemen, consider the machine gun"? Du Picq himself might conceivably have done so, had he been alive, but Foch's generation scorned it. Had not Napoleon III relied overmuch on a machine gun, his famous *mitrailleuse*? The basic hallmark of the school which again reveals the romantic element in their thinking, was the subordination of the material to the moral. The Prussians, insisted Foch, had beaten the Austrians at Sadowa in 1866 not because of the needle gun, but because of superior generalship, and for the same reason they had beaten the French in 1870 "despite being outclassed in ordnance." The latter view, incidentally, is only partially correct. There is no doubt that the French were beaten in 1870 because of their inept generalship, but it is not true that they possessed the superior ordnance. The French had in their *chassepot* a breech-loading rifle superior to the German needle gun, but their field artillery was markedly inferior in quantity and quality to the German. However, whether correct or not, Foch's views helped guarantee that the French would enter World War I with an allotment of two machine guns per battalion as compared with the Germans' six, which also turned out to be inadequate.

In at least one place Foch did indeed acknowledge that "moral superiority, resulting from numbers, formations, etc., is no longer sufficient today with modern weapons: their effects are too demoralizing."[15] But this is a statement such as authors sometimes throw in for the record without any intention of letting it influence the argument. Concerning

[15] F. Foch, *The Principles of War*, trans. by de Morinni, Fly, New York, 1918, pp. 370f.

its effect on his offensive theory, this acknowledgment was nullified by Foch's remarkable dictum that "all improvements in firearms add to the strength of an offensive intelligently planned because the attackers, choosing their ground, can concentrate on it so much greater a volume of fire."[16]

Foch did not deny that on the battlefield the attacker might lose more men than the defending opponent. In one telling passage he pointed with approval to Napoleon's conduct at Wagram, where the Emperor sent Macdonald to charge the Archduke Charles' center with fifty battalions of densely massed infantry, that is, some 22,500 men, of whom barely 1,500 survived. Foch emphasized with enthusiasm that the attacking mass was powerless to act by fire, because of the formation it had assumed, and that during the advance it did "absolutely no harm to the enemy, while suffering much itself. . . ." He then summed up the results thus: "In short, the decimated troops beat the decimating troops, and they decide the army's advance, that is victory on the March-feld. The result was obtained not from material effects—they are all in favor of the defeated side—but from a purely moral action."[17]

It may be a slight digression from our present theme, but useful in other respects, to indicate how other historians, free of the need to prove a point, have summed up the same battle. According to standard accounts, among the factors that Foch neglected to mention were the following: (1) Napoleon's whole force at Wagram, comprising over 180,000 men on the battlefield, outnumbered that of Charles by a ratio of at least three to two; (2) the Austrian retirement was forced not by Macdonald's "decimated" battalions, which were quite uselessly destroyed by the Austrian artillery, but

[16] *Ibid.*, p. 33.   [17] *Ibid.*, p. 322.

by the movement of the undecimated divisions under Davout on the right wing, which threatened to envelop the Austrian flank; (3) Charles retired to a new position a short distance away in perfect order, full of fight, unmolested by any pursuit, after imposing far more casualties than he suffered; and (4) the strain on French morale was revealed by a widespread panic at the appearance of the advance patrols of the Archduke's reinforcements, who arrived too late to take part in the battle.

It is interesting, too, to see how Foch treats the conduct of Napoleon at Borodino which, as we noted above, Clausewitz mentioned with such approval: "Remember Bonaparte engaging the very last soldier at Aboukir, and Napoleon in 1812 saving his reserve at the Moskova, because instead of being a young and ambitious general with nothing to lose and all to gain, he has become an Emperor with much to lose."[18] How sublimely contemptuous! There is no room here for the thought that while the general may be commendably reckless with his own career, the nation he serves has much more to lose than that.

The phrase "history teaches," when encountered in argument, usually portends bad history and worse logic. But seldom has it resulted in such brazen and portentous distortions as it did in the hands of Foch and his followers.

Scores of battles in the century after Napoleon demonstrated conclusively that, even before the modern machine gun, the massed frontal attack upon a dug-in and fairly determined defender resulted almost invariably in massive but useless casualties for the attacker.[19] The American Civil

[18] *Ibid.*, p. 355.

[19] See, in this connection, the article by "Athos" entitled "Defense Against Mass Attacks," *Journal of the Royal United Service Institution,* xcviii (February 1953), 76-81.

War began with the leaders of both sides worshipping at the shrine of Austerlitz, but Lee's losses at Malvern Hill in the Seven Days Battle taught him better (except for a lapse at Gettysburg), and the northern leaders absorbed the lesson shortly thereafter at Second Bull Run and Fredericksburg. Near the end, when Grant's overwhelming superiority caused him at Cold Harbor momentarily to abandon maneuver and resort to bold frontal assault, he achieved only a costly and very sobering repulse.

If Foch and his school insisted on regarding the American Civil War as a mere backwoods affair (as du Picq had also done), they had plenty of examples involving European armies. Even the Franco-Prussian War, the maneuvers of which Foch had presumably studied with thoroughness, had tactical lessons that he ignored. The French reliance on the bayonet (*l'arme blanche*) and on "irresistible French *élan*" had provided the invaders with the "advantages of a strategic offensive combined with the tactical defensive."[20] When at last at Gravelotte-Saint Privat the French leaders found themselves sufficiently bereft of *élan* to use entrenchments and natural cover in a defensive battle, they administered a severe tactical defeat to the enemy. The French military historian, Colonel Jean Colin, later deduced the lesson of 1870: "Well-chosen and well-arranged defensive positions, even when very weakly held, could not be carried." This lesson was again confirmed at Plevna in the Russo-Turkish War of 1877. In several major battles of the Russo-Japanese War of 1904-1905, which saw the first important use of a modern machine gun, it was demonstrated that the attacker could carry entrenchments only by dint of great superiority and at the cost of considerable time and disproportionately

[20] L. Montross, *War Through the Ages*, Harper, New York, 1946, p. 649.

heavy losses. This lesson, incidentally, was one which Count Schlieffen in Germany thoroughly absorbed and which completely dominated his famous plan.[21]

There was another component to the French conviction. "We, the French," Foch had said, "possess a fighter, a soldier, undeniably superior to the one beyond the Vosges in his racial qualities, activity, intelligence, spirit, power of exaltation, devotion, patriotism." This was neither the first nor the last time that bad anthropology contributed to bad strategy. The Germans paid dearly in two world wars for their contempt of the Slavs, as Napoleon had a century earlier. One recalls also the American conviction, even after Pearl Harbor, that the Japanese were congenitally "imitative"; yet these supposedly unimaginative people, who had demonstrated the offensive use of aircraft carriers at Pearl Harbor, had the wit at Leyte Gulf to put all their remaining and by then useless carriers into their decoy force, and thereby completely fool their American adversary. What a really marvelous idea!

The Loss of the War Aim

What we must finally notice about Foch's formulas for waging war is that something important is absent from them, something which if present would have compromised his entire theoretical structure. What is absent is any consideration of the problem of relating tactics and strategy to war aims and objectives. With Foch war became altogether an end in itself.[22] In this respect he reflects only too faith-

[21] E. Bircher and W. Bode, *Schlieffen, Mann und Idee*, Nauck, Zurich, 1937, pp. 191f.

[22] By one of those odd quirks of distortion that result from the handing-down of isolated quotations, Foch is often quoted in the literature today as having asked the question, *De quoi s'agit-il?*—"What is it all about?"

52

fully the bent of his entire generation of soldiers. Lost completely is the cast of thought that makes Clausewitz both timeless and profound, his constant awareness that war is a political act, fought for a purpose outside itself. True, Clausewitz had cautioned against unduly tempering violence lest it render one weak against the ruthless, but he nevertheless insisted that the end must govern the means. The generation that was to fight World War I remembered only the injunction against tempering violence. "Blood is the price of victory" was the one dictum of Clausewitz they quoted everlastingly.

Less arresting, but infinitely wiser, was the admonition they forgot: "No war is begun, or at least no war should be begun if people acted wisely, without first finding an answer to the question: what is to be attained by and in war?" The influence of this question, Clausewitz insisted, "manifests itself down to the smallest details of action."[23] Foch gives little indication in his writings of having thought about the matter at all.

He even descends in one place to the old "honor of the battlefield" conception, for he refers to the conquest of the enemy's ground as "the visible sign of victory."[24] For the rest, it is mostly a matter of making the enemy "feel defeated." The destruction of the enemy's armed forces, of course, he regards as a good thing, and one may credit him with assuming that the general must at the same time avoid

---

This is usually interpreted as showing his profound concern with the objective of war. Another quoted remark of his is, "War is not the supreme aim, because after war there is peace." See, for example, Sir John Slessor, *Strategy for the West*, Morrow, New York, 1954, p. 9. In such quotations from Foch it is always necessary to ask whether the statement was made before, during, or after World War I.

[23] Clausewitz, *op.cit.*, p. 569.   [24] Foch, *op.cit.*, p. 312.

the destruction of his own forces. But he nowhere asks the question that Clausewitz forced himself to ask: what if I *cannot* destroy the enemy's forces, or cannot do so without also destroying my own?[25]

One also has to assume that in the backs of their minds Foch and his contemporaries coupled their conception of ruthless and unqualified violence on the battlefield with one of magnanimity in the peace terms offered, for only an enemy government that need not fear losing much by a negotiated peace could indulge the luxury of letting itself "feel defeated" at an early stage in the proceedings.

It is true that the determination of war objectives is a high policy function that, in theory, is or should be reserved to the civilian leaders. But in practice military leaders inevitably enjoy immense authority over all phases of the conduct of the war. They do so in all their peacetime military planning, when few others in authority seem to be much interested in their thoughts and decisions or in the operations of war. It really cannot be otherwise. Regardless of where ultimate authority resides—and in the American democracy there is no question about that—it is a matter of great moment that only the military and their immediate retainers brood persistently during peacetime upon the prob-

[25] See especially Clausewitz, *op.cit.*, bk. 7, ch. xxii. The title of this chapter, "The Culminating Point of Victory," refers to the point at which a successful offensive begins to incur excessive losses and undue risk of ultimate defeat. It might be regarded as the qualifying corollary to the so-called principle of pursuit, i.e., as the principle of knowing when to stop. There are many examples from recent military history of a belligerent permitting his successes to carry him to overcommitment and thence to disaster (e.g., Japanese conquests between Pearl Harbor and the Battle of Midway; Hitler's offensives in Russia; MacArthur's rush to the Yalu in 1950). Yet I have never observed in a contemporary strategic essay any reference to or development of Clausewitz's concept of the "culminating point." One finds, of course, plenty about the "principle of pursuit."

lems of war. Those who have done the thinking and controlled the preparations will at the moment of crisis be ready to invoke the decisions they have long since made. The capacity to say them nay depends not alone on the enjoyment of higher authority, but much more on the possession of an alternative idea.

The Test in World War I

Let us now touch briefly on the application in World War I of the theories we have examined. We have already intimated that the first of the world wars may well contain more lessons for the future than the second. Perhaps that assumption is only the result of the greater perspective with which we view the first war. Yet if the total war of the future is fated to be one where victory is pursued blindly, and therefore at wholly incommensurate costs which destroy its meaning, it will be more akin to the first than the second of the two world wars. World War II also had plenty about it that was tragic, and some have even called it an "unnecessary war." But Hitler clamored to be destroyed with an insistence that could not be denied, and to destroy him and his Fascist colleagues justified a war in a way that the destruction of the Hohenzollern and Hapsburg dynasties never could. Also World War II mercifully entailed for the western powers—largely because of the strategic "misfortune" of their having been ejected from the Continent at an early stage—much less carnage than did World War I.

World War I was the purposeless war, which no one seemed to know how to prevent and which, once begun, no one seemed to know how to stop. The world it changed was for a generation a much worse place politically than it was before. If the second World War enhanced the power of the great communist state, the first World War created it and also gave rise to the corruptions of Fascism and Nazism.

World War I was also a war which, because of technological changes of much lesser degree than those which are new to us now, completely baffled the military leaders who had to fight it. They were not incompetent men, but they had been reared under a regime of maxims and precepts which bore no relation to the situation in which they found themselves. Their ability to make reasonable deductions from the events in which they were caught up seemed to be paralyzed by the very magnitude of those events. It was such a situation as Clausewitz had described where "man, who in great things as well as in small usually acts more on particular prevailing ideas and emotions than according to strictly logical conclusions, is hardly conscious of his confusion, onesidedness, and inconsistency."[26] Their bafflement and confusion contributed enormously to the tragedy. For while all major wars are bound to be costly in lives and wealth, World War I proved that it makes a great deal of difference how they are fought.

During World War I the British military leaders, who had not been tutored by Foch and seemed hardly aware of his writings, were hardly less enamored of the strategic offensive than the French. What distinguished the French school on the doctrinal level was its utter disregard of contextual circumstances, such as enemy strength and intentions. As Churchill was later to say (concerning the Nivelle offensive): "However absorbed a commander may be in the elaboration of his own thoughts, it is necessary sometimes to take the enemy into consideration." The French were to

[26] Clausewitz, *op.cit.*, p. 570.

fight even their defensive battles with such violently offensive and unyielding tactics that they alone of the three great armies on the western front managed to lose more men than their opponents even when they were on the strategic defensive, as at Verdun.

The Germans also approached World War I with an offensive plan, but it depended upon an enveloping movement which marshalled overwhelming superiority (three to one in the original plan) in the vital area of maneuver. For the sake of gaining the necessary local superiority the German planners were ready to exploit the intrinsically greater strength of the tactical defense against enemy frontal attacks in order to hold with the barest minimum of forces not only the eastern frontiers but also that large portion of the western front south of Metz. They looked upon the possibility that the French might launch an offensive of their own in Lorraine, as in fact they did, as a "favor" (*Liebesdienst*) not to be relied upon.

The single French general who wished to deploy the French army to counter the Schlieffen movement, which he accurately predicted, was none less than the Commander-in-Chief-designate in the event of war, General Michel; but in 1911 he was dismissed from his post as Vice-President of the Superior Council of War because his singular views had cost him the confidence of the General Staff. Under his successor, Joffre, there was adopted the egregious Plan xvii, which, since it proposed to make the Germans dance to the French tune, could disregard German intentions. The device to accomplish this was a simple headlong attack eastward of the whole French field army.

When the test came in 1914, both the German Schlieffen Plan and the French Plan xvii failed. Both sides had been utterly confident of success, as staffs are wont to be about their laboriously prepared plans. The whole rationale of the commitment on each side had depended on a quick decisive victory. Normally in war the failure of one side spells the success of the other, but by a supreme irony of fate, largely abetted by the machine gun which both sides had in different degrees underrated, the plans of both had now miscarried. What was to be done?

Schlieffen himself had intimated one answer: call off the war! But Schlieffen was now dead, and whatever influence he might have had if alive (assuming he had retained the same conviction) would have been restricted to the German side. The Germans had won a great victory over the Russians in East Prussia and held a position in the west deep within French territory. The desirability of making concessions could not impress itself strongly upon them. The Allies, on the other hand, had suffered a tremendous loss of prestige, position, and blood, but yet had averted total disaster. The situation could hardly have been less favorable for negotiations.

The will on both sides to continue the war to "victory" was just as strong among the civilians in the respective governments as among the military, but the latter had to provide the ideas about how to continue. On the Allied side the conclusion was simple: continue as before. At each stage the attitude was that the last offensive had failed but the next one would surely succeed. What happened in the next year of the war has been eloquently summed up by Sir Winston Churchill:

In the series of great offensive pressures which Joffre delivered during the whole of the spring and autumn of 1915, the French suffered nearly 1,300,000 casualties. They inflicted upon the Germans in the same period and the same operations 506,000 casualties. They gained no territory worth mentioning, and no strategic advantage of any kind. This was the worst year of the Joffre regime. Gross as were the mistakes of the Battle of the Frontiers, glaring as had been the errors of the First Shock, they were eclipsed by the insensate obstinacy and lack of comprehension which, without any large numerical superiority, without adequate artillery or munitions, without any novel mechanical method, without any pretence of surprise or manoeuvre, without any reasonable hope of victory, continued to hurl the heroic but limited manhood of France at the strongest entrenchments, at uncut wire and innumerable machine guns served with cold skill. The responsibilities of this lamentable phase must be shared in a subordinate degree by Foch, who under Joffre's orders, but as an ardent believer, conducted the prolonged Spring offensive in Artois, the most sterile and prodigal of all.[27]

Let us remember about the soldiers of World War I that it was their horizons rather than their skills which proved so disastrously limited. They were confident they had the right answers. And there is nothing in the stars that guarantees our own generation against comparable errors.

[27] Churchill, *op.cit.*, p. 568. The extraordinary chapter which contains this statement is entitled "The Blood Test." See also the volume written to correct some of the "extravagances" of Mr. Churchill, *The World Crisis by Winston Churchill: A Criticism*, by Lord Sydenham of Combe, Admiral Sir Reginald Bacon, General Sir Frederick Maurice, General Sir W. D. Bird, and Sir Charles Oman, Hutchinson, London, 1928. Mr. Churchill's chapter cited above aroused the particular ire of his military critics. While they exposed some definite errors on Mr. Churchill's part (and committed some serious errors of their own), it is clear from our present perspective that he was basically right in contending (1) that all the Allied offensives on the western front prior to August 1918 accomplished nothing commensurate with the terrible losses sustained, and (2) that in all of them the attacking Allies suffered far heavier casualties than the defending Germans. This point is confirmed by final statistics of total losses by both sides on the western front. See, for an opposing view, Maj. Thomas R. Phillips, "Attack or Defense," *Infantry Journal*, XLVII (March-April 1940), 38-111.

The years 1916-1917 saw a comparable series of great, costly, and futile "pushes" at the Somme, at Arras, on the Aisne, and at Passchendaele. During this period there was only one great German offensive, that of Verdun in the spring of 1916. It is hard to see any gain to the attackers in these fierce tests, since they almost invariably lost far more heavily than the defenders and since the "offensive spirit" which they were so desirous of preserving could hardly be kept alive in men who were consumed in the process. In addition, the failure of the Nivelle offensive in the spring of 1917 resulted in the demoralization of the French Army, with open mutiny in no fewer than sixteen separate Army Corps.

Perhaps the ultimate emptiness of the attachment to the offensive idea is revealed in the words which Sir William Robertson, Chief of the Imperial General Staff, wrote to the British field commander, Sir Douglas Haig, during the latter stages of the Passchendaele offensive: "I confess I stick to it [i.e., support of Haig's current offensive] more because I see nothing better, and because my instinct prompts me to stick to it, than because of any good argument by which I can support it." Churchill's comment is stern: "These are terrible words when used to sustain the sacrifices of nearly four hundred thousand men."[28]

Finally, in the spring of 1918 came the great Ludendorff offensive, which seemed to come the closest to success of any that had thus far been launched on the western front, but which in its ultimate failure spelled the final ruin of the German army. Then Foch, now effectively supreme commander of all the Allied forces, faced with a sprawled

[28] Churchill, *op.cit.*, p. 739. See also Leon Wolff, *In Flanders Fields*, Viking, New York, 1958.

and exhausted enemy, aided by fresh American divisions, and strengthened with large numbers of tanks as well as huge stores of ordnance and munitions of all kinds, confronted a situation where his offensive theories, somewhat modified by brutal experience, could at last be applied with success. So came "vindication."

The Object Was to Win

It must be asked: what were these men after that they were willing to pay so high a price for it? Strangely, this question has rarely been asked in all the years that have since passed. The high commands of both sides in World War I have often been condemned for their methods, as well as for their arrogance, insensibility, and what not, but almost never for their lack of objective! Clearly, each side was trying to achieve "victory." But what did that mean? It is abundantly evident that for the commands of both sides the term was a mere symbol, almost devoid of content save that it determined who asked whom for an armistice. In a very literal sense it concerned simply the question of who was to cry "uncle"!

The relevant thoughts of Field Marshal Sir Douglas Haig, commander of the B.E.F. during the last three years of the war, have come to us through his intimate diaries. His references there to war aims are sparse and indeterminate. One of the first reports an attitude of his predecessor in command of the British field armies, Field Marshal Sir John French. In an entry for September 28, 1915, while French was still in command, Haig says: "He seemed tired of the war, and said that 'in his opinion we ought to take the first opportunity of concluding peace, otherwise England would be ruined'! I could not agree, but said we cannot make peace till the

German military power is beaten."[29] A year later, on September 6, 1916, during the Battle of the Somme, Haig writes: "For several reasons Derby is afraid Asquith may be willing to discuss peace terms in November or December, if Germany were to offer to give back Alsace-Lorraine, etc., to France." This is to Haig a dismal thought, but from his own conversation with Mr. Asquith he is convinced that the latter "seems fully determined to fight on until Germany is vanquished."[30]

Another year later, on August 28, 1917, during the Passchendaele offensive, Haig remarks to his American visitor, the elder Henry Morgenthau: "My chief fear [is] that Germany might offer in October or November terms of peace which the Allied Governments might accept, though not giving all that we ought to receive."[31] It is not indicated that he has anything specific in mind either as to the terms likely to be offered or as to those that might be acceptable. On March 19, 1918, on the eve of the great German offensive, he replies to Churchill's query about his views on making peace: "From the point of view of British interests alone, if the enemy will give the terms Lloyd George recently laid down, we ought to accept them at once; even some modification of our demands for Alsace-Lorraine might be given way on. At the present moment, England is in a stronger position than she has ever been and by continuing the war she will get weaker financially and in manpower. On the other hand, America will get stronger and finally will dictate *her* peace which may not suit Great Britain."[32]

Finally, on October 19, 1918, Haig recommends to Prime Minister Lloyd George that the terms of the imminent

---

[29] *The Private Papers of Douglas Haig, 1914-1919,* ed. by Robert Blake, Eyre & Spottiswoode, London, 1952, p. 104.
[30] *Ibid.,* pp. 163f.   [31] *Ibid.,* p. 252.   [32] *Ibid.,* p. 294.

armistice should require Germany to evacuate Belgium, occupied France, and Alsace-Lorraine and to return Belgium and French rolling stock. As for making further demands, he comments: "But why expend more British lives—and for what?" He does not identify himself with Field Marshal Sir Henry Wilson's view that the Germans should be required to lay down their arms, nor with Lord Milner's that the west bank of the Rhine should be temporarily occupied until the Germans complied with the peace terms. He is dead set against permitting the French to enter Germany "to pay off old scores."[33]

Thus after two years, during which he has presided over the liquidation of British lives at a greater rate than has ever occurred before or since in history, he recommends *in victory* the imposition of exactly those terms which in September of 1916 he feared might become a basis for a negotiated peace. It is not that his ideas about a proper peace have meanwhile changed. They were chivalrous at the end, and must have been so all along. As is abundantly evident throughout, the question of *who* states the terms, and how, is to Haig much more important than the question of *what* the terms are. To have an ally like America state them is almost as disagreeable as having the enemy do so. And then there is that special, quite separate purpose of having Germany "vanquished"—a purpose which has almost nothing to do with the severity of the terms contemplated!

On the French side, Foch was bent on somewhat larger goals, but was also on the whole markedly restrained. When Clemenceau asked Foch what he thought of the proposal of President Poincaré and of the American Generals Pershing and Bliss to deny the Germans an armistice and to fight for

[33] *Ibid.*, pp. 333f.

unconditional surrender all the way to Berlin, the Marshal replied: "To continue the struggle longer would incur great risk. It would mean that perhaps fifty or a hundred thousand more Frenchmen would be killed, not counting the Allies, and for quite problematic results. . . . Enough blood, alas! has already been shed, and that should suffice." Clemenceau emphatically agreed: "Marshal, I am entirely of the same opinion."[34] There is no reason to suppose that the politicians were any more clear-headed than the soldiers about the goals towards which they had been driving their peoples and their armies. For them too the symbol of "victory" was self-sufficient. It is clear that they were much less interested in being able to dictate terms, having no clear conception of what they wanted to dictate, than in avoiding being dictated to.

The politicians did show themselves much more sensitive than their military brethren to the price being exacted for the undefined "victory." They sensed that the common soldier was not merely a means for fighting but also one for whom the fight was being waged. They recognized that the state is its people, and not some disembodied abstraction. In the beginning no one had any idea what the ultimate price would be, but as the war progressed the generals tended by and large to accept, and the politicians by and large to resist, the notion that competitive attrition in manpower could be adopted as a valid standard of military success. The military contemptuously dismissed the misgivings of the politicians as a mere "squeamishness about casualties" stimulated by a concern for the next election.[35]

[34] Jere Clemens King, *Generals and Politicians*, University of California Press, Berkeley, 1951, pp. 238f.

[35] One example among many is to be found in the following excerpt

In a "secret committee" of the French Parliament, which met in June of 1916 to discuss the current events at Verdun, the first speaker was a Deputy who had been wounded in the early months of the war. If the French forces, he said, "melt away at the same rate as in the preceding months, France may emerge victorious from the struggle, but she will be exhausted and condemned to become a nation of second rank." He pointed out that Germany had experienced on two fronts hardly more deaths than France had suffered on one, though France was far below Germany in population and birth rate. He condemned the madness of "uninterrupted partial offensives which result in no appreciable change of strategic importance, but only in murderous losses." The name of the Deputy, incidentally, was André Maginot.[36]

Two years later this protest was in effect echoed by Winston Churchill, then Minister of Munitions, when in a minute to the War Cabinet early in March of 1918 he asserted that the British were "merely exchanging lives upon a scale at once more frightful than anything that has been witnessed before in the world, and too modest to produce a decision."[37] In the previous winter, Lloyd George, appalled by what had been happening at Passchendaele, had deliberately withheld in England troops which Haig was demanding as re-

---

from Haig's diary entry for April 15, 1916: "For the first hour of the meeting, the 'Civilians' and the 'Military' wrangled over certain [manpower] figures. This really did not interest me, and I felt the real issue of the war in the 'Civilians'' minds was votes, and not the destruction of the German military power." *Op.cit.*, p. 139. The Prime Minister at this time, it may be noted, was still Asquith, and Haig had much greater contempt for the person and presumed motives of Asquith's successor, Lloyd George, whom he regarded as a "thorough impostor."

[36] King, *op.cit.*, pp. 116f.
[37] Churchill, *op.cit.*, p. 570.

inforcements and which might have helped to stem the Ludendorff offensive.[38] These, however, were merely confused efforts on the part of the politicians to halt or retard what they regarded as a willful wastage of men and thus to force upon the commanders a change of military strategies. Committed as they were by promises they had made in order to gain new allies, especially to secure the participation of Italy, they could hardly do more.

It remained for Hans Delbrück in Germany, a student and disciple of Clausewitz, to argue publicly for a union of military and political strategies, in accordance with his constant emphasis on the interrelationship of war and politics. In a series of monthly commentaries in the *Preussische Jahrbücher* he urged the German government to acknowledge a willingness to negotiate coupled with a disclaimer of territorial ambitions in the west, which he reasonably concluded would make the western allies far less resolved upon the tremendous sacrifices they were making.

His arguments helped secure the passage by the Reichstag of the Peace Resolution of July 1917, which substantially expressed his views. During the debate on the resolution, Hindenburg and Ludendorff threatened to resign if it was adopted, and after its passage they effectively kept the government from identifying itself with it, thus enabling the western powers to dismiss the Reichstag's professions as insincere. In despair Delbrück wrote: "Athens went to her doom in the Peloponnesian War because Pericles had no successor. We have fiery Cleons enough in Germany." After the war Delbrück testified before the Reichstag Commission on the Causes of the German Collapse that Germany had lost because the high command had disregarded the most important

[38] *Ibid.*, p. 787.

lesson of history, the interrelationship of politics and war. "To come back once more to that fundamental sentence of Clausewitz, no strategical idea can be considered completely without considering the political goal."[39]

True, the Allies had disregarded the point about as much, and they had nominally won. Yet what they won, and what they lost, prove that Delbrück was in fact putting his finger on the most ominous lesson of World War I. It is that the vast advance in the technology of war which distinguishes the twentieth century from the nineteenth has been attended by *suppression of rational concern with the political aims of war*. During World War I the "national interest" seemed to require that no one should question where that interest lay or what it was. Thus a war that was clearly not being fought for total objectives, such as the political extirpation of the enemy state, was allowed to become total in its methods and intensity.

"That the political point of view should end completely when war begins," Clausewitz had said, "would only be conceivable if wars were struggles of life or death, from pure hatred." In reality, he added, wars were not of that character. "Policy is the intelligent faculty, war only the instrument, and not the reverse. The subordination of the military point of view to the political is, therefore, the only thing that is rationally possible."[40] The war aims entertained by both sides during most of World War I, and the relatively mod-

[39] See Gordon A. Craig's chapter, "Delbrück: The Military Historian," in *Makers of Modern Strategy*, especially pp. 275-282. In this connection, one should not forget the efforts in England of Lord Lansdowne, who circulated in the War Cabinet towards the end of 1916 a confidential letter urging the ending of the war. His famous letter on the same subject to the *Daily Telegraph* in November 1917, caused his repudiation by the government.

[40] Clausewitz, *op.cit.*, p. 598.

erate terms actually imposed by the victors even after the most terrible and desperate of ordeals, proved that Clausewitz was right in maintaining that modern European wars were *not* "struggles of life or death, from pure hatred." But the war was fought as though it were such a struggle, and the subordination of the political point of view to the military, which Clausewitz regarded as not "possible" (meaning not "permissible"), actually took place.

The causes of the decline in rational control of war situations by those responsible for state policy are several and varied, and the attempt to examine them in any systematic way would carry us far beyond the proper confines of this book. The reasons are no doubt largely political and social and yet the great increase in the volume and power of the means of fighting also had much to do with it. For when the whole resources of the nation entered into the scale, "the means available—the efforts which might be called forth— had no longer any definite limits; the energy with which the war itself could be conducted had no longer any counterpoise, and consequently the danger for the adversary had risen to the extreme." Extreme danger obviously requires extreme counter-measures.

The last quotation is not from someone writing after 1918, as one would expect, but is again from Clausewitz, speaking here of the effect of the French Revolution. He immediately goes on to predict, correctly as it turned out, that "it is just as improbable that wars henceforth will all have this grand [absolute] character as that the wide barriers which have been opened to them will ever be completely closed again."[41] Clearly Clausewitz was counting on some continuance of the

[41] *Ibid.*, pp. 582-584.

restraint of reason, which did manifest itself during most of the wars in the century after Waterloo.

The explosion of 1914 revealed trends of which Clausewitz could hardly have dreamed. The soldiers, challenged by the increasing technical and logistic demands of their craft, had been growing increasingly and perhaps excessively professional; but no comparable development had been taking place among politicians, who showed themselves by and large more amateurish in their approach to statecraft than their nineteenth century predecessors. Far from maintaining a firm grip on national policy during wartime, the frightened and often inexperienced ministers fairly abdicated control to the military leaders. The latter, in their increasing preoccupation with means, had abandoned whatever modest concern they had ever felt about ends and objectives.[42]

Thus it was possible for great nations to proceed to battle with an energy previously undreamed of, and almost no sense of direction. "Events," as Churchill put it, "passed very largely outside the scope of conscious choice. Governments and individuals conformed to the rhythm of the tragedy, and swayed and staggered forward in helpless violence, slaughtering and squandering on ever-increasing scales, till injuries were wrought to the structure of human society which a

---

[42] The governments of the Central Powers and of Czarist Russia were sufficiently militarist to begin with, but it is not generally appreciated how much the high commands of democratic countries like France and Britain took into their hands control over a broad range of policy issues. The virtual dictatorship of the General Staff in France is the subject of Prof. J. C. King's previously cited *Generals and Politicians*. For the British side one should read the superb account of the Passchendaele campaign in Leon Wolff's, *In Flanders Fields*, previously cited. Mr. Wolff's book did not become available before the above chapter was completed, and the similarity of views between him and the present author, especially with respect to the lack of war aims of the British leaders, is entirely accidental.

century will not efface, and which may conceivably prove fatal to the present civilization. . . ."[43]

This same war, however, also saw the forging of an instrument destined to be put forward as a means of avoiding in the future any similar insensate and futile blood-letting. This instrument was air power. In 1914 it existed in the form of a few frail craft suited only for observation, but before the war's end it realized or in some measure anticipated every use to which it was to be put in World War II. Even the philosophy that was to govern its uses in the later war had already received before the end of World War I a fairly explicit formulation and expression at the highest levels of authority. The systematic development of that philosophy was to be the work of an Italian officer bent on restoring reason to war and art to strategy. He would attempt to do this by inculcating a closer examination, not indeed of man's purposes, but of the potentialities of his machines and weapons and particularly of those machines which permitted him to overfly the barriers that had so frustrated and exhausted his offensive ardors for the four long years of World War I.

[43] *The World Crisis, 1915*, Scribner's, New York, 1929, pp. 1-2. This passage is not contained in the one-volume edition previously cited.

‹3›

THE HERITAGE OF DOUHET

BRIGADIER GENERAL GIULIO DOUHET possessed the largest and most original mind that has thus far addressed itself to the theory of air power. The few basic ideas which he elaborated were not altogether his own creations—the general merits of strategic bombing were being advanced in British and American official circles more than a year before World War I ended[1]—but he was the first to weave them into a coherent

[1] During World War I a committee under the nominal chairmanship of the Prime Minister, but actually headed by Lt. Gen. Jan C. Smuts, presented to the War Cabinet a report, its second, dated August 17, 1917, which successfully recommended the formation of a separate Air Ministry without waiting for the war's end. The memorandum contained also the following observation: "As far as can at present be foreseen there is absolutely no limit to the scale of its [air power's] future independent war use. And the day may not be far off when aerial operations with their devastation of enemy lands and destruction of industrial and populous centres on a vast scale may become the principal operations of war, to which the older forms of military and naval operations may become secondary and subordinate." This memorandum is reprinted as Appendix II in the semi-official history of the British air arm in World War I, *The War in the Air*, Volume of Appendices, ed. by H. A. Jones (Oxford University Press, Oxford, 1937), pp. 8-14. The British officer usually credited with prompting the kind of advanced thinking reflected in the above-quoted report was Hugh M. Trenchard, then commander of the Royal Flying Corps with the rank of major general, later Marshal of the Royal Air Force Lord Trenchard. Trenchard is supposed to have greatly influenced Brig. Gen. William A. Mitchell, who as a young major visited him in May 1917.

The effect of this new thinking on Americans was also absorbed and exercised through the Bolling Mission (after Col. R. C. Bolling) which left for Europe in the middle of 1917 to gather information about military aviation in Britain, France, and Italy. One member of that mission, Lt. Col. Virginius E. Clark, produced a summary of the theory of strategic bombing in a memorandum dated October 15, 1917. Another member, Lt. Col.

and relatively comprehensive philosophy. That philosophy is fairly completely presented in his first book-length publication, *The Command of the Air*, published originally in 1921. His later writings, particularly his polemic ones, did little more than reiterate his ideas, with some additional clarification and occasional modification but with little in the way of further development.[2]

He was much too busy pressing home those ideas upon

Edgar S. Gorrell, also produced a notable memorandum on the subject, dated November 28, 1917. Both Clark and Gorrell were considerably influenced by the Italian plane designer Gianni Caproni, who was a close friend of Douhet and also of another Italian air theorist, Nino Salvaneschi. Salvaneschi, obviously sponsored by Caproni, whose commercial and intellectual interests apparently coincided, had already published in 1917, in Milan, a little book in English advocating strategic bombing as a means of ending the war. It was entitled: *Let Us Kill the War: Let Us Aim at the Heart of the Enemy*. See "Italian Influence on the Origins of the American Concept of Strategic Bombardment," by Dr. J. L. Boone Atkinson, *The Air Power Historian*, IV (July 1957), 141-149; also "An American Proposal for Strategic Bombing in World War I" (the text of the Gorrell memorandum), *ibid.*, V (April 1958), 102-117; "The Army and the Strategic Bomber, 1930-1939," by Robert W. Krauskopf, *Military Affairs*, XXII (Summer 1958), 83-94; "Development of Air Doctrine, 1917-41," by James L. Cate, *Air University Quarterly Review*, I (Winter 1947), 11-22; W. F. Craven and J. L. Cate, *The Army Air Forces in World War II*, vol. I, *Plans and Early Operations*, University of Chicago Press, Chicago, 1948, chs. I and II; and I. B. Holley, Jr., *Ideas and Weapons*, Yale University Press, New Haven, 1953, especially Part III, "Heritage of the Air Weapon from World War I."

[2] Douhet's principal writings are: *Il Dominio dell' Aria: Saggio Sul' Arte della Guerra Aerea*, Stab. Poligr. per l'Amministrazione della Guerra, Rome, 1921 (2nd ed., with addition of Part II, Instituto Nazionale Fascista di Cultura, Rome, 1927); "La Guerra del'19—," *Rivista Aeronautica* (March 1930), 409-502. The above works, along with a monograph of 1928 and a long polemical article published in the *Rivista Aeronautica* for November 1929, have been translated into English by Dino Ferrari and published in a single volume with the title, *The Command of the Air* (the original title of the first of the works included), Coward McCann, New York, 1942. Subsequent page references to Douhet's writings will be to the Ferrari translation.

a generally hostile audience to have the time or stimulus within his comparatively short lifetime to develop and refine his thoughts, and very likely he lacked the temperament. His demonstrable errors are therefore considerable and sometimes very crude. But his insights remain impressive. Since time has rescued him from his first and gravest error—his gross overestimate of physical effects per ton of bomb dropped—by introducing the nuclear bomb, Douhet's thoughts are for any unlimited war more valid today than they were during his lifetime or during World War II.

Douhet's Success With Airmen

If that is considered insufficient reason for examining Douhet's ideas, there is also the fact that he had and continues to have enormous influence on air forces generally and especially on that of the United States. This is not to say that Douhet, or any other theorist, is widely read among today's air force officers. But we know that his views influenced American officers, who were already leaning towards a strategic bombing philosophy years before his written work became available in English.[3] We know that the development

[3] A French translation (1932) of a substantial part of the second edition of *The Command of the Air* was in turn translated into English in 1933 and put into mimeographed form for officers of the United States Army Air Corps. The late General H. H. Arnold had the following to say about Douhet's influence in the U.S.A.A.C. of the thirties: "As regards strategic bombardment, the doctrines were still Douhet's ideas modified by our own thinking in regard to pure defense. We felt, out in the 1st Wing, that we were doing much to furnish the practical tests for, and proofs of, the Maxwell Field theories. A different attitude from Douhet's toward bomber escort and a very different view of precision bombing resulted." *Global Mission*, Harpers, New York, 1949, p. 149. Incidentally, it is difficult to see how the views of American airmen could have been significantly different from Douhet's on either of the issues mentioned. On the question of fighter escort for bombers, Douhet assumed somewhat different posi-

of American air doctrine followed Douhet not merely in its broad emphasis on strategic bombing, but also through most of the finer ramifications of his philosophy. It adopted Douhet's de-emphasis of fighters, whether for defense or for escort of bombers, and a corresponding emphasis on destroying the enemy air force at its bases. A disdain for the battle in the air was distinctively Douhet's and certainly characteristic of U.S. Army Air Corps thinking prior to World War II. There are other comparably striking examples of identity and, in fact, no important instances of difference. When American Air Force officers have talked about "understanding air power," they have usually meant what is actually the Douhet thesis on air power, practically *in toto*.

Air officers would not have embraced Douhet's philosophy so warmly, one might almost say so uncritically, had it not been peculiarly congenial to them. Ground force and naval officers have rarely regarded that philosophy, either generally or in its particulars, as self-evidently reasonable and true. To air force officers, however, its emphasis upon an independent mission for a national air force and upon the overriding importance and sufficiency of that mission could hardly be unwelcome.

Douhet's success with one arm of the military services was perhaps the most immediate and striking in the annals of strategic thinking. One is reminded of the great prestige and authority accorded Mahan at the end of the last century and the early decades of the present, but Mahan was after all a

---

tions at different times and generally conveyed the idea that it was desirable but not necessary. On the question of bombing accuracy, he had almost nothing to say except that aerial bombing could never be as accurate as naval gunfire.

reinterpreter of old strategic concepts rather than a creator of new ones. Douhet's strategic philosophy was by contrast wholly revolutionary.

His success was immediate and complete, not only in the United States Army Air Corps (renamed Army Air Forces on June 20, 1941) but in every major air force that had the administrative and intellectual freedom to follow him. The Royal Air Force of Great Britain had, like its American counterpart, already anticipated his views and was therefore all the more readily won over.[4] The German Air Force also fell into line. We have the word to that effect of General-leutnant Adolf Galland, and it confirms something we might have suspected from the nature of German air operations following the defeat of France:

Douhet's ideas met with a great deal of approval in Luftwaffe leading circles before the war. Although in the first phase of organization it was the fighter arm which stood in the foreground, in the second it was unequivocally the bomber. I still remember clearly a period when the talk was all of strategic bombers and one referred with something of pitying condescension to "home defense fighters."[5]

Of course the German Air Force, like all continental air forces, was bound to the ground forces by the tremendous prestige and insistent demands of the latter, but its conduct

[4] In a published lecture, Marshal of the Royal Air Force Sir John Slessor scoffs at the idea that Douhet had had any special influence on R.A.F. doctrine, but his subsequent remarks unwittingly confirm that influence. He attributes to Lord Baldwin the dictum: "The bomber will always get through," which, whether or not Baldwin ever actually voiced it, is certainly near the heart of the Douhet thesis. Slessor's lecture is reproduced in "Air Power and the Future of War," *Journal of the Royal United Service Institution* (August 1954), 343-358.

[5] "Defeat of the Luftwaffe: Fundamental Causes," *Air University Quarterly Review*, IV (April 1953), 23.

in the battle of Britain, which was supposed to be a preparation for the intended cross-channel invasion (Operation Sea Lion), shows how restive it was under German Army and Navy demands. Its leaders were determined to fight their own war and to the best of their ability did so.

The only major air forces at the time of World War II that seemed not to be inoculated with Douhet's ideas were the Japanese and the Russian, and the reasons for these two exceptions are fairly obvious. In Japan, not only were there two air forces under the army and navy respectively, as they were nominally in the United States, but also the conservative army and navy leaders were in fact in control of the government, which was certainly not true of the United States. Besides, the heart of any great enemy power was bound to be a very long distance away, so that Douhet's ideas about strategic bombing were largely inapplicable to Japanese policy.

In the Soviet Union, the control of the armed services by the government was absolute and complete. There had been an enormous purge of leading military officers in the late thirties, and among those eliminated was Corps Commander (i.e. Lieutenant General) V. V. Khripin, Deputy Air Force Commander up to 1937 and chief Soviet air theoretician. The author of numerous articles on air power, he had also written in 1935 the introduction to the Russian translation of Douhet's *Command of the Air*. Shortly before the end of his career, he had been named First Commander of the short-lived "Army of Special Designation" (A.O.N.), a combined long-range bombing and airborne forces organization. His successors probably associated his fate to some extent with the cause he had espoused, and in any event a purge environment does not favor the development of new ideas.[6]

Douhet's influence on the United States Air Force has actually been much greater than that of its own great leader, Brigadier General William A. Mitchell. Mitchell's fame rests more on his qualities and conduct as a man and officer than on his stature as a military philosopher, though he certainly saw the future more clearly than did those senior officers in the Army and Navy with whom he fought. He was full of ideas, some of them brilliant and original, but they were largely dedicated to the proposition that the airplane is a much better missile carrier than any other vehicle, especially the battleship. He developed as early as 1918 the idea of creating an airborne parachute division, for which he even obtained General Pershing's approval. He also inspired the development of very large bombs. But his thinking was almost entirely tactical, and the book that comes closest to presenting his military thought has only a few pages on what might be called the strategic use of air power. Those pages are pure Douhet.[7]

Comparison With Mahan

The popular idea held of Douhet as "the Mahan of air power" prompts a comparison of these two distinguished figures in twentieth century military thinking. Although

[6] See Raymond L. Garthoff, *Soviet Military Doctrine*, The Free Press, Glencoe, Ill., pp. 343-345.

[7] See his *Winged Defense*, Putnam's, New York, 1925, especially pp. 126-128. It must be acknowledged that, although he published several books and many articles and left some unpublished manuscripts, writing was decidedly not Mitchell's forte. He is portrayed to better advantage by his biographers than by himself. An excellent biography is that by Isaac Don Levine, *Mitchell: Pioneer of Air Power*, Duell, Sloan & Pearce, New York, 1943.

Douhet and Mahan were both gifted with incisive and logical minds, which they applied to the use of military power, they could hardly have been more unlike in temperament and in their approaches to their respective fields of interest.

Rear Admiral Alfred Thayer Mahan was essentially a scholar and historian. The aspects of naval strategy that interested him most were those that had remained relatively unaffected by the transition from sail to steam and the other colossal technological changes that occurred during his lifetime. His treatise entitled *Naval Strategy*, published in 1911, was only a summarization of the points he had made and developed in the voluminous histories that had brought him fame.[8] He quite ignored the submarine, which was already a highly efficient instrument at the time of his death in December 1914. In fact his dictum that "the *guerre de course* [commerce raiding] can never be by itself alone decisive of great issues"—a view he derived mainly from his study of the War of 1812—contributed, because of his great prestige, to the general underestimation on the eve of World War I of what the submarine could do. Mahan significantly acknowledged as "my best military friend," Jomini, source of the maxim that in war "methods change but principles are unchanging."

To Douhet such a maxim was plain nonsense. To his mind,

[8] The ubiquitous references to Mahan's most famous work almost invariably omit the dates which are an essential part of the title: *The Influence of Sea Power Upon History, 1660-1783*, Little, Brown, Boston, 1890. The other of his major historical works are, *The Influence of Sea Power Upon the French Revolution and Empire, 1793-1812*, 2 vols., 1892; *The Life of Nelson*, 2 vols., 1897; *Sea Power in its Relations to the War of 1812*, 2 vols., 1905; and *The Major Operations of the Navies in the War of American Independence*, 1913, all published by Little, Brown. His very first published work, in 1883, was the little-noticed *The Gulf and Inland Waters*, one volume of a three-volume history (the other two by different authors) of the naval aspects of the American Civil War.

the changes he saw taking place around him in the methods of waging war changed the basic character of war, and principles which remained "immutable" despite such changes seemed to him to border on the frivolous or irrelevant. For that reason he was totally uninterested in military history prior to World War I. "It is always dangerous to keep looking backward when marching forward, and still more so now when the path is full of sharp detours." Even with respect to World War I, in which he had served and which had provided at the time he was writing the only real experience in the military use of aircraft, he was moved in one instance to exclaim: "In the name of charity, let us forget the last war!"

Douhet on World War I

Nevertheless, he wrote an appreciation of that war which in its penetration and its grasp of the larger issues is a model of historical insight and is eminently worth reading quite apart from any special interest in air power.[9] To Douhet the first World War demonstrated how general staffs composed of technically proficient and industrious men could be isolated from the realities of battle and of national interest, not only before the war but even while they were waging it. On these and related matters he wrote with an eloquence and a passion to which the more sedate Mahan (who prob-

[9] This appreciation comprises the first two chapters of his monograph, originally published in 1928, which is included in the Ferrari translation under the title, "The Probable Aspects of the War of the Future." The relevant chapters comprise pp. 148-177. Douhet began in 1915 to keep a war diary, subsequently published, and it was his outspoken criticism of his seniors during World War I which resulted in his conviction and imprisonment. He completed his one-year sentence before the disaster of Caporetto, which was later officially construed as confirming his charges. In 1920 a military court formally reversed the original verdict.

ably would have shared his views) would not have succumbed.

With respect to the military use of aircraft, Douhet believed that World War I provided no guidance whatsoever for the future. He apparently deplored the great emphasis in that war on the aerial duels of fighter aircraft, an emphasis largely forced by the technological circumstances of the time, when a single advance in fighter performance could bring one side or the other virtual domination of the skies.

Unfortunately, Douhet reached a quite different conclusion about the lessons to be derived from the land campaigns of that war, a conclusion that was proved by the events of World War II to be the first cardinal error in his philosophy. To Douhet the first World War proved that on land the defensive had gained a marked and *permanent* ascendancy. Since this result had followed from the great increase in fire power in the hands of the infantry, he concluded that the future, which must continue to improve that fire power, would confirm and expand the superiority of the defensive. One of the several things he overlooked, because of his preoccupation from first to last with what we now call strategic bombing, was the effectiveness of aircraft used tactically. This error reflects his shortcomings as a student of military history, including for that matter the history of World War I. He was not the only student of World War I, either lay or professional, who deduced the same lesson from the experience of that war without somehow taking into account such events as the German offensive of March 1918, in which remarkable advances were achieved without benefit of tanks or of any great numerical preponderance, or the fluid nature of the eastern front during most of the period when it was active.

Douhet's insistence upon the inevitably static nature of the front in any future war has helped perpetuate the legend that his primary if not exclusive interest in advocating his ideas was the defense of Italy, which after all has its land frontiers in the Alps. Marshal Henri Pétain stressed this point in a friendly but skeptical preface to the French edition of Douhet's major work, and one of the most intelligent and objective of American interpreters of Douhet rested his interpretation predominantly on this view.[10]

It is true that Douhet, as a patriotic Italian and an officer in his country's armed forces, was especially concerned with the application of his ideas to Italy. In one place he even asserted that his "first thought" was for the situation of Italy and that his theories "therefore should not be considered applicable to all countries." And he added: "In all probability, if I were specifically considering a conflict between Japan and the United States, I would not arrive at the same conclusions." That he should confine his exception to a war between these two powers is significant. They were on opposite sides of the globe from each other. With the limited ranges of aircraft in his day (and for that matter in World War II as well), he would have had to be a fool or a fanatic to apply his ideas without great modification to a war between the United States and Japan. Besides, as he pointedly remarked in more than one place, the United States was the only world power rich enough to be predominant in more than one element of military strength, and was therefore not obliged for economy's sake to concentrate on air power.

[10] Louis A. Sigaud, *Air Power and Unification*, Military Service Publishing Co., Harrisburg, Pa., 1949, pp. 21f., 44, 47.

When he wrote his imaginative account of a future war that would test his ideas, "The War of 19—," the two countries he postulated to be at war with each other were France and Germany, with Italy playing no part at all. Douhet's mind and ideas were much too big to suffer confinement to a single country's military problems, particularly those of a second-class power like Italy.

Unlike most extremists, including many of his own followers, Douhet both preached and practiced the strict discipline of logical reasoning. In his polemical writings he liked to expose and exploit the *illogicality* of the opposing argument. If there are basic errors in the Douhet thesis—and World War II, which was the "war of the future" of his constant reference, certainly revealed such errors—they are to be discovered not in the deductions he drew from his premises but in the premises themselves, in what he called "present realities." We have already mentioned what the major ones were: his extreme overestimate of physical effects per ton of bombs dropped, and his utter confidence in the great and permanent ascendancy of the defensive in ground warfare.

Essential Elements of the Douhet Thesis

In its broad outline, Douhet's philosophy is fairly well known. His basic argument is twofold: first, the nature of air power requires that "command of the air" be won by aggressive bombing action rather than by aerial fighting, and second, an air force which achieves command thereby ensures victory all down the line. The bulk of his theory is concerned with what he means by "command of the air" and how it is attained, and with demonstrating its all-conclusive effects.

To Douhet it was not that other things like ground and

82

naval superiority do not matter; it was rather that these other things follow almost automatically from command of the air. The nation that has lost air command loses also the means of regaining it, because of the destruction by bombing of her aircraft industries, and immediately thereafter she loses the means of mobilizing and maintaining her armies and navies, if indeed she has not already lost her will to fight. The ascendancy of the defensive in ground warfare guarantees that there will be no decision prior to that won by the air arm, which in fact comes with incredible swiftness. Hence Douhet's maxim for the allocation of military resources: resist on the ground in order to mass for the offensive in the air.

Douhet did not deny the utility of armies and navies. But he held that their functions are defensive and can be carried out with forces considerably inferior to those of the enemy. Only the air force has to be superior to its antagonist. In this special way he applied the old concept of "concentration of force" to the allocation of strength among the services.

Douhet took considerable pains to explain what he meant by "command of the air," the phrase he used as a title for his major published work. He borrowed heavily from the older concept of command of the sea, which is basic to naval strategy, and he several times defined the character and functions of air command in terms which could serve, by changing a few words, as an orthodox definition of command of the sea. But Douhet was troubled by some obvious differences between the vehicles of sea and air power which tend to work against the transferability of the idea of command.

Sea command, at least in the days of battleship supremacy, was won by the ability of a superior fleet *to intercept* and destroy an inferior fleet when the latter sortied for an attack within the area in dispute. But no one protested more than

Douhet himself the low probability of decisive interception in the air. The swiftness and the tridimensional movement of aircraft, combined with their relatively low endurance or "air-keeping" qualities, put them in marked contrast to naval vessels. Douhet emphasized repeatedly that a determined bomber attack would get through to its target even in the face of a much larger defending air force.

He redressed this difference in capabilities by stressing another advantage peculiar to air power. On the seas the superior fleet could attack an inferior one only when the latter offered itself for battle or put to sea to effect some militarily useful purpose. The former was incapable of attacking with its guns, save at undue risk, the heavily defended naval base within which the inferior naval force could hide between sorties. An air force, on the other hand, could fly over any ground defenses and, for that matter, through air defenses as well, to destroy whatever forces might be lurking behind them. Thus an air force that seizes and holds the initiative does not have to patrol the skies waiting for the enemy to offer himself for battle; *it can seek him out on his bases, where he is most vulnerable, and destroy him forthwith.* This was one of the most daring, and enduring, of Douhet's conceptions.

Since the superior air force can accomplish destruction more rapidly than an inferior one, even if the latter adopts the same strategy, its superiority must grow by some geometrical progression, leading swiftly into that position of complete ascendancy which may be justly termed "command of the air." The inferior force has no alternative but to follow the same strategy, its only hope for ultimate success lying in its being more aggressive than its opponent, and in striking first with all its strength.

Douhet's reasoning required him to place an enormous premium upon hitting first with all one's might, and he did not shrink from the implications of this requirement: "Whatever its aims, the side which decides to go to war will unleash all its aerial forces in mass against the enemy nation the instant the decision is taken, without waiting to declare war formally. . . ."[11]

Douhet made clear that by "command" he did not mean such totality of control that "even the enemy flies are prevented from flying." But it is essential to the idea of command that the enemy be put in a position where he finds it impossible "to execute aerial actions of any significance." Or in language which again borrows heavily from orthodox naval strategy: "To have command of the air means to be in a position to prevent the enemy from flying while retaining the ability to fly oneself."[12] Such a degree of mastery, he held, is within the capability of any air force that enjoys a superiority in bombers over its opponent and, more important, possesses a properly aggressive spirit.

Clearly such a view implied a poor regard for the effectiveness of defenses against aerial attack. Douhet left his readers in no doubt on the matter. For antiaircraft artillery he expressed contempt mixed with anger at the prodigal waste that this form of defense entailed in World War I. "How many guns lay waiting month after month, even years, mouths gaping at the sky, on the watch for an attack which never came!" A system that depended upon dispersion for its execution was inherently bad. The guns were not only futile when hostile planes did come into view but added by their own fire to the projectiles falling from above.[18]

[11] Douhet, *op.cit.*, p. 202. [12] *Ibid.*, pp. 24, 96f., 220.
[18] *Ibid.*, pp. 17f., 55, 112.

Nor did he have much greater esteem for the defensive work of fighter aircraft. He believed that their poor air-keeping capability effectively prevented their massing to patrol the avenue of threatened attack. The inherent requirement for dispersal of combat units is less extreme and less conspicuous with defensive fighters than with antiaircraft guns, but no less real. Attacking bombers (and their escorting fighters, if any) can shoot back at defending fighters, assuming the latter achieve interception. Living in an age that knew nothing of radar, Douhet did not assign high probabilities of success to interception. These considerations led Douhet to propound the paradox that an effective defense by fighter aircraft "would require a defensive force equal to the total combat strength of the attacking air force, multiplied by as many times as there are defensive positions to be protected"— in short, an impossible or absurdly wasteful allocation of military resources.[14]

The only way to destroy an enemy air force is to strike at it on its own bases, and the only force that can accomplish such destruction is a bomber force. This was Douhet's constant refrain. A determined attack in mass will always get through. For air forces, attack is not simply the best defense, it is the only defense. In Douhet's view the attitude of the superior bomber force to the air battle is one almost of indifference; it will neither seek combat nor let itself be deflected from its target in order to evade it. If enemy fighters intercept a bomber mission, some bombers will be lost, perhaps many; but the interceptors will suffer proportionate damage and (for reasons which Douhet did not make clear) even greater disorganization. "The pursuit unit [is] fated by its very nature to lose most of its offensive power in of-

[14] *Ibid.*, pp. 52-55.

fensive action." In addition, those interceptors which miss or survive battle will suffer heavy losses at their bases between sorties. Following the first exchange of blows, therefore, the scale and effectiveness of air defense activities must go into a rapid and drastic decline.

The proper function of fighter planes, insofar as they are used at all, is not to defend one's territories against enemy bombers but to support one's own bombers in the attack on enemy targets. "Viewed in its true light, aerial warfare admits of no defense, only offense. *We must therefore resign ourselves to the offensives the enemy inflicts upon us, while striving to put all our resources to work to inflict even heavier ones upon him.* This is the basic principle which must govern the development of aerial warfare."[15] It is the principle which airmen have favored and, by and large, continue to favor to this day.

Douhet's total commitment to the aerial offensive did not stem from that mystique of the offensive which has marred the thinking of so many other military officers before and since his time. We must remember that he considered the only proper attitude for an army to be a defensive one. He was persuaded, however, that an air force was pitifully weak in defense and incomparably powerful in offense. Some of his most eloquent pages were devoted to an indignant castigation of the Allied generals in World War I for their insistence, at the outbreak of war, on "plunging in like a bull after a red cloth waved by the enemy" and continuing to plunge thereafter for no other reason than that they were "dazzled by the myth of the offensive." He cited with sorrow and contempt the prewar maxim of the French General

[15] The italics are Douhet's. *Ibid.*, p. 55. See also pp. 59, 61, 194.

Staff, unaffected as it was by the enemy's plans and the size of his forces: " 'Forward, and trust in victory!' "[16]

The Exaggeration of Bomb Damage

It is clear that Douhet's system for winning and exploiting command of the air depended upon a very high estimate of the physical and moral effects produced by each ton of bombs dropped. A bomber force can afford Douhet's sublime disdain for interception and attrition only if the bombs getting through are effecting large and immediate results, especially on the enemy's air power. He emphasized the modesty of the resources necessary to achieve command and the marvelous payoffs that must follow, at least until his precepts were so generally followed in practice that the price of command would be raised by sheer competition.

Douhet adduced as his basic "unit of bombardment" a force of ten planes carrying two tons of bombs each. These twenty tons, dropped in a uniform pattern, he concluded (how or why is never made apparent) ought to destroy any targets over a surface which "should be exactly the area of a circle 500 meters in diameter." With a penchant for standardization that is supposed to be more characteristic of Americans than Italians, Douhet suggested that this area be considered a "unit of destruction."[17]

Concerning what kinds of bombs ought to be used, we have only a hint from his last written work, "The War of 19—." Here the imagined belligerent of the future (a pro-Douhet Germany) adopts three types of bomb, all weighing 50 kg. (110 lbs.) each but varying in content: high explosive, incendiary materials, or poison gas. These three types were loaded in each squadron in the proportions 1, 3, and 6 re-

[16] *Ibid.*, pp. 10f., 155-165, 263.   [17] *Ibid.*, pp. 20f.

spectively—high explosive bombs thus being only 10 per cent of the whole! With regard to bomb weight, World War II was to show that high explosive bombs of ten to twenty times the 50 kg. stipulated by Douhet were often insufficient for the destruction of vital parts of significant industrial systems.

Throughout his work Douhet indulged in recurring fantasies about what his twenty-ton "bombing units" could accomplish. "An air force of 50 bombing units (500 planes), each capable of destroying a surface 500 meters in diameter, could in a single flight completely destroy 50 enemy objectives, such as supply depots, industrial plants, warehouses, railroad centers, population centers, et cetera."[18] Speculations representing roughly the same arithmetic occur again and again, except that in his "The War of 19—" he had such things as railroad centers being quite effectively attacked with as little as ten tons each. In the same paper he had 150 railroad centers being simultaneously bombed with an *average* of twenty tons of bombs each. These figures presumably made full allowance for limitations on the accuracy of aerial bombing, which Douhet in one place admitted could never be as accurate as artillery fire. They must be interpreted in the light of a "guiding principle" he had expressed earlier: *"The objective must be destroyed completely in one attack, making further attack on the same target unnecessary."*[19]

To be sure, accuracy of bombing is of lesser moment when the target is a large population center, but even then the requirements for proper distribution of bombs set certain minimum standards of accuracy. Nevertheless, Douhet considered 500 tons of bombs (mostly gas) quite sufficient to

[18] *Ibid.*, p. 50.
[19] *Ibid.*, pp. 19f. The italics are Douhet's.

destroy a large city and its inhabitants.[20] If Douhet had applied basic arithmetic to his large-scale predictions, he would have realized that a circular area "unit of destruction" of 500 meters diameter, for which he allocated a unit of twenty tons of bombs, comprises only about one-twelfth of a square mile, and that 500 tons is equal to twenty-five of his own destruction units. Thus, even if his assumptions of required bombing density were correct, he could expect 500 tons to destroy only about two square miles, which is a fairly minor portion of any large city. Unfortunately, Douhet never pushed himself so far in his calculations, nor was he induced to do so by the superficial and usually irrelevant kinds of criticism he received in his lifetime. It is therefore not remarkable that, in his "The War of 19—," the conflict he described was for all practical purposes decided in a single morning.

Neglect of Target Selection

Related to his exaggeration of the physical effects of bombing was his general vagueness with respect to selection of targets. One of his utterances on the *importance* of target selection, however, is a classic statement on the subject. Immediately following an enthusiastic survey of what an air force of fifty bombing units could do, he added this cautionary note:

All this sounds very simple, but as a matter of fact the selection of objectives, the grouping of zones, and determining the order in which they are to be destroyed is the most difficult and delicate task in aerial warfare, constituting what may be defined as aerial strategy. Objectives vary considerably in war, and the choice of them depends chiefly upon the aim sought, whether the command of the air, paralyzing the enemy's army and navy, or shattering

[20] *Ibid.*, p. 393.

the morale of civilians behind the lines. This choice may therefore be guided by a great many considerations—military, political, social, and psychological, depending upon the conditions of the moment.[21]

Few ideas in Douhet are more profoundly true or better stated. It is only a pity that he gave the matter little further thought.

One must give him due credit for avoiding simple conclusions in this area. He properly insisted that "no hard and fast rules can be laid down on this aspect of aerial warfare," and significantly added: "It is just here, in grasping these imponderables, in choosing enemy targets, that future commanders of Independent Air Forces will show their ability." Lesser minds than his have been all too ready to give final answers to what was, prior to thermonuclear weapons, the terribly difficult problem of selecting targets for the bombers. In some respects it is still a difficult problem. Nevertheless, it is disappointing and astonishing that Douhet contented himself with only the most general observations on the subject. How could one who had so little idea what one must hit after the enemy air force is destroyed be quite so sure of the tremendous results that would inevitably follow from the hitting? That kind of intellectual hiatus has remained characteristic of Douhet's more enthusiastic followers down to the present.

Douhet by implication put the enemy air force and his aircraft production industry at the top of the priority list among target systems to be attacked, though he allowed for certain exceptions to the rule, as for example "when the enemy's aerial forces are so weak it would be a waste of time to devote men and materials to so unimportant an objective."[22]

[21] *Ibid.*, pp. 50f.   [22] *Ibid.*, p. 51.

Granting, however, that Douhet would in most cases desig-
nate enemy air power in all its forms as the first objective
for one's bombers, the question remains: what next? Command of the air is, after all, only a means to an end. Douhet
favored strategic bombing over tactical, and on the tactical
side he clearly favored "interdiction" targets (i.e., targets af-
fecting supply and transportation, or "communications" in
the military sense of the term) rather than front line targets.
But he too scrupulously followed his own advice to avoid
hard and fast rules. His preoccupation with poison gas, which
he was certain would be used on a vast scale in the next war,
his insistence on the devastating morale effects of bombing,
his conviction that civilians are far less able than soldiers to
endure the blows that air power can deal, and his references
to the greater vulnerability of the targets exposed to air attack as compared with those exposed to naval or land artillery fire all confirm the impression that fundamentally
Douhet reposed his faith on the bombing of cities per se, on
the attack against urban populations. Certainly there is no
evidence of his having devoted any study to what is actually
involved in the attack on an industrial system, as for example
the aircraft industry, which is almost the only industry
Douhet mentioned in his few allusions to targets.[23]

There is, however, one dictum that Douhet was willing
to assert without qualification: "*Inflict the greatest damage in
the shortest possible time.*" This he presented as a "basic
principle, which is the same one which governs warfare on
land and sea." The defensive attitude he himself advocated
for land and sea warfare was in a sense a rejection of this
principle, but no matter. He was quite certain it applied to

[23] See *ibid.*, pp. 20, 22, 50, 57, 58, 59f., 61, 126, 128, 140, 201, 362, 363,
391.

aerial bombardment. "A really strong Independent Air Force," he said, ". . . could inflict upon an unprepared enemy such grave damage as to bring about a complete collapse of his forces in a very few days." On this basis he considered the value of the surprise attack prior to a declaration of war to be "obvious." One must quickly annihilate the enemy or be annihilated oneself.[24]

Other Facets of the Douhet Thesis

Most of the rest of Douhet's thinking is plainly derived from the general principles already reviewed. Nevertheless, it is interesting to recall some of his ideas on the equipping and operation of air forces, and to observe how these too have persisted into the present.

The grand mission he assigned to air power obviously permitted no subservience of the air forces to the demands or requirements of the land and naval arms. The nation's air force must be independent and at least coequal to the other services. But Douhet went further and insisted that *all* the nation's military aviation must be contained in the Independent Air Force, that "auxiliary" aviation—that is, aviation integrated with ground and naval forces—was "worthless, superfluous, harmful." It was "worthless" because it could not contribute to winning command of the air and yet could not operate unless command was achieved. It was "superfluous" because after the indispensable command was won and its major benefits exploited, the Independent Air Force would be in a position to divert a substantial part of its strength to ground and naval support if needed. It was "harmful" because it diverted aerial force from the essential

[24] The italics earlier in the paragraph are Douhet's, *ibid.*, pp. 51, 60.

93

purpose of that force and put the achievement of this purpose into needless jeopardy. Thus Douhet's slogan for the allocation of the national military resources was a dual one: the major national military resources must be concentrated in the Independent Air Force, and *all air* resources must be concentrated in the Independent Air Force.

It must be added that Douhet put himself to few pains to explore how the Independent Air Force, after it had carried out its major mission, would devote itself to direct ground force and naval support. An air force properly used would bring about the disorganization and collapse of enemy armies and navies—if the enemy homeland did not collapse first— and that was all there was to it.[25]

As might be guessed from his emphasis on the inherently offensive nature of air power, Douhet stressed the value of the bomber as compared with the fighter. The latter, which he considered useful merely as an escort to the bomber, need only exist in numbers proportionate to the enemy's, whereas the more bombers the better. Certainly if one must choose between the two types, the lack of fighter or pursuit planes is much the lesser evil.

In Part II of his *Command of the Air*, which he added in 1926, Douhet rejected the fighter altogether in favor of what he called the "battleplane," which was simply a bomber with sufficient armament and armor to enable it to defend itself against enemy fighters. The battleplane was, as he put it, "the only type of plane which should make up the operating mass of an Independent Air Force—the *only* organism necessary,

[25] For Douhet's few comments on the influence of air power on armies and navies, see especially *ibid.*, pp. 198f., where he speaks not of the utilization of air power by armies and navies but rather of the need of those services to make themselves less vulnerable to enemy air power used against their bases.

because sufficient in itself, to wage aerial warfare."[26] On the other hand, in his very last written work, "The War of 19—," he has the Germans effectively using very fast fighters, not indeed as escorts but in "explorer squadrons" flying separate offensive missions in support of their bombers. Whether this represented a further modification of his views back to something like his original position or was simply a dramatic device to make his fictional portrayal more vivid is not clear. Neither is it important. His conception of the bomber as a plane *capable* of operating independently and of giving an adequate account of itself when attacked by enemy fighters remained to the end, and incidentally played no small part in inspiring American bomber types from the B-10 onward.

With respect to aircraft performance, Douhet first argued (no doubt with the idea of the battleship in mind) that the bomber type must sacrifice speed to fire power; later he decided that the bomber (battleplane) must have a speed equal to fighters'. However, he always deplored what he conceived to be an overemphasis on speed in both types of combat aircraft, which prevented a stabilization of weapons and hence a build-up in numbers. The only type of plane whose speed he conceded to be important was the reconnaissance type, which he felt should have superior speed and no armament. As far as the bomber was concerned, it would depend for its security not only on its own armament and armor but also

[26] *Ibid.*, pp. 117-120. Readers of Alexander de Seversky's *Victory Through Air Power*, Simon & Schuster, New York, 1942, will recall that he presented the "battleplane" as his own bold new concept, adding to Douhet's original idea the startling insistence that distance was no impediment to bombing operations since a bomber could have all the range designed into it that its user wanted, up to the ultimate round-the-world range of 25,000 miles (which he prophesied as becoming "inevitable" five years from the publication of his book).

on the tactic of flying in large masses and dense formations. An air force so equipped in material and doctrine, Douhet held, could and should operate in daylight.

Mr. Edward Warner, the distinguished aeronautical engineer, considers Douhet's depreciation of the importance of speed in combat aircraft to be "the worst of all of Douhet's failures in dealing with technical development."[27] Today of course the minimum acceptable speed in bombers is several times greater than it was in Douhet's time. Nevertheless, the question of how much speed to design into bombers is still a very live one, speed being costly not only in other performance characteristics, especially range, but also in the numbers of aircraft available for any given expenditure. Multiplicity of units may, within limits, provide a better guarantee of successful penetration than speed.

Views on the Broader Aspects of War

In considering the national aspirations and objectives that give meaning and direction to any issue of arms, it must be acknowledged that Douhet was no Clausewitz or Mahan.[28]

[27] Edward Warner, "Douhet, Mitchell, Seversky: Theories of Air Warfare," ch. xx of *Makers of Modern Strategy*, ed. by E. M. Earle, Princeton University Press, Princeton, 1943, p. 494. Mr. Warner is too harsh with respect to Douhet's insights into technological advances. Douhet's ability in 1923 to foresee the need not only of armor in combat aircraft (which Warner acknowledges) but also of all-metal construction and of the use of superchargers and pressurized cabins argues a vision in this regard which is more than a little exceptional. See Douhet, *op.cit.*, pp. 45, 65f.

[28] Mahan's stature as a political scientist has not been generally appreciated. Those of his essays gathered together in the volume *Armaments and Arbitration: The Place of Force in International Relations*, Little, Brown, Boston, 1912, show a thoughtfulness about international politics that would have done credit to some of his critics, who in the interwar period generally followed the fashion set by the late Charles A. Beard of denouncing Mahan as a simple reactionary. He was, however, enough

Yet neither does he wholly belong to that far more numerous genre of strategic thinkers and writers who are content to leave politics to the politicians, who disdainfully dismiss as "idealistic" a concern to make the means fit the ends.

The opening sentences of Douhet's second major work, *Probable Aspects of the War of the Future* (1928), expressed a humane sentiment against which modern military men normally steel themselves:

The study of war, particularly the war of the future, presents some very interesting features. First is the vastness of the phenomenon which makes whole peoples hurl themselves against one another, forgetting for a time that they belong to the same family of humanity striving toward the same goal of ideal perfection, to become wolves and throw themselves into torment and a bloody work of destruction as though possessed by blind folly.[29]

Now to Clausewitz the notion of fighting a war in any such compulsive manner as this was totally inadmissible. It represented the negation of what is basic and timeless in his philosophy, the idea that war is designed to further political objectives and must be governed from first to last by those objectives.

Douhet's severe criticism of the French General Staff for its handling of World War I was based, at least implicitly, on a revulsion against the terrible bloodletting that attended the futile offensives, which besides being militarily stupid and dangerous could not but sacrifice the long-term political and social interests of France. Apparently he saw no comparable problem, however, in the conduct of air operations.

---

imbued with the Darwinism of his times to have reached the conclusion that war, as a way of selecting the fittest, was in general good for nations. See Francis Duncan, "Mahan: Historian With a Purpose," *U.S. Naval Institute Proceedings*, LXXXIII (May 1957), 498-503.

[29] Douhet, *op.cit.*, p. 145.

He felt that air war by its very nature had to be concentrated and unrestrained violence. Judgment and choice were to be exercised only in determining the order of things destroyed, but not the speed or magnitude of destruction.

Douhet was not driven to this conclusion by any undue respect for the traditional "principles of war" with their emphasis on concentration in time and space. On the contrary, he went out of his way to express contempt for those principles.[30] But he was impressed, according to his own image of air warfare, with the contrast between the gigantic potency of the offensive and the impotence of the defensive. He concluded that air war is a race against annihilation, in which the only way to escape that end is to be swifter than the enemy in dealing out destruction.

To be sure, a few points in the scoring were left to endurance or ability to sustain the initial blows:

Tragic, too, to think that the decision in this kind of war must depend upon smashing the material and moral resources of a people caught in a frightful cataclysm which haunts them everywhere without cease until the final collapse of all social organization. Mercifully, the decision will be quick in this kind of war, since the decisive blows will be directed at civilians, that element of the countries at war least able to sustain them. These future wars may yet prove to be more humane than wars in the past in spite of all, because they may in the long run shed less blood. But there is no doubt that nations who find themselves unprepared to sustain them will be lost.[31]

This is all so simple, so straightforward, so inexorable. Every war *must* be a total war, regardless of the character of the powers waging it, the causes of the conflict, or the original objectives of the statesmen who have let themselves

[30] See *ibid.*, p. 149.
[31] *Ibid.*, p. 61.

be drawn into it. In fact, there can be no meaningful objectives other than survival through the elimination of the threat-posing rival. War must be total because the decision "must depend upon smashing the material and moral resources of a people . . . until the final collapse of all social organization." This is a long way indeed from Clausewitz, and the distance reflects not so much the profound changes since his time in the political and social structure of the world as the development of a mechanical instrument, the airplane. Douhet regretted it, but he had to "accept realities." Like the poet Housman, he lived "in a world I never made." One senses here the final and frightening abandonment by the soldier of any sense of responsibility for the political and social consequences of his military acts, not only abroad but at home as well.

It is useless to delude ourselves. All the restrictions, all the international agreements made during peacetime are fated to be swept away like dried leaves on the winds of war. . . . The purpose of war is to harm the enemy as much as possible; and all means which contribute to this end will be employed, no matter what they are. . . . The limitations applied to the so-called inhuman and atrocious means of war are nothing but international demagogic hypocrisies.[32]

This is different from Ludendorff's glorification of total war, but the results are the same. Incidentally, the last two sentences quoted are clearly wrong. The purpose of war is something other than "to harm the enemy as much as possible," and while historical efforts to limit the means of waging war have often been illusory and possibly naïve, they usually reflected the earnest aspirations of responsible statesmen. They have rarely been merely "demagogic hypocrisies." Subject as

[32] *Ibid.*, p. 181.

99

he was to such nihilistic convictions, Douhet was scarcely able to consider how the strategy of air power could be adjusted to different political and geographical situations.

When Douhet in "The War of 19—" projected into the future the application of his principles to a specific imaginary war, he made a significant departure from his own previous axioms. He had the German air force deliberately holding back its attacks and permitting the French bombers to strike at Germany first, in order that the Germans should have a better position before "world public opinion" for their own planned "reprisals." Indeed, the Germans go so far as to warn the French of the day and hour at which they will begin "the disintegration of the enemy's national resistance." It is the civilian foreign minister who remonstrates that such warning means giving up the advantage of surprise, and the military commander who replies that it is "the Independent Air Force which would constitute the real surprise, and not the hour at which it would go into action."[33]

If this seems like a small concession for Douhet to have made to the utility of a good propaganda position, one must remember the enormous importance he had attached, and presumably still attached, to hitting first. According to his own lights, the kind of surprise he had his hero cast away was no trifle. Had he not felt that the course of the war was not worth further describing once the command of the air had been decided, and had he not therefore terminated his account with the second morning of the conflict, his mature insights might well have continued to play tricks with his own dogmas.

Douhet's writings are not voluminous, and what there is of them is markedly repetitive. Perhaps because he did not

[33] *Ibid.*, pp. 353, 365f., 372.

live long enough, probably also because he was too deeply immersed in controversy over his basic ideas, and certainly also because he was so far in advance of his contemporaries in a completely new field of thought, Douhet did not attempt to amplify some ideas that seem to the modern student of air power to cry for development.

The Test of Experience

How did Douhet's theses fare in the one great test they have received? While the next chapter will provide a detailed answer, a few anticipatory comments here will not be amiss. If one disregards for a moment the over-all vision and considers only specific assertions and theses, one has to conclude that in World War II Douhet was proved wrong on almost every salient point he made. To assert the reverse, as is often done, is to engage in propaganda, not analysis.

World War II was clearly a fair test. It began a full eighteen years after the publication of his *Command of the Air*. Although none of the belligerent governments was anything like fully committed to his ideas and therefore ready to apply them without reservation—a point which has often been used to argue the "unfairness" of the test—it is nevertheless a fact that the bomber fleets which ultimately took to the air, especially on the Allied side, were larger by whole orders of magnitude than those which Douhet thought sufficient to win a decision in a single day. In performance the aircraft almost certainly exceeded his expectations. The tonnage of bombs dropped on Germany alone, and on specific targets within Germany, were in ranges of figures that Douhet never dreamed of. Surely we should not put ourselves in the position of saying that 1,000 times the weight of bombs Douhet called for was not a fair test, but that 2,000 or 3,000 times would have been! Also, the facts that huge tonnages of bombs were necessary and that the war lasted long enough to permit their delivery demonstrate that the strategic results of bombing did not come nearly as quickly as Douhet had expected. The delay was bound to mean, among other things, that land and naval action was to count for far more than he had predicted.

We are here considering the experience of World War II as a test of Douhet's specific doctrines, not as a test of the value of strategic bombing *per se*. Experience may convince us that strategic bombing is decidedly worth while but still oblige us to reject Douhet's exclusive preoccupation with it. If that happens, we must find a new philosophy or "doctrine" which is more compatible with experience and reason.

Certainly some of the basic premises upon which Douhet built his conclusions were proved wrong *under the conditions of World War II*. Some of those same premises, however, may be restored to validity under the new conditions of today and tomorrow, especially because of nuclear weapons. We shall come to that presently, but for the moment we are reviewing past history.

In one respect World War II provided a test tremendously weighted in Douhet's favor. For four long years there was, along the English Channel, as static a "front" as could be imagined, but for reasons the exact opposite of those which Douhet advanced. The surface stalemate in the west resulted not from the strength of the ground defensive but from the rapid and overwhelming offensive in 1940 of the German armies, which forced the collapse of France and the Low Countries and the ejection of the British armies from Europe. The swift invasion of Poland in the previous year, and the enormous advances of German armies in southeast

Europe and in Russia during 1941, also proved the invalidity of one cornerstone of the Douhet philosophy—the assumption of static land fronts.

Another way in which the scales were weighted in Douhet's favor provides a corollary to the point just made. The gigantic land and naval operations taking place in eastern Europe, Africa, and later in France gave enormous assistance in two ways to the effectiveness of Allied strategic bombing. First, that fighting absorbed huge German resources which otherwise would have gone into expanding the defenses against strategic bombing. The existing defenses were costly and painful enough to the Allies as it was. True, the British and the Americans also put into land operations resources that might have gone into advancing their strategic bombing offensive; but until the last year of the war they were far less deeply involved in ground campaigns than the Germans. Second, the great German land campaigns greatly burdened the German military economy, making it considerably more sensitive to the effects of destruction from the air than it might otherwise have been.

The Allies learned after the war that the attack on enemy morale had been on the whole a waste of bombs, which means a waste of about half the total tonnage dropped. That error Douhet also helped to propagate, though not through carelessness or willful ignorance. In the years following World War I, persons far more expert in the social sciences than he developed exaggerated expectations of the potentialities of "psychological warfare." In World War II the effects of bombing on civilian morale were certainly not trivial, but it seems clear that the lowered morale resulting from bombing did not importantly affect military operations or the outcome of the war.

Because strategic bombing did not produce results as swiftly as Douhet expected, and because vastly greater tonnages than he called for were necessary to produce any results at all, defenses against air attack proved far more effective than he predicted. Douhet did not deny that fighters could shoot down invading bombers; he simply could not consider the attrition they inflicted as important. In his "The War of 19—," he postulated a situation where an attacking force loses one third of its strength on the first day of war and still goes on to win. In World War II, where the bombing campaigns were virtually trucking operations requiring repeated hauls by individual aircraft and crews, attrition rates of 5 to 10 per cent could be most serious to the attacker. They strained his physical resources and the combat aggressiveness of his air crews.

The Battle of Britain resulted in an outright victory for the defense. The later Allied air assault on Germany resulted in a complete Allied victory; but it was touch and go during more than one phase of the operation. There are grounds for believing that if the Germans had played their hand better they could have turned the Allies back in the air by making their losses prohibitive. They might, among other things, have pushed the use of the jet engine in fighters instead of diverting it at Hitler's orders to bombers, which were bound at that time to be too few and too late to carry out a successful counteroffensive. Anyway, the U.S.A.A.F. found before its air offensive was well begun that it would have to provide long-range escort fighters, which, in accordance with the Douhet philosophy, had been previously neglected. Even the antiaircraft gun, which Douhet so much despised, won the respect of bomber crews. It turned out that the military worth of a target could be appreciated by the defender as well as the attacker, and that antiaircraft guns could be distributed accordingly. There was point as well as poignance in the comment of an R.A.F. officer written during the war: "If it is true that 'the bomber will always get through,' as it is popularly stated, it is equally true that 'not all the bombers will get through' against adequate defenses. . . ."[34]

The American air assault on Japan came closer in some ways to confirming Douhet's position than that on Germany, for it achieved much greater effects per ton of bombs dropped. But as a test of his ideas it was vitiated by the fact that Japan was a defeated power—and recognized to be such by her military chiefs, especially of the Navy—before the strategic bombing campaign was well begun.

Nevertheless, after noting these important discrepancies between prediction and performance, we must still honor Douhet's over-all vision. However knocked about they were by the test of World War II, his ideas nevertheless fared better than those of most of his critics. Strategic bombing did pay large military dividends, and, as we shall see in the next chapter, could have paid much larger ones if its limitations as well as its real capabilities had been more adequately understood. Douhet provided a framework for such understanding. It is not altogether his fault that his followers were too content with what he gave them to develop and refine his insights further.

Yet, because of a revolution in weapons which Douhet could never have dreamed of, his philosophy is less challenged today than ever before. People may still reject strategic bombing, but not because they doubt its efficacy. Quite

[34] Ft. Lt. V.E.R. Blunt, *The Use of Air Power*, The Military Service Publishing Co., Harrisburg, Pa., 1943, p. 39.

the contrary. It is probably true that without the nuclear bomb Douhet's theses would by now have succumbed to those other technological developments since World War II which have made strategic bombing far too costly and uncertain for ordinary bombs. It is also true, however, that the framework of strategic thought he created is peculiarly pertinent to any general war in the nuclear age.

⤙4⤚

STRATEGIC BOMBING IN
WORLD WAR II

AIR POWER had a mighty vindication in World War II. But it was Mitchell's conception of it—"anything that flies"—rather than Douhet's that was vindicated. It was in tactical employment that success was most spectacular and that the air forces won the unqualified respect and admiration of the older services. By contrast, the purely strategic successes, however far-reaching in particular instances, were never completely convincing to uncommitted observers. Against Germany they came too late to have a clearly decisive effect; against Japan they were imposed on an enemy already prostrated by other forms of war. If airmen were like laboratory animals running a maze, they would seek to repeat successes and to recoil from frustrations. They would now be all in favor of tactical as against strategic uses of air power. But being instead very human, and knowing also the power of nuclear weapons, they have remained intensely loyal to their original strategic ideas.

The conditions of any future war in which nuclear weapons are used will be critically different from those of World War II in almost every significant respect. Nevertheless, because the experience of World War II is often appealed to as having "proved" this or that about air power, there is value in summarizing that experience briefly and objectively. It is, for all practical purposes, the only experience we have with strategic bombing. Small wonder that it has influenced importantly the ideas we still carry around on the subject,

especially with respect to the amount of destruction necessary to win a war by strategic bombing.

The Allied strategic bombing campaigns against Germany
and Japan in World War II are, despite their complexity and
magnitude, among the most brilliantly illuminated military
campaigns of all time. The United States Strategic Bombing
Survey (U.S.S.B.S.) carried out its survey of Allied bombing
in Europe on the heels of the advancing Allied armies, in
the hope of applying the resulting lessons to the strategic
bombing of Japan. However, the victory over Japan followed soon thereafter, and the Survey organization proceeded at once to make a comparable study of the campaign
against Japan.

The resulting work comprises 208 separate published items
for the European war and 108 items for the Pacific war. The
Survey staff was in most fields marked by very high competence and talent, and the manner in which the members
were selected provided about as good a guarantee against
bias as could be found. There were also some complementary
studies carried on by other organizations or individuals,
some of which benefited from being under less pressure of
time than was imposed on the authors of the Survey.[1] Thus,

[1] The British work most nearly comparable to the U.S.S.B.S. is that
by the British Bombing Survey Unit (called during the war the RAF
Bombing Analysis Unit). However, the publications of that organization—
most of them classified—have had only the most limited distribution within
the United States. The basic volume in the series is entitled *The Strategic
Air War Against Germany, 1939-45*. In America, there have been some
distinctive publications (also originally classified) by an agency of the
Air Force called the AAF Evaluation Board, which was rather more concerned with tactical targets and operations, such as those incident to the
Normandy landing, than with strategic air operations. The British Bombing Survey Unit tended to straddle both strategic and tactical operations.
It was, unlike the other surveys mentioned, very largely directed by persons
who had made heavy commitments to operational decisions. With respect

the relevant facts of any importance are available. All one has to do is read the appropriate publications carefully with an open mind.

The Attack on the German War Economy

With respect to the German campaign, study of the survey findings leads to three major conclusions: (1) our strategic bombing brougnt the German war economy to the point of collapse; (2) that result came very late in the war, too late to develop its full potential effects on the ground and naval campaigns, which were already proceeding to a decisive conclusion; and (3) given only the air power actually in Allied hands, but assuming better understanding of the capabilities of strategic bombing and especially a wiser choice of targets, the positive results achieved by bombing could have come much sooner than they did. Had they come sooner by six months, their beneficial influence for shortening the war and saving Allied lives would have been unequivocal.

Let us examine the first conclusion. The oft-repeated argument, based on U.S.S.B.S. statistics, that German war production in almost all categories increased drastically between the middle of 1942 and the middle of 1944, is beside the point, because the scale of bombing which brought about the final significant results had barely begun by mid-1944. The weight

___

to targets within France, one must mention also the work of the French Operational Research Group.

The general, semi-official histories which might be studied in conjunction with the above-cited reports are, for the United States, W. F. Craven and J. L. Cate, *The Army Air Forces in World War II*, 7 vols., University of Chicago Press, Chicago, 1948-1955; and for the British, Denis Richards and Hilary St. George Saunders, *Royal Air Force, 1939-1945*, 3 vols., H. M. Stationery Office, London, 1953-1954. See also Burton H. Klein, *Germany's Economic Preparations For War*, Harvard University Press, Cambridge, 1959.

of Allied attack, which in 1942 averaged under 6,000 tons monthly, rose in 1944 to an average of 131,000 tons monthly—a more than twenty fold increase. The greatest rate of increase occurred just prior to the Normandy invasion, which itself absorbed in tactical operations for many months the major part of our strategic-bombing capabilities. Along with this increase in tonnage of bombs dropped came a great improvement in operational techniques, especially in the use of radio direction devices. And beginning only in February 1944, large numbers of P-51 long-range fighters became available for escorting bomber sorties practically anywhere within Germany.

Also, until mid-1942 the German war economy contained a large amount of slack. Contrary to general opinion, that economy was far from fully mobilized for war either in the kind of commodities produced or in the rate of production. The labor force was essentially on a single-shift basis and included relatively few women. The great increases in German war production over the next two years, despite our bombing, resulted mostly from the taking up of this slack. Even so, judged by the standard of British industrial mobilization, the German economy never attained anything like its full war potential.[2]

In any case, from our point of view it would not matter whether or not production as a whole diminished if the Germans had been denied even one truly indispensable war commodity, such as liquid fuel. In the final stages of the war, that is just what happened. Allied bombers knocked out the German industries producing liquid fuels and chemicals.

[2] See U.S.S.B.S., *The Effects of Strategic Bombing on the German War Economy* (Item #3 for European War), especially pp. 6-11. See also Klein, *op.cit.*

In an overlapping campaign they also effectively knocked out the German transportation services, upon which everything else depended.

German oil-production facilities were recommended as a top-priority target on March 5, 1944, and officially designated as such in a directive of June 8, two days after the Normandy landing. There had meanwhile been two days of attacks on the industry during May, but the full-scale attack started at the end of June and continued until March 1945. There were 555 separate attacks on 135 different targets, including every synthetic-fuel plant and major refinery known to be in operation.

The beginning of the onslaught started a precipitous drop in German oil production. From an average of 662,000 tons per month, it went down to 422,000 tons in June, 260,000 tons in December, and 80,000 tons—or 12 per cent of the preattack level—in March 1945. As for aviation and motor gasoline, the results were even better. Practically all German aviation gasoline was made by the hydrogenation process in synthetic-oil plants, and those plants were the first to be hit. Aviation gasoline production declined from 170,000 tons per month to 52,000 tons only one month after the oil bombing offensive began, and it had been eliminated completely by the following March.

The effect on Luftwaffe operations was tremendous. German gasoline stocks had been tight to begin with, and production losses meant immediate curtailment of consumption. Flight training was steadily shortened, and toward the end of the war pilots were sent into action who had had only forty to forty-five hours in the air. Their inexperience made them easy marks for our highly-trained air crews. Germany's large reserve of military aircraft was grounded with empty tanks. Only fighter missions against our bombers were permitted, and even those became few and ineffective.

Effects on ground combat were somewhat slower. Use of gasoline was restricted first in motor transport, but in the last stages of the war huge numbers of German tanks were unable to reach the fighting areas, or were abandoned on the battlefields, for lack of fuel. Before the end, wood or coal-burning gas generators, such as had been only moderately successful on buses and trucks, had been put on some fifty tanks.

Chemicals were never singled out as a target, but since most of the chemical industry was closely integrated with synthetic-oil production, attacks on the latter served to damage the former as well. When two plants (Leuna and Ludwigshafen) were shut down as a result of air attacks, Germany lost 63 per cent of its synthetic-nitrogen production and 40 per cent of its synthetic-rubber production. Damage to five additional oil plants brought the loss in synthetic nitrogen to 91 per cent. Nitrogen is essential for all explosives and powder propellants. As early as August 1944, Albert Speer was reporting to Hitler that the attacks on chemicals were threatening Germany's ability to carry on the war. Before V-E Day the Germans were filling their artillery shells with as much as 70 per cent inert rock salt.[3]

German transportation, including the extensive canal network as well as the railways, became a strategic target system in March 1944, although heavy attacks did not start until September 1944. By the end of October, carloadings were declining rapidly and showing immediate effects in

[3] U.S.S.B.S., *Ordnance Industry Report* (Item #101 for European War), p. 29; also *Oil Division Final Report* (Item #109 for European War), pp. 40-47. Incidentally, the latter item is one of the most illuminating reports in the entire series.

over-all production. By late November and early December all munitions production had been severely affected by the failure to move critical materials.

Even as early as August 1944, the Germans could no longer supply coal to the steel plants of Lorraine and Luxembourg. By February 1945, the Ruhr was just about completely isolated. Such coal as was loaded was often confiscated by the railroads for locomotive fuel; even so, by March, locomotives were standing idle for lack of coal in districts where some traffic could otherwise have moved. On March 15, when almost the whole of the Allied army was still west of the Rhine, Speer reported to Hitler: "The German economy is heading for an inevitable collapse within four to eight weeks." At that time over-all carloadings were 15 per cent of normal and moving toward zero.[4]

It was the collapse of transportation which caused the Strategic Bombing Survey to state in one of its most often-quoted passages: "Even if the final military victories that carried the Allied armies across the Rhine and the Oder had not taken place, armaments production would have come to a virtual standstill by May; the German armies, completely bereft of ammunition and of motive power, would almost certainly have had to cease fighting by June or July."[5] But these results of the bombing of Germany came late.

On the credit side, the fact that our ground forces during the last year of the war had little enemy air opposition to contend with, while our own planes were making things very rough for the German armies, owed much to our strategic bombing, especially to our bombing of enemy air fields (al-

[4] U.S.S.B.S., *The Effects of Strategic Bombing on German Transportation* (Item #200 for European War).
[5] U.S.S.B.S., *Effects on German War Economy*, p. 14.

ways considered good unloading spots for planes coming home with unused bombs) and to the air battles that attended our bombing forays. Moreover, the shortage of materials, especially oil, which our bombing was imposing on the Germans, did in fact hasten the final collapse of their armies. More important, the Germans in the last year of the war were devoting at least a third of their total war resources to air defense, resources which would otherwise have been available to their armies. We must remember also that some of our attacks, like that on the German V-weapon program, had important defensive results.

Nevertheless, the fact remains that the ultimate destruction of the German armies was practically assured from the time of the successful Allied break-out west of St. Lo late in July 1944, at which time the tangible battlefield results of our strategic bombing, apart from its important contribution to suppressing enemy air activities, added up to very little. By the time those results were making themselves felt seriously, the Battle of the Bulge was a thing of the past and the Allied armies were well into Germany.

If prior to mid-1943 we had put into our strategic air force some of the resources used in building up a great army and invasion armada, as some argued we should have done, we would no doubt have got our strategic bombing results faster. However, that is not the same as saying that the war would have ended sooner. The fact is that we did put into strategic bombing a colossal effort. We were also committed to an invasion of France, and there were at the time few grounds for calling that a bad commitment. At the time we made the relevant decisions, our government feared, probably wrongly, that if we limited ourselves to an air and naval effort the

Russians would make a separate peace. If, as is more likely, the Russians had gone on fighting, and if our bombing had guaranteed the success of Soviet ground forces, it would have been their armies and not ours that would have "liberated" western Europe, and that might very well have been there now.

The strategic bombing of Germany during World War II was almost totally a new experiment, in which much had to be learned the hard way. We steadily tried to reach out after greater capabilities, especially in carrying capacity, depth of penetration, and accuracy of bombing; and we sought, partly and inescapably through trial and error, to find good target systems. In both respects we can now see many critical and perhaps unnecessary errors which delayed our success.

The U.S.A.A.F. paid dearly for the prewar conviction, inherited from Douhet, that fighter escort was unnecessary for bombers like the B-17, unhappily called the "Flying Fortress." The disastrous second Schweinfurt raid of October 10, 1943, in which the attacking squadrons lost 30 per cent of their aircraft, indicated that deep daylight penetrations into Germany had to await the availability of large numbers of long-range fighters. Starting in early 1944, the P-51s played a major part in destroying the German Air Force. Similarly, the British paid heavily for their early conviction that night bombing could be precise enough for specific industrial targets. When that was disproved, they adopted in 1942 Chief of Bomber Command Sir Arthur Harris' compensating conviction that area bombing was the most promising method of aerial attack anyway, since the search for specific target systems was only a futile search for "panacea targets." Sir Arthur, incidentally, had not lost that conviction even when he wrote his memoirs after the war's end; nor had some of the senior officers who had served under him.[6]

The basic strategy for the Combined Bomber Offensive was laid down in the Casablanca Conference of January 1943, where the relevant directive stated the primary objective of the strategic air offensive: "the progressive destruction and dislocation of the German military, industrial, and economic system, and the undermining of the morale of the German people to a point where their capacity for armed resistance is fatally weakened." The directive went on to name five primary target systems in the following order: (1) submarine construction yards, (2) the aircraft industry, (3) transportation, (4) the oil industry, (5) generalized targets in the enemy war industry. In the absence of specific instructions to the contrary, air force commanders retained the authority to alter the order of priority for individual raids according to their own judgment.

On June 10, 1943, a new and much more pointed directive from the Combined Chiefs of Staff set down the "Pointblank" target system, and created the so-called "Jockey" Committee as an advisory body on targets; this Committee carried out its function until it merged with the Combined Strategic Targets Committee in September 1944. Under "Pointblank," German fighter plane production and existing strength were made unequivocally top-priority targets for the American bomber forces. The governing considerations were: (a) air dominance had to be established in the face of increasing German fighter strength, which threatened the con-

---

[6] See Marshal of the R.A.F. Sir Arthur Harris, *Bomber Offensive*, Collins, London, 1947, especially pp. 75, 220-234. Sir Arthur's Senior Air Staff Officer (or Chief of Staff), now Air Marshal Sir Robert Saundby, has espoused the same views in his numerous articles in British professional journals.

tinuance of the bomber offensive; (b) destruction of the German Air Force would provide the best short-term strategic-bombing contribution to the planned invasion of the Continent; and (c) the immediately preceding months, with their brilliant victories at sea, had brought the submarine menace under control and had shown, moreover, that the destruction of submarine yards and bases along with the other desired target systems was simply beyond the capabilities of existing bomber forces. The June 1943 directive thus recognized the need for adjusting to limited capabilities by ordering concentration on a single specifically-designated target system. All other systems were made secondary, and individual force commanders were given minimum discretion with regard to choice among systems to be attacked.

In principle, the selection of the German Air Force as a target system, and especially of its fighter contingent, was right. It placed first things first according to common sense as well as to the well-known Douhet dictum that command of the air must be won before it can be exploited. However, the offensive against the German aircraft industry, which reached its greatest intensity in the period February-April 1944, was a failure. Attacks upon airframe plants simply induced the Germans to disperse their facilities, which proved relatively easy to do since the tools mainly used were fairly mobile. The temporary loss of production resulting from such movement of equipment was about all that could be chalked up to the credit of the attacks.

The fact remains that front-line German fighter air strength increased sharply during the Allied offensive against it. No doubt the increase was less than it would have been but for our bombing. The Aircraft Division of the U.S.S.B.S. estimated that some 18,000 aircraft of all types were denied the German Air Force in the period between July 1943 and December 1944.[7] That figure, based on the disparity between planned and actual production, is ventured against an alleged total production for the same period of 53,000 aircraft—a quite improbable figure. The economists who prepared the over-all economic-effects report of U.S.S.B.S. were more cautious, offering the opinion that "it is possible that production would have been 15-20 per cent higher in the absence of bombing."[8]

In short, the attack on airframe production paid dividends —any diminution of enemy strength is a dividend—but they were not in the category of "decisive." They did not bear out what had been promised for a concentrated offensive by air forces of the size we were operating in early 1944. Moreover, we do not know how effectively the German Air Force could have used those "lost" aircraft, in view of shortages in fuel and pilots. The moment we started our attacks upon oil production in May 1944, the Germans began to find themselves with more planes than they could fly. Their aircraft production began to lag only in the fall of 1944, after the aircraft industry had ceased to be a primary target for the Combined Bomber Offensive. And, as we have noted, the major losses of German aircraft, together with trained pilots, occurred as a result of air battles which our bombing forays forced upon them and of our attacks on enemy airfields.

Possibly it was our method of attacking the aircraft target manufacturing rather than the choice of the system itself that was wrong. Hermann Göring and Albert Speer argued after their capture that aircraft-engine production would

---

[7] U.S.S.B.S., *Aircraft Division Industry Report* (Item #4 for European War), p. 6.
[8] U.S.S.B.S., *Effects on German War Economy*, p. 12.

have made a better target system than airframes, because the engines were made in a much smaller number of factories. But others pointed out that engine-manufacturing plants were of much lower physical vulnerability than airframe factories, especially to the light bombs (maximum 500 lbs.) we were then using.[9]

The marked and immediate success achieved against the oil-producing industry seemed to indicate that the enemy air force was far more vulnerable through denial of liquid fuel than through direct attack upon it. The great fuel-producing plants could not be dispersed, their essential producing facilities were quite vulnerable to blast and incendiary damage, and they were difficult to conceal. Yet only about 1 per cent of the half-million tons of bombs dropped on Germany before May 1944 had been aimed at the oil industry. This omission resulted from the belief that the major fuel-producing plants lay beyond our range capabilities, from our consistent overestimation of the reserves of fuel which the Germans had in storage, and from our anxiety to get quick results. The total weight of bombs ultimately aimed at oil-production facilities and storage depots was about 240,000 tons, or about half the total tonnage that had been dropped on Germany proper prior to May 1944.

Our failure to make a direct and comprehensive attack on the German chemical industry, including the synthetic-rubber plants, was also a serious error. The fact that that industry collapsed as a wholly unexpected result of our attack on oil reveals how vulnerable it was. Had we elevated it to the status of a target system in itself, we could have demolished it much earlier in the war than we did and with only a small percentage of the bombs ultimately aimed at oil. The German

<hr>

[9] U.S.S.B.S., *Aircraft Division Report*, pp. 53f.

General Heinrici told our U.S.S.B.S. interrogators that if Allied effort had been concentrated on ammonia plants, Germany could have been knocked out of the war a full year earlier.[10] That may not be so, but it is an interesting opinion.

The Failure of City Bombing in Germany

The bombing of cities turned out to be a great waste of effort. To be sure, cities were easier to find and hit than were particular industrial plants, and the kind of weather encountered over Germany often left no choice. Also we must remember the special limitations imposed on the R.A.F. by the fact that it was built and equipped as a night-bombing force:

Prior to the development of long-range fighters and the discovery and improvement of non-visual bombing aids and techniques, the RAF could not undertake daylight bombing without prohibitive losses, nor could it achieve sufficient accuracy in night bombing to attack other than very large targets. Even with the earlier forms of radar, an attack on a target smaller than a city area of at least 100,000 population was not economical.

For example, using "GEE," the first radar navigational aid (which became available in March 1942), Bomber Command of the RAF, in attacks on towns in the Ruhr, could drop approximately 50 per cent of its bombs within five miles of the aiming point and 10 per cent within two miles. This meant that only 5 to 10 per cent of the tonnage dispatched could be dropped on a town the size of Essen and only two to three per cent on the Krupp works within Essen. Thus, economy required that attacks be aimed at the city center, ensuring that the maximum tonnage of bombs would fall somewhere on the target.[11]

[10] U.S.S.B.S., *Powder, Explosives* . . . (Item #111 for European War: Oil Division; Ministerial Report No. 1), p. 4; see also *Oil Division Final Report*, pp. 40-73.

[11] U.S.S.B.S., *Area Studies Division Report* (Item #31 for European

Bombing accuracy was greatly improved later on, especially during the summer of 1944. Nevertheless, the limitations described above could be accepted, and a campaign carried out despite them, only if the attacker expected substantial results from area bombing. Air Marshal Sir Arthur Harris of Bomber Command did expect such results, because, despite his utter disdain for what we now call "psychological warfare," he shared Douhet's faith in the critical vulnerability of civilian morale. We shall consider the effects of bombing on civilian morale in a separate section, though it should already be obvious that whatever morale decline took place was of limited effect upon the over-all strategic situation. There was immense destruction and damage wrought on the buildings in German cities, and it is really surprising that the war industries gathered in those cities should have suffered so little impairment or loss of production.

The tonnages expended on city bombing were enormous. Prior to our oil offensive, 53 per cent of the bombs dropped on Germany were aimed at area targets, and only 13 per cent at specific industries. Even during the oil offensive, over 27 per cent of the million-and-a-half tons dropped were aimed at cities and only 22 per cent at specific industries, the latter including the 16 per cent assigned to oil targets.

What were the results? The Report of the Area Studies Division of the U.S.S.B.S. opens with the following paragraph:

The major cities of Germany present a spectacle of destruction so appalling as to suggest a complete breakdown of all aspects of

---

War), pp. 3f. This kind of inaccuracy, incidentally, is one reason why electric power stations, which Speer and others considered an extraordinarily choice target system, were not in fact targeted. The vulnerable portions of electric power stations generally take up a very small area.

urban activity. On the first impression it would appear that the area attacks which laid waste these cities must have substantially eliminated the industrial capacity of Germany. Yet this was not the case. The attacks did not so reduce German war production as to have a decisive effect on the outcome of the war.

The reasons for this indecisive effect were several, and we can only mention a few. One was the fact that in most German cities the industrial areas were on the perimeter, and area attacks on previously unbombed cities were always aimed at the centers. Even with the considerable improvement in nonvisual bombing aids between 1943 and 1944, it was practically impossible to concentrate bombing attacks upon the industrial portions of built-up areas. Where industrial plants were hit, the nonessential as well as the essential were affected. The halting of the former only helped to speed the flow of labor and other resources to the latter. Such essential services as electricity, gas, and water were disrupted by heavy attacks, but in most cases they were readily restored. The cutting of the Ruhr gas lines in 1944 shut down important plants in Düsseldorf, Essen, Krefeld, and Berlin and contributed to the collapse of German steel production, but that was an exceptional occurrence. It must be remembered too that the same bombing which inevitably reduced some of the supply of essential utilities also reduced some of the demand.

Another important fact about city bombing is that the damage was done primarily to buildings rather than to the machines or machine-tools which some of those buildings housed. Not more than an estimated 6 to 7 per cent of all machine tools in Germany were damaged or destroyed by air attack, and not all of those had to be replaced. "In 1944, the year of the heaviest bombing, it is estimated that it was necessary to devote only 10 to 12 per cent of machine tool production to the repair of machine tools damaged as a result of air attack."[12] If the buildings which housed machines important to war production were too severely damaged, the machines often could be moved to other locations. Otherwise the structures were roughly patched up and the workers prevailed upon to continue.

We should not assume that the damage done to over-all production was trivial. An area raid could drive production in a city down by as much as 55 per cent in the month immediately following the attack. But recovery was rapid; most cities were back to 80 per cent of normal within three months, and had recovered completely within six to eleven months. Naturally the recovery was most rapid in the most essential industries. No doubt the "cushion" in consumer goods was being eroded away. No doubt, too, indirect effects, as expressed in absenteeism of workers, were growing steadily more serious.

Certainly the terrible shock given to the entire German state by the series of extremely heavy attacks directed at Hamburg at the end of July and the beginning of August 1943 suggests what might have happened if attacks of comparable intensity could have been directed also against a substantial number of other German cities at about the same time and in rapid succession. *There is clearly no basis at all for assuming that conclusions about German urban bombing in World War II would apply to war in the atomic age.* A different result, as we shall see, obtained even in the same war in the case of Japan. But the fact remains that "the over-all index of German munitions production increased steadily from 100 in January 1942 to 322 in July 1944,"[13] a period that included a tremendous amount of general city bombing.

[12] U.S.S.B.S., *Area Studies Division Report,* p. 22.
[13] *Ibid.,* p. 19.

The bombing of German cities cost the Germans much in production and more in the diversion of military resources to defense; but we must nevertheless state that no critical shortages in war commodities of any kind are traceable to it. To cause inconvenience and unhappiness to the enemy is a reasonable military aim in war, but in view of the promises made by Douhet and his followers, and in view also of the great military resources invested in it, the urban-area bombing of World War II must be set down unequivocally as a failure.

Trial and Error in Bombing Tactics

For World War II types of bombs it was necessary not only to pick the right target systems but also to find the right facilities within those systems and the right target centers within those facilities. In our attack upon railroad transportation, for example, a large proportion of the bombing was directed against freight-car marshalling yards, and usually we aimed at the center of the yards in order to hit the greatest amount of trackage. As a result, such bombing usually left some fairly intact stump yards near the entrance to the original yards, which the Germans could use for high-priority traffic while proceeding with repairs. The entrance, or throat, of the yard would have been a far better target center, but was rarely so designated. Moreover, the Germans not only had a large surplus capacity in yards, but some of the important traffic, including troop movements, tended to use complete trains which did not require the use of marshalling yards at all. By far the most effective way of interdicting railroad transportation, at least with the H.E. (high explosive) bombs of World War II, proved to be by way of line cuts at bridges, underpasses, viaducts, tunnels, and the like.[14]

[14] At least this is the conclusion of the Transportation Division of

Even in the successful offensive against the oil industry there was a generally poor selection of "ground-zeros"[15] within the plants selected for attack. Although accuracy in general was far below the "pickle-barrel" precision advertised before the war, vulnerable areas when chosen consistently as the bull's-eye were invariably destroyed. In only a small minority of the cases, however, were the most critical and vulnerable sections of the plant so chosen.

Also, the bombs used were usually too light for the job. The U.S.A.A.F.'s attacks were "based on the observation that it is easier to hit an elephant with a shotgun than with a rifle." The average weight per unit of the bombs we dropped on oil and chemical targets was 388 pounds, but it was the heavy bombs of two to four thousand pounds each, used toward the very end of the war, which were alone able to do really permanent damage to heavy industrial installations. The British, incidentally, were considerably more advanced than we in this respect, the average weight of the bombs dropped by the R.A.F. during our oil offensive being something like 660 pounds. A considerable improvement in effec-

U.S.S.B.S. The British Bombing Survey Unit credited much greater effectiveness to the bombing of marshalling yards, but, as we have noted, the Survey was directed by persons who had been deeply involved in the operational decisions.

[15] This awkward term is forced upon me by shifts in terminology since World War II. What for bombing would correspond to the "bull's-eye" in pistol or rifle target shooting used to be called the "aiming point," which is the sense in which the latter term is used through most of the U.S.S.B.S. However, with the development of bombing sights that permitted offset bombing, the "aiming point" might well be miles from the center of the target (making it rather like the offset "aiming point" used in archery target shooting). The atomic bomb has encouraged the habit of using the term "ground zero" to indicate the point on the surface immediately under the center of burst, and "designated ground zero," often abbreviated D.G.Z., is therefore comparable to "bull's-eye." In short, it is the point aimed at, not the "aiming point"!

tiveness could also have been obtained through cutting down the proportion of bombs in both forces which failed to explode.

One does not have to think in terms of perfect planning, perfect intelligence, or perfect anything else to admit that better planning and testing before the war and more flexibility of doctrine would have brought vastly better results than were achieved. The bombs aimed at what proved to be the right targets, the destruction of which caused the collapse of the German economy, comprised only a minute percentage of the total tonnage dropped on Germany and German-occupied territory.

In this brief résumé of the strategic bombing of Germany, we have *not* been concerned with whether the campaign was worth its cost. If we were trying to appraise the total payoff of the campaign, we should have to sum up the direct and also all the indirect results which we can find, including the great effort which the Germans put into active military and non-military defenses against our bombing. We should especially have to take into full account the fact that, from Dunkirk to the time of the invasion of Italy, there was no way other than bombing by which the British and ourselves could strike at Germany in Europe. The question whether strategic bombing on the scale applied represented the *optimum* use of the resources expended in it is essentially unanswerable; but there is a strong prima-facie case for its having been a good use of those resources.

The questions to which we have addressed ourselves are, first, whether the campaign produced *decisive* results, and, secondly, whether such results could have been achieved earlier with a better use of the resources actually available. The answer to the first question is a qualified "yes," and to the second a clear affirmative. But that such a campaign could have been decisive even in the absence of ground opererations—with all the freeing of resources for the air battle that such a situation would have implied *for both sides*—must be regarded as neither proved nor provable. Assertions to the contrary, on either side of the argument, can be only declarations of faith.

The Strategic Bombing of Japan

Any appraisal of results of the strategic bombing of Japan must start from consideration of the military conditions prevailing at the time the campaign really got under way, which was quite late in the war. The raids that began in the fall of 1943 by B-29's based in China, and supplied entirely by air transport over the "hump" from India, were on much too small a scale to have strategic significance. The U.S.S.B.S. report suggests that with their limited sortie rate, those forces would have been more effectively used in the campaign against Japanese shipping. The inauguration of the strategic air offensive against Japan is reasonably dated not earlier than November 1944. Toward the end of that month bomber attacks were initiated from recently won Saipan, and later from Tinian and Guam.

However, the intensive air attack on the Japanese that marked the latter stages of the war began only in March 1945, at which time some radically new tactics worked out in General Curtis LeMay's headquarters were introduced. These tactics involved "maximum effort" low-level attacks at night, with great compression of force in space and time. The intensity of attacks increased gradually, until an attack occurred on the southwest portion of Tokyo on May 23, 1945 in which 520 bombers dropped 3,646 tons of incendiary bombs on an area of about eleven square miles. For two hours during that attack the bombs were dropping at an average rate of 1,000 pounds per second.[16]

The plight of the Japanese Empire at the time this campaign began is summarized by a single sentence from the U.S.S.B.S. report: "By March 1945, prior to heavy direct air attack on the Japanese home islands, the Japanese air forces had been reduced to Kamikaze forces, her fleet had been sunk or immobilized, her merchant marine decimated, large portions of her ground forces isolated, and the strangulation of her economy well begun."[17]

At that time, moreover, the Japanese had already lost the Philippines and Iwo Jima, and were suffering the investment of Okinawa. They were sending no further supplies to their ground forces outside the home islands, and they were concentrating solely on defense against invasion. How long they would have continued to endure even in the absence of a concentrated strategic-bombing campaign is questionable, because the blockade resulting from destruction of the Japanese merchant marine had, among other things, brought the national diet to below subsistence levels. The situation was thoroughly understood by many Japanese military leaders. Some of the senior naval officers had been secretly working since the previous September, that is, since before the Battle for Leyte Gulf, to take the country out of the war.[18]

So long as the American goal was unconditional surrender,

[16] I am indebted for this information, and for much more that I have not been able to include, to my colleague Dr. Alexander W. Boldyreff.

[17] U.S.S.B.S., *Summary Report (Pacific War)*, p. 9.

[18] U.S.S.B.S., *Japan's Struggle to End the War*, p. 4. See also Robert J. C. Butow, *Japan's Decision to Surrender*, Stanford University Press, Stanford, 1954, which effectively supersedes the U.S.S.B.S. document and which provides an excellent and fascinating narrative of relevant events.

and especially so long as we were eager to achieve it as quickly as possible, there seemed at the time to be no question that some kind of direct assault on the Japanese home islands was necessary. A full-scale invasion was accordingly being projected for the following November. It is unequivocally to the credit of the strategic-bombing offensive that it secured all the objectives of the planned invasion before the latter could be mounted. It did so at immeasurably less cost in American lives, and no doubt also in Japanese lives, than might otherwise have been the case. Nothing can diminish or gainsay the value and importance of this accomplishment, which had no parallel in Europe. By the same token, it is both unreasonable and ungracious to the other services—as well as to the tactical air forces which conducted four years of marvelously successful and effective operations over land and water—to equate that accomplishment with the winning of the war.

The strategic air offensive against Japan was remarkably different from that against Germany in character as well as result. It was much more concentrated in time, and had the benefit of the more advanced technology then available. Japan was more urbanized than Germany, its cities were more vulnerable to fire, and its active defenses at the time of the campaign were of a low order of effectiveness, being almost confined to antiaircraft guns.[19] Thus, more was accomplished with fewer bombs. Only 160,800 tons of bombs were dropped on the home islands of Japan, compared with 1,360,000 tons dropped within the borders of Germany. Sixty-six Japanese cities received 104,000 tons of bombs (mostly incendiaries) as compared with 542,554 tons dropped on

[19] Of which, however, there were some 500 heavy guns (88 mm. or larger) in the Tokyo area alone.

sixty-one German cities. Also, a disproportionately large part of the Japanese tonnage was dropped on a very few large cities. Of the sixty-six Japanese cities attacked, only six were struck before the last three months of the war.[20] Yet some 40 per cent of the built-up areas of those sixty-six cities was destroyed.

In Japan, unlike Germany, the urban-area bombing seems to have contributed more to achieving the desired results than did the precision bombing of specific industries. This was due not alone to the fact that there was less opportunity for recuperation among Japanese cities than there had been in Germany, but more importantly to the fact that in Japan economic objectives counted for less than psychological ones. The precision bombing was, as in Germany, much more effective per bomb in reducing Japanese war production, and immeasurably more discriminating about the kind of production reduced, than was the urban-area bombing. But Japan had already lost the battle of production; her economy had already proved grossly inadequate to the political and strategic ambitions of her leaders; her losses in a merchant fleet that had been inadequate from the start had already caused, through denial of raw materials, a sharp contraction in production. Greater contractions would have followed inevitably, even without bombing.[21] It must be added that her overwhelming military defeats, by practically wiping out her navy and isolating most of her army, had greatly re-

[20] U.S.S.B.S., *Effects of Air Attack on Japanese Urban Economy, Summary Report*, pp. ivf.

[21] The U.S.S.B.S. estimated that by August 1945, "even without direct air attack on her cities and industries, the over-all level of Japanese war production would have declined below the peak levels of 1944 by 40 to 50 per cent solely as a result of the interdiction of overseas imports." (*Summary Report* [*Pacific War*], p. 15.)

duced the demands which the military forces were making upon the economy.

Japan was already defeated. It was necessary only to make her government develop a clear consensus on that fact, and then openly concede it. The U.S.A.A.F. may not have correctly appreciated the situation, but it acted as if it had. What was wanted was not a discriminating pruning out of this or that kind of military production, but simply the maximum of direct military pressure upon the population and the government. The awful terror of the great fire raids on the cities, culminating in the two atomic attacks, copiously provided that pressure.

The Attack on German Morale

It is difficult to tell just what proportion of the bombs dropped on Germany in World War II was deliberately aimed at German morale, but it was unquestionably very large. A good deal of the area bombing of cities was so directed, especially by the R.A.F. Although Sir Arthur Harris in his *Bomber Offensive* speaks sarcastically of "psychological" objectives as among the "panaceas" thrust upon him by uncomprehending but meddling civilians, it is abundantly clear from the whole text of his memoirs that the "German will to resist" was precisely what he was most interested in attacking. Douhet too, as we have seen, had considered it the most important target after the enemy air force.

The huge share of Allied bombs spent in the attack on German morale failed to achieve any important end results. Bombing did indeed seriously depress the morale of German civilians. The oft-expressed view that the bombing of cities stiffens the will of the populace to resist finds no support in experience. But in Germany the depressed morale had no critical effects—at least until the very last months of the war, when all was lost anyway—on either the political structure or the capability of the German war economy to support the troops in the field.

The reason that this was so is to be found largely in a distinction, which the German Internal Security Service consistently emphasized throughout the latter part of the war, between *Stimmung* (attitude or feeling) and *Haltung* (behavior). It was one of the important discoveries of the war that the influence of the former upon the latter was much less immediate and direct than had been generally supposed. Some degree of influence there was bound to be, but from the Allied point of view it was disappointingly small.

The attack upon *Stimmung* or attitude was remarkably successful, but this success did not have much meaning for the things that counted. Depressed morale, *plus* the problem of coping with the physical deprivations resulting from bombing, significantly increased absenteeism of industrial workers beyond the normal. It also significantly lowered the productivity of those who reported for work. In combination, these effects—and notice that morale was depressed by defeats in the ground battles as well as by air raids—resulted in a loss of output of at least 25 per cent during the last year of the war. That looked serious enough to those responsible for keeping the war machine going. But as for stopping or vitally impairing the functioning of that machine, the effects were spread too broadly across all industries, were at best marginal, and therefore counted as nothing compared to the knocking out of a single essential industry such as oil production or transportation.

From at least the beginning of 1944 the average German had become disillusioned with the Nazi leadership, increasingly frightened by the war's toll and its potential threat to himself and his family, and persuaded with growing certainty that all would end in defeat. Yet he stuck to his job and his machine for as long as it was physically possible to do so, and in so doing kept a disastrous war going to its ultimate ruinous conclusion. Why did he do so? The answer is to be found in need combined with habit, in coercion, and in propaganda—in descending order of importance—all adding up to the plain circumstance that the German worker had no real alternative open to him.

The effect of habit is in part reflected in the fact that unauthorized absenteeism was much more marked among women than among men, especially in those occupations in which female labor was strictly a wartime phenomenon. The man kept to his job largely because that was what he had always done, in calm and in crisis, and because he and his family needed his wages in order to eat.

The coercion of the government extended to all sorts of restrictions about changing or leaving one's job without permission, and applied with special vengeance to overt expression of feeling—let alone action—against the regime. More telling was the fact that over the years the regime had succeeded in eradicating practically all organized political opposition, so that no means existed for giving direction to and translating into action the feelings of disaffection which undoubtedly developed. There could be no *peace party* in Germany (outside the army, where the dissident group was liquidated after the abortive *putsch* of July 1944) simply because there could be no *party* outside the control of the Nazi leadership.

This absence of organized opposition is the feature of totalitarian countries that must give pause to those who would count heavily on defeating them by psychological means. In that connection, a critical difference between wartime Germany on the one hand and Italy and Japan on the other was that the latter two countries, though quasi-totalitarian, had in their monarchial systems a latent means of crystallizing an effective and legal opposition to the war party. Those countries surrendered before hostile troops had effectively invaded their main territories, while Germany did not surrender until Hitler was dead and the eastern and western fronts had merged in the center of the Reich.

Although habit and coercion worked exclusively for the benefit of the German government, propaganda was the one means by which the Allied governments could hope to compete with the Nazis in giving guidance to the German workman and soldier. The Allied bombing helped induce Germans to listen to enemy radio broadcasts, partly because its success gave the lie to so many Nazi claims, and also because German stations had to go off the air to avoid serving as beacons. The invading aircraft themselves dropped millions of leaflets. Allied propaganda during the last year or more of the war concentrated on the hopelessness of the German military position, something which the huge formations of British and American bombers ranging freely over Germany effectively drove home. That was all right so far as it went, but it left a hiatus into which Goebbels and Company promptly moved.

The great propaganda achievement of Goebbels, in which he was aided and abetted by Allied word and actions, was to exploit sheer desperation as a means of keeping the Germans fighting. There was no "will to win" because, especially after the collapse of the hopes based on "secret weapons," there could be no expectation of winning. What took the place of a will to win was an apathy about politics combined with a driving fear of what defeat would bring. One of the grimmer aphorisms then current in Germany was *"Geniess den Krieg; der Friede wird schrecklich sein"* (Enjoy the war; the peace will be terrible). The number of Allied casualties in the last year of the war testifies to the effectiveness of this combination of negative incentives.

One lesson the bombing attack on morale brought home was that a people accustomed to responding to authority— and all peoples are, in modestly varying degrees—will continue to respond even under very great physical stress. As physical conditions approach chaos, the population becomes more dependent upon authority, because of greater need for guidance and succor combined with the absence of alternative. Besides, the person of independent mind who forms his own opinions on the evidence of his senses and the fruits of his logic is an ideal form of human being which, like other ideal forms, rarely exists in nature. Even most intellectuals— always a small minority in a population—tend in their thinking merely to follow more refined fads. Moreover, it takes a very profound revolution of the mind and spirit to accept those cues for behavior provided by the acknowledged enemy as against those offered by one's own leaders.

Granting that it is behavior rather than morale that most interests both attacker and defender, there are nevertheless a few features about the response of German morale to Allied bombs which are especially interesting in view of the new weapons that have appeared since World War II.

One surprising finding of the U.S.S.B.S. was that the most heavily-bombed cities did not necessarily show lower morale than those less severely hit. As between unbombed towns and lightly-bombed ones, morale was much lower in the latter. It suffered a further but less sharp decline as the status of bombing progressed from "light" to "medium." But as the weight of bombs progressed from "medium" to "heavy," the morale of the target population appeared, if anything, to recover somewhat.[22] Much, of course, depends on how one measures morale, and the returns used in the survey were undoubtedly too gross to confirm a real upturn in morale. But what is firmly established is the absence, after a relatively modest weight of bombing, of any significant correlation between additional bombs dropped and further depression in morale.

Why is this so? One reason, no doubt, is the simple fact that the person preoccupied with dodging enemy missiles does not find much time to think about other matters which might otherwise disturb him. He is unlikely to be brooding on the historic sins and errors of a government to which he can scarcely conceive an alternative. He is politically apathetic, and his apathy may look a good deal better to those whose job it is to control him than did the discouraged restlessness that perhaps preceded it. Besides, if he has been bombed out of house and home, he is grateful for small offerings, and he may acquire a more favorable attitude toward

[22] The following classification for degrees of bombing was adopted by the Morale Division of U.S.S.B.S.: Group I (heavily bombed), cities receiving 19,100 tons to 47,200 tons (average: 30,000 tons); Group II (medium bombed), cities receiving 1,700 to 13,100 tons (average: 6,100 tons); Group III (lightly bombed), cities receiving 300 to 800 tons (average: 500 tons). Since these figures and categories ignore the size of the city concerned, they cannot give a good index of the *intensity* of bombing for any one city. However, a recheck of the results described in the text above according to the *percentage of destruction* for each city confirms the general conclusions reached. See *The Effects of Strategic Bombing on German Morale*, vol. I, Morale Division, U.S.S.B.S. (Item #64b for European War), pp. 24, 27.

the regime merely from being given coffee at the refugee station.

On the other hand, we learned also that depression in morale, while not necessarily proportional to weight of bombs dropped, does vary with degree of personal involvement, such as the death or severe injury of members of one's family, or the destruction of all one's worldly goods, or forced evacuation. Despite the large amount of physical destruction in German cities, the statistics of personal involvement were quite different from what one would expect—certainly different from what one would have to expect with nuclear weapons. Only one-third of all Germans lived in cities that were subjected to bombing. One-half of 1 per cent of all Germans were killed by bombing, and 1 per cent were injured; that is, only 5 per cent of that minority of Germans *actually subjected to bombing* were killed or injured. One-fifth of all civilians were at one time or another deprived of water, gas, or electricity. And one out of fifteen civilians was evacuated.

These figures are impressive when converted to absolute numbers of people, and it is also true that virtually no German escaped some measure of hardship or suffering as a result of the bombings. But the great majority of Germans escaped the more serious kinds of heartbreak or horror. Under atomic weapons, even ignoring the effects of fallout, the proportion of persons exposed to risk in the cities would be much greater, the incidence of casualties and of lost homes would be multiplied, and the disorganizing effects upon the surrounding countrysides would be immeasurably more immediate and direct. Certainly the amount of warning permitted by missiles and by attacking cells of planes moving at or above the speed of sound would be much less.

It is true that the effects of reduced morale upon German production look very different if one concentrates on the last two months of the war rather than on the entire two years of heavy bombing. In the end, the overwhelming conviction that there simply was no use in going on did indeed control events. The efforts to restore damaged facilities finally collapsed for complete want of incentive. With nuclear bombs such a state of affairs would occur within days or hours of the onset of the attack.

The Attack on Japanese Morale

The physical and social context of the bombing attack on Japanese morale was sufficiently different from that of Germany to provide distinctive instruction; yet it serves also to emphasize the striking similarity of the results. The bombing of urban areas in Japan was both more concentrated in time and more intense than in Germany, and it resulted in a higher incidence of both physical destruction and casualties. Also, the campaign reached its awesome and dreadful culmination in two atomic explosions.

As in Germany, only more so, the effect of the bombing on Japanese morale was to produce, by whatever kind of measurement one adopts, an immediate and precipitous decline. In Japan as in Germany, low morale was reflected in loss of the people's confidence in their leaders and in one another, as well as in their becoming, as the U.S.S.B.S. puts it, "more and more obsessed with finding individual solutions to their own severe and urgent personal problems." In Japan there was no more tendency than there was in Germany for the low morale to find expression in any organized popular movement to revolt, or in manifest pressure upon the government to surrender. On the contrary, the

Emperor's announcement of the surrender was apparently greeted by a majority of the population with stunned disbelief and dismay. Only a relatively small minority of the whole population later admitted to their American interrogators a feeling of relief at hearing that the war was over. Even among those who had personally experienced ten or more air raids, barely 52 per cent were ready to cite cessation of such raids as a sufficient reason for satisfaction at the ending of the war.[23]

That is not to say that the low state of public morale played no part in bringing about the surrender. In the peculiar oligarchical system by which wartime Japan was ruled, the peace faction which gradually emerged and moved toward ascendancy had to proceed most cautiously—even conspiratorially—with respect to the die-hard faction. The leaders of the peace-seeking party, ostensibly led by the Premier, Admiral Kantaro Suzuki,[24] had to assure themselves that the people knew enough of the general state of affairs to accept a surrender decision and to refrain from supporting a possible *coup d'etat* by the army die-hards. The latter faction also had to be persuaded that the mood and condition of the people made absurd any talk of a last-ditch defense in which civilians would fight off the invaders with bamboo spears. Even so, the maneuvers of the peace group were delicate in the extreme, and required finally the personal intervention of the Emperor.

The part played by the two atomic bombs cannot be un-

[23] See *The Effects of Strategic Bombing on Japanese Morale*, U.S.S.B.S. (Item #14 for Pacific War), pp. 150f.

[24] The real leader of the movement was Shigenori Togo, whom Admiral Suzuki had selected as Foreign Minister, knowing that he had been opposed to the war from the beginning; but Togo on one or two critical occasions had to stiffen Suzuki's determination to end the war. See Butow, *op.cit.*, chs. III and VII.

equivocally determined by what was said or not said in cabinet meetings and comparable conferences. It would be hard to believe that they failed to have a positive and powerful effect on the surrender deliberations, but very little seems to have been said about them in those deliberations. So far as the populace was concerned, few people outside the target areas had any real comprehension of what the bombs meant, and those within the areas seem to have been psychologically affected in no significantly different way from the people of other cities who had experienced severe HE or incendiary attacks.[25]

The cabinet had already initiated peace proposals to the Soviet government before the atomic bombs were dropped, and there is no reason to suppose that acceptance of the Potsdam Declaration would have been long delayed in the absence of such bombing. In the meeting of August 9-10 (after the second bomb had exploded) the cabinet was still deadlocked on the minimum terms under which Japan could agree to quit the hopeless fight, and it was this deadlock that the Emperor personally resolved. No doubt the atomic bombs affected him; but they could hardly have affected him decisively, because he had impressed upon the new Premier as early as the preceding April the need for finding the quickest possible means of ending the war.[26]

[25] *Ibid.*, p. 94. See also Part 1 of *Air War and Emotional Stress*, by Irving L. Janis, McGraw-Hill, New York, 1951. A remarkable document in this connection is Dr. Michihiko Hachiya's *Hiroshima Diary: The Journal of a Japanese Physician, August 6–September 30, 1945*, University of North Carolina Press, Chapel Hill, 1955.

[26] See Butow, *op.cit.*, pp. 63f. My RAND colleague, Dr. Paul Kecskemeti, argues cogently in his *Strategic Surrender: The Politics of Victory and Defeat* (Stanford University Press, 1958) a position very close to the one that I have presented here, based on a completely independent examination of the same evidence. He tends, however, to allow even less

In summary, we can say that, insofar as the low morale of the Japanese people influenced the governmental decision to surrender, it did so in a quite passive way. The leaders who spearheaded the peace movement had been convinced for more than a year before the end that Japan had lost. The terrible destruction and death rained down on Japan in the summer of 1945 naturally compelled a mood of urgency on the part of the peace-seekers, and made speedier and easier the acceptance by the erstwhile die-hards of almost-unconditional surrender. No reasonable observer can deny that the aerial bombardment hastened the end of the war and sufficed to make invasion unnecessary. But what must be denied, for the sake of clarity in strategic thinking, is that this process operated to any important degree through the direct pressure of public feeling.[27]

All this must of course be related to the singular political and social structure of wartime Japan. But under any form of government, an orderly surrender usually requires the initiative of political leaders who are already in authority or close enough to it to acquire it without waiting upon popular revolution.[28] Popular revolutions do not thrive under

---

weight than I do to the influence of the two atomic bombs in ending the war (*Strategic Surrender*, pp. 199-206).

[27] The authors of the above-cited U.S.S.B.S. morale report go so far as to insist, in their ch. xi, that the Japanese leaders ended the war when they did to conserve not lives but rather their own special privileges under the existing class structure of Japan. The authors, however, produce no evidence in support of that view, for the insistence upon the retention of the Imperial institution cannot be so regarded. No doubt the Japanese leaders, conservatives all, were interested in preserving as much as they could of the social and political structure of Japan, but we have no reason to assume they were callous in the face of the miseries being inflicted on the populace.

[28] A much qualified exception is the Bolshevik Revolution of 1917, followed by a Russian withdrawal from the war under peace terms (at

conditions of wholesale destruction from the air. The kind of extreme destruction that can be envisaged with nuclear weapons is rather more likely to dissolve all government than to cause the replacement of an incorrigible regime by an amenable one.

The Japanese experience suggests also that to compel huge evacuations is more profitable as well as more humane than to produce corpses. During the American air campaign, some eight and one-half million Japanese left their homes to become refugees. This figure must be considered not only in relation to the whole national population but even more to the populations of those larger industrial cities which mainly fed the exodus. Although evacuations also took place in Germany, the flight of urban dwellers from Japanese cities was more concentrated in time and hence more disorganized, and it included very much larger proportions of workers previously engaged in war industries. These panicked humans not only spread throughout Japan the full account of the horrors occurring in the cities, but they also created for the government burdens with which it showed itself unable to cope.

This rout of citizens would no doubt have resulted in any case from the fury of our attack, but it was given strong additional impetus by an American practice introduced in the last months of the war. That was the explicit warning of impending bombing attack, which was done chiefly by dropping leaflets (scarcely 2 per cent of Japanese civilians ever heard enemy radio broadcasts) listing cities to be destroyed "in the next few days." Each list was designed to be

---

Brest Litovsk) that were comparable to surrender. On conditions of surrender in general see the aforementioned study by Paul Kecskemeti.

short enough to impress the reader with its specificity, four or five cities usually being named in each series, yet long enough to avoid giving any marked assistance to the Japanese air defenses. The attendant commentary took care to stress that other cities besides those named might also be hit.

Unfortunately, the U.S.S.B.S. interrogators failed to question people seriously on what they had *done* as a result of hearing or reading about such warnings. They asked instead how many had seen the warnings or heard of them, and how many of those who did had believed them. But the evidence indicates (1) that the warnings were received by most of the targeted populations, (2) that they were generally believed, and (3) that they were acted upon through flight. Relatively few people left their homes until the cities in which they lived had received some bombing, but after such bombing the warnings had a most receptive audience. Many were unquestionably stimulated to move who would otherwise have tarried.

The military situation peculiar to the closing months of World War II in the Pacific was as favorable as it could be to the use of warnings, which literally cost us nothing in planes or air crews. Nevertheless, the warning technique could undoubtedly be applied even in the future under a wide variety of military circumstances. Whether it would be employed, however, in that massive interchange of blows which is the usual mental image of the onset of World War III is another matter.

Relevance for the Future

The World War II experience with strategic bombing was the first of its kind in the history of warfare, and also, we can be reasonably certain, the last. No campaign on a comparable scale is likely ever again to be carried on between great belligerents with HE or other chemical bombs, not only because of the availability of nuclear weapons but—in the unlikely event that nuclear weapons could be outlawed and stay outlawed in an otherwise total war—also because technological developments have made long-range sorties with bombers or missiles far too costly to be acceptable as means of delivering bombs of such very limited capability.

We have offered the above chapter out of the conviction that relevant experience is always valuable, the more so as it is scarce, but insofar as our interest is not purely historical, we have to acknowledge that in this instance the relevance is qualified. There are, however, hints about the future to be found in it, perhaps the most obvious and also the most important being the reminder that men's predictions about the outcome of a wholly new kind of campaign are likely to prove highly fallible.[29]

[29] For a systematic effort to apply the lessons of various disaster studies, including the strategic bombing of World War II, to future war, see Fred C. Iklé, *The Social Impact of Bomb Destruction*, University of Oklahoma Press, Norman, 1958.

⊰ PART II ⊱

NEW PROBLEMS AND NEW APPROACHES

⊰5⊱

THE ADVENT OF NUCLEAR WEAPONS

PEOPLE often speak of atomic explosives as the most portentous military invention "since gunpowder." But such a comparison inflates the importance of even so epoch-making an event as the introduction of gunpowder.

Those who lived through the first military use of gunpowder, sometime in the early part of the fourteenth century, seem to have been quite unexcited about it, and actually failed to record the occasion. Not until a century later, at the siege of Orleans in 1428-1429, do we find firearms, in this case siege guns, playing a major part in battle, though still an indecisive one. In leading the final storming of that city, Joan of Arc was wounded by an arrow.

Gunpowder is often said to have established the superiority of the infantryman over the armored knight, and thus to have helped spell the death of feudalism. But the ascendancy of the infantryman, even without firearms, was in fact demonstrated effectively by English archers at Crécy (1346), Poitiers (1356), and Agincourt (1415), and during the same period by other foot soldiers elsewhere in Europe. A shrewder interpretation has held that it was not firearms but the reintroduction of discipline on the battlefield—lost since Roman times—that caused the demise of the armored, mounted knight.

When in 1605—three centuries after the introduction of firearms—Cervantes published the first part of his great novel that buried in mockery the Age of Chivalry, the flintlock had not yet been invented.[1] Field artillery did not become important until the Seven Years War, in the middle of the eighteenth century. As late as the American Revolution, so sensible a man as Benjamin Franklin was able seriously to consider the wisdom of arming the Continental soldiers with bows and arrows rather than with the cumbersome, slow-firing, unreliable, and grossly inaccurate muskets. Not until the middle of the nineteenth century—five centuries after the first military use of gunpowder—did we enter the age of modern firearms, with the development in all arms of breech loading and rifling and, in artillery pieces, of explosive projectiles.

In short, when we speak of the revolution wrought by gunpowder, we are talking about something that required centuries to accomplish. It required also centuries of perspective to discern. Yet the gradualness of the development, with all the opportunities it permitted for doctrinal adjustment in the military arts, is still not the crux of the matter. The gun and its relatives remained from first to last strictly *tactical* weapons, gradually displacing weapons such as the battering ram, the arrow, the sword, and the lance, but only by proving superior in the same functions that those weapons had exercised on the battlefield.

At least until World War I, which for the first time produced the phenomenon of nationwide continuous lines that could not be outflanked, the study of military strategy and of the grand tactics of battles, whether of land or sea, could

[1] However the art of the armorer for man and horse had only recently come into its greatest glory. One especially magnificent specimen of a full suit of armor in the collection of the Metropolitan Museum of Art in New York City is dated 1590. Rather more intriguing is one, dated 1527, made for Galiot de Genouilhac, who was Master of Artillery to Kings Louis XII and Francis I.

profitably proceed from the study of campaigns going back to antiquity. The thesis that "methods change but principles are unchanging" had much to justify it, because methods did not change very much, or at any rate not too abruptly. Certainly they were not changing very rapidly in the time of Jomini, from whom that maxim is derived. The application of lessons of the past to current and predicted military issues always required a proper appreciation of changed technological conditions, but not until the latter half of the nineteenth century did the problem of adjustment offer any difficulties. In the twentieth century it became increasingly critical, and with the advent of nuclear weapons the entire value of past military experience as a guide to the future was called basically into question.

Even before the atomic bomb the airplane threatened to take war away from the battlefield, and Douhet and his followers proclaimed that it had done so. But because of the limitations of the high-explosive and incendiary weapons fired and dropped from aircraft in two world wars, it took time to achieve decisive results. During that time aircraft had to fight for command of the air, and land and naval campaigns unfolded in their old accustomed fashion, profoundly affected by the new arm as they had always been by each other, but nevertheless retaining their essential and distinctive characteristics.

Instead of taking war away from the battlefield, the airplane only added a new area of battle behind the fronts, and a third dimension to those already prevailing on land and at sea. The science of strategy, which had always been divisible into two parts, was now divisible into three. For the two traditional forms of war, the basic treatises had been written and needed only to be modified. Air strategy still awaited its Mahan—for Douhet's philosophy, however far-sighted, had proved critically deficient—but the early appearance of the new air philosopher could be confidently expected. The air experience of World War II was sufficient in bulk and variety to provide him with the necessary materials. Then the atomic bomb came and changed everything.

Few people were unexcited or unimpressed by the first atomic weapons. That something tremendously important had happened was immediately understood by almost everyone. Interpretations of the military significance of the new weapons naturally varied greatly, but even the most conservative saw nothing inappropriate or extravagant in such extraordinary consultations and decisions as resulted in the Truman-Attlee-King Declaration of November 15, 1945, or the Baruch Proposals before the United Nations in the following year. Then the MacMahon Act set up the Atomic Energy Commission, an autonomous government agency hedged about by all sorts of special provisions, for the manufacture and development of atomic weapons. Nothing of the sort had ever happened before; but photographs of the destruction wrought at Hiroshima and Nagasaki had been spread across the land, and few persons were unaffected by the thought that the damage had in each case been done by a single aircraft.

This was the response evoked by the explosion of two atomic bombs over Japan, plus the simultaneously released news of the test shot at Alamagordo, at a time when few additional ones were presumed to exist. We can now see that the more conservative of the opinions then expressed on the implications of atomic weapons were in the main wedded to presumptions that were soon to be disproved; for example, that the bomb was fated to remain scarce, extremely costly, bulky and therefore difficult to deliver, and limited to about the same power (20,000 tons of TNT equivalent or 20 kilotons) and spatial effectiveness as the Nagasaki bomb.[2]

In an age that had grown used to taking rapid advances in military technology for granted, how remarkable was this immediate and almost universal consensus that the atomic bomb was different and epochal! Equally striking was the fact that the invention caused the greatest forebodings in the hearts of the people who first possessed it and benefited from it. The thought that it represented a fabulous and mostly American scientific and engineering accomplishment, that it had apparently helped to end World War II,[3] and that the United States had for the time being a monopoly on it seemed to cause no exhilaration among Americans.

Subsequent events did not undermine the early consensus on the importance of the new weapon, nor did they qualify the misgivings. On the contrary, the first decade of the atomic age saw the collapse of the American monopoly, of the myth of inevitable scarcity, and of reasonable hopes for international atomic disarmament. It saw also the development of the thermonuclear weapon in both major camps. If at the end of that decade one looked back at the opinions

[2] At an early date in the nuclear era, the AEC adopted the 20 kiloton (K.T.) yield as a standard, referring to it in the literature of the time as the "nominal" atomic bomb. The book prepared under the direction of the Los Alamos Laboratory entitled *The Effects of Atomic Weapons* (Government Printing Office, 1950) based all its quantitative data on the "nominal" bomb. A later version of this book, under the title *The Effects of Nuclear Weapons*, was prepared by the same editor, Dr. Samuel Glasstone, and published by the AEC in 1957. The later book contains effects calculated up to 20 megatons, or 1,000 times greater than the earlier volume.

[3] In the previous chapter we pointed out that postwar researches oblige us greatly to depreciate the influence in ending World War II of the two atomic bombs dropped upon Japan. See above, pp. 139f.

expressed so voluminously at the beginning of it, one found almost none that had proved too extravagant. Only the conservative guesses had proved to be hopelessly wrong.

It is no longer possible to distinguish between the new weapons on the one hand and the "battle-tested" or "tried and true" ones on the other, because in this new world no weapons are tried and tested. The hand rifle, the field gun, and the tank, as well as the infantry division or combat team that uses them, are at least as much on trial in the age of atomic warfare as is the atomic bomb itself; indeed, they are more so.

The Thermonuclear Bomb

Since we are now well launched into the thermonuclear age, we might first ask what differences, if any, the thermonuclear or fusion or hydrogen bomb must make for our strategic predictions. We have been living with the fission bomb for more than a decade, and it may well be that the fusion type introduces nothing essentially new other than a greater economy of destruction along patterns already established. Unfortunately, that is not the case.

No doubt the strategic implications of the first atomic bombs were radical in the extreme, and it was right at the time to stress the drastic nature of the change.[4] The effectiveness of strategic bombing as a way of war could no longer be questioned. It at once became, incontrovertibly, the dominant form of war. A strategic-bombing program could be carried through entirely with air forces existing at the out-

[4] See Part 1: "The Weapon," in *The Absolute Weapon: Atomic Power and World Order*, ed. by Bernard Brodie, Harcourt, Brace, New York, 1946, pp. 21-110. See also Bernard Brodie and Eilene Galloway, *The Atomic Bomb and the Armed Services*, Library of Congress: Legislative Reference Service, Public Affairs Bulletin No. 55 (May 1947).

set of a war, and at a speed which, however variously estimated, would be phenomenal by any previous standard. Also,
because any payload sufficient to include one atomic bomb
was quite enough to justify any sortie, strategic bombing
could be carried out successfully over any distance that might
separate the powers involved. If the limited ranges of the
aircraft made a refueling necessary, it was worthwhile. These
conclusions represented change enough from the conditions
of World War II. They served, among other things, to end
completely American invulnerability.

Nevertheless, fission bombs were sufficiently limited in
power to make it appear necessary that a substantial number
would have to be used to achieve decisive and certain results.
That in turn made it possible to visualize a meaningful even
if not wholly satisfactory air defense, both active and passive.
It was therefore still necessary to think in terms of a struggle
for command of the air in the old Douhet sense, hardly
shorter in duration than what he imagined. It was also still
necessary to apply, though in much modified form, the lore
so painfully acquired in World War II concerning target
selection for a strategic-bombing campaign. Even with fission
weapons numbering in the hundreds, there was still a real—
and difficult—analytical problem in choosing targets that
would make the campaign decisive rather than merely
hurtful. It was possible also to distinguish between attacks
on population and attacks on the economy. Finally, the functions of ground and naval forces, though clearly and markedly
affected by the new weapons, still appeared vital.

Even these tenuous ties with the past were threatened
when it became known that thermonuclear bombs were not
only feasible but apparently also inexpensive enough to justify

their manufacture in substantial numbers.[5] Possibly the feeling that the H-bomb was distinctively new and significantly different from the A-bomb argued in part an underestimation of the A-bomb. But when one has to confront a basic change in circumstances, it helps if it is unequivocal.

The "Mike" shot of the Operation IVY series, set off on November 1, 1952, caused the complete disappearance of the small island of Elugelab on which the thermonuclear device was placed. In its place was left an underwater crater over one mile across and about 175 feet deep at the center, or, as was later publicly stated, large enough to hold fourteen buildings the size of the Pentagon. It was announced that the amount of energy released was over five million tons (or five "megatons") of TNT equivalent, and the fireball itself was about three and one-half miles across, compared to about one-sixth of a mile for a "nominal" 20 K.T. bomb.

At the time this information was released, almost a year-and-a-half after the event, at least one other American thermonuclear explosion had taken place (the "Bravo" shot in the CASTLE series on March 1, 1954), and it was reported to have been several times more powerful than "Mike." Small wonder that the AEC Chairman, Rear Admiral Lewis L. Strauss, stated on that occasion that the H-bombs that the United States could build and deliver would be individually capable of wiping out any city in the world! Later the world learned that the March 1954 shot had also produced an unexpectedly large amount of radioactive debris, which was

[5] Information which was first officially revealed in the many references to Dr. Edward Teller's special contributions to H-bomb technology in the published transcript of the Oppenheimer hearings—an investigation designed to tighten security. See *In the Matter of J. Robert Oppenheimer: Transcript of Hearing before Personnel Security Board*, U.S. Government Printing Office, Washington, 1954.

deposited as "fallout" of dangerous and even lethal intensity over thousands of square miles and up to distances of 200 miles or more downwind from the explosion.

One immediate result of the new development was the realization that questions inherited from World War II concerning appropriate selection among industrial target-systems were now irrelevant. Only a few industries tend to have important manufacturing facilities outside cities, these being notably in steel and oil production. Since a large thermonuclear bomb exploded over a city would as a rule effectively eliminate all its industrial activities, there is hardly much point in asking which industries should be hit and in what order, or which particular facilities within any industry. New and important kinds of discrimination are still possible —for example, between disarming the enemy and destroying him—but henceforward attacking his industrial economy is practically indistinguishable from hitting his cities, with obvious consequences for populations. Cities are in any case the easiest targets to find and hit. Of course the enemy's strategic retaliatory force must be the first priority target in time, and possibly also in weight of bombs, but destroying that force, if it can be done, is essentially a disarming move which seems to await some kind of sequential action.

There is nothing in logic to require such a sequence. It is likely, however, in view of traditional attitudes, to be considered a practical necessity. The attacker may feel he cannot count with high confidence on fully eliminating the enemy air force, even if he strikes first. He might, therefore, feel obliged to begin the counter-economy competition before he knew the results of the counter-air-force strike. At any rate, decisions of the sort we are implying would have to be made well before hostilities began. The plan which goes into effect at the beginning of a war, insofar as circumstances permit its going into effect, is the emergency war plan, which is prepared in peacetime and periodically revised. In view of existing habits of thinking, one would expect that even where a counter-air-force attack was given top priority in such a war plan, a counter-economy attack would probably be to some degree integrated with it.

There could indeed be a significant difference in ultimate results between a strategy aimed primarily at the enemy air force and one aimed chiefly at population, even if a lot of people were killed in both. However, it must be remembered that in striking at an enemy strategic air force, an attacker will normally feel obliged to hit many more airfields than those indicated to be major strategic air bases, because he must assume in advance that some dispersion of enemy aircraft will have taken place as a result either of warning or of routine operating procedures. In striking at airfields near cities, he might, especially if he entertained conventional attitudes about maximizing effects, choose to use some quite large thermonuclear weapons.

Thus the distinction in priority could turn out to be an academic one. It is idle to talk about our strategies being counter-force strategies, as distinct from counter-economy or counter-population strategies, *unless* planners were actually to take deliberate restrictive measures to refrain from injuring cities. They would have to conclude that it is desirable to avoid such damage, which would be a reversal of the traditional attitude that damage done to enemy installations or populations in the vicinity of the primary target is a "bonus." Otherwise it can hardly matter much to the populations involved whether the destruction of cities is a by-product of the destruction of airfields or vice versa.

The number of cities that account for the so-called economic war potential of either the U.S. or the U.S.S.R. is small: possibly fifty or less, and certainly not over two hundred. The range in these figures is the result of the varying weight that can be given to certain tangible but difficult-to-measure factors, such as interdependence. The leading fifty-four American "metropolitan areas" (as defined by the Census Bureau) contain over 60 per cent of the nation's industrial capital, and a population of over 80,000,000, including a disproportionate number of the people whose special skills are associated with large-scale production.[6] Altogether the Census Bureau lists 170 metropolitan areas in the United States, which together contain over 75 per cent of industrial capital and 55 per cent of the nation's population. We must note that far the greater portion of these cities are concentrated in the eastern and especially the northeastern part of the United States, where urban and non-urban populations alike may be subject to overlapping patterns of radioactive fallout.[7] The concentration of industry in Russian cities, and the concentration of cities and populations in the western part of their national area, make of the Soviet Union a target complex roughly comparable to the United States, though less urbanized. The Soviet Union has only four cities of over a million population, as compared with fourteen such cities in the United States.

The great Hamburg raids of July 1943, which were so

[6] See Margaret B. Rowan and Harry V. Kincaid, *The Views of Corporation Executives on the Probable Effect of the Loss of Company Headquarters in Wartime*, The RAND Corporation, Research Memorandum RM-1723 (ASTIA No. AD 105967), May 1, 1956, p. 86.

[7] See S. M. Greenfield, R. R. Rapp, and P. A. Walters, *A Catalog of Fallout Patterns*, The RAND Corporation, Research Memorandum RM-1676-AEC, April 16, 1956, p. 91.

tremendous a shock to the whole German nation, caused the destruction of about 50 per cent of the city's housing and resulted in casualties amounting to about three per cent of its population. A single H-bomb of anything above one megaton yield bursting within the confines of a city such as Hamburg would cause a degree of housing destruction much higher than 50 per cent; and unless the city had been evacuated in advance the proportion of casualties to housing destroyed would certainly be far greater than it was at Hamburg.

The latter fact underlines one of the distinctive features of nuclear weapons. There are at least four reasons why casualty rates with nuclear weapons are likely to be far greater in relation to property destroyed than was true of nonatomic bombing: (1) warning time is likely to be less, or nonexistent, unless the attacker deliberately offers it before attacking; (2) the *duration* of an attack at any one place will be literally a single instant, in contrast to the several hours' duration of a World War II attack; (3) shelters capable of furnishing good protection against high-explosive bombs might be of no use at all within the fireball radius of a large ground-burst nuclear weapon, or within the oxygen-consuming fire-storm that such a detonation would cause; and (4) nuclear weapons have the distinctive effect of producing radioactivity, which can be lingering as well as instantaneous, and which causes casualties but not property injury.[8]

[8] The direct gamma radiation of any nuclear detonation is of extremely brief duration, and its lethal radius depends roughly on the size of the explosion and on the amount of shielding people in the target area have. Since air itself provides shielding, the limit of direct radiation effects is likely to be a very few miles in radius (probably under five) even for the larger thermonuclear bombs. On the other hand, the radioactive products

There are a few very large metropolitan centers in the United States and in other countries which are wide enough in area to be able to escape complete destruction by a single large thermonuclear weapon. For such areas, two or three such weapons, or half a dozen, can easily be made available. The difference in cost between large and small warheads will not be great enough to be the critical factor in determining the choice between them for distant targets.[9] The weight factor will matter, especially in missiles, but even ICBMs can carry multi-megaton weapons. What all this means is that "overkilling" will be cheap and therefore, according to the military considerations normally brought to bear, no longer to be shunned.

The problem of getting nuclear weapons delivered to some scores or hundreds of widely spaced points may not, especially with aircraft, look simple to those who have to plan

---

of the nuclear reaction, if deposited on the earth's surface, remain as a lingering though decaying hazard. The amount created varies not only in direct proportion to the bomb yield, but also according to the physical constitution of the bomb. The significance of whether the bomb is air- or ground-burst is that in the latter the soil and rock particles carried into the air in huge volume capture the condensed fission products and deposit them within a matter of hours over an area of ground which in size and shape is governed by the winds aloft as well as by the spreading force of the explosion itself. This constitutes the "fallout" effect. An air-burst bomb, on the other hand, quickly sends its volatilized fission products to extremely high altitudes, beyond the reach of rain and without the larger particles necessary to bring them down quickly. This eliminates the hazard of the short-lived radioactive products and spreads out the distribution of the longer-lived ones which ultimately drift down, though the latter will include the extremely noxious strontium 90.

[9] We are of course using the cost index as a gage of availability, with the knowledge that doing so presupposes some reasonably intelligent planning decisions in the past. Once the shooting begins the dollar cost of a weapon in the stockpile is in itself an absolutely irrelevant historical datum so far as the use of that weapon is concerned.

the operation. Enemy strategic airfields and missile launching sites must be hit within minutes of each other. On the other hand, we should be clear that with missiles there is nothing intrinsically impossible about getting hundreds of bombs to detonate on their targets more or less simultaneously. In any case, after the enemy retaliatory force is accounted for, the number of bombs that have to be dropped on other targets in order to put any nation out of business as a producing or even functioning organism is, when measured against the standards of World War II, absurdly small.

The Theory of "Broken-Backed" War

The British in their 1954 *Defence White Paper* used the expressive phrase "broken-backed war" to describe what presumably would happen after the first huge exchange of thermonuclear weapons, assuming the exchange itself failed to be decisive.[10] Various Americans have adhered to the same conception without necessarily using the phrase.[11] The

[10] "In this event [global war], it seems likely that such a war would begin with a period of intense atomic attacks lasting a relatively short time but inflicting great destruction and damage. If no decisive result were reached in this opening phase, hostilities would decline in intensity, though perhaps less so at sea than elsewhere, and a period of broken-backed warfare would follow, during which the opposing sides would seek to recover their strength, carrying on the struggle in the meantime as best they might." *Statement on Defence, Presented by the Minister of Defence to Parliament . . . February, 1954*, Command Paper #9075, Her Majesty's Stationery Office, London, p. 5.

[11] "Presumably massive blows would continue as long as either side retained the capability. . . . With the passing of that initial phase, and if the issue is still unresolved, tough people would carry on across the radioactive ashes and water, with what weapons are left. Sea control will be an elemental consideration in accomplishing either the follow-through phase of atomic war or the better appreciated chores of a prolonged nonatomic war." Admiral Robert B. Carney, then U.S. Chief of Naval Operations, in a Cincinnati speech of February 21, 1955, as reported in the *Washington Post and Times Herald* for the following day.

essential feature of the idea is the insistence, usually implicit, that war resources, human and mechanical, will continue to be drawn from the national "mobilization base" and that the margin of advantage that one side or the other enjoys in this respect is what will prove decisive in the end. Although the conception of "broken-backed war" appeared to be entirely abandoned in the *Defence White Paper* for 1955, which tended instead to rest everything on "deterrence," it has nevertheless continued to underlie and to confuse the basic structure of American and Allied defense planning.

One can easily conceive of conditions in both contending camps so chaotic, following the opening reciprocal onslaughts, that the war issue will not be immediately resolved and hostilities not formally concluded. One can also picture surviving military units, including some possessing thermonuclear weapons and the means of delivering them, continuing to hurl blows at the enemy to the utmost of their remaining though fast-ebbing capacity. But it is difficult to imagine such intensive continuing support from the home front as would enable "conventional" military operations to be conducted on a large scale and over a long enough time to effect any such large and positive purpose as "imposing the national will on the enemy," or, to use the words of our own former Army Chief of Staff, General Matthew B. Ridgway, "carrying the fight to the enemy and defeating him."[12]

[12] In his speech before the National Press Club in Washington, D.C., March 19, 1954. This speech was reproduced in full in the *Congressional Record, Appendix*, March 24, 1954, pp. A2254-6 (under "Extension of Remarks of Hon. Dewey Short"). It is noteworthy that at this time General Ridgway still found himself able to conceive of a future war in which we would "reduce the other side's industrial potential and military bases" but would nevertheless succeed in carrying out on our own side "not merely the mobilization and training of men but also the conversion of industry to full war production." In other words, General Ridgway was

The major premise of the "broken-backed war" conception was that the result of the initial mutual nuclear violence would be something like a draw. Otherwise it could hardly fail to be decisive. Moreover, the nuclear phase would have to end cleanly, or diminish to a trivial magnitude, early in the hostilities and at about the same time for both sides! The second and related premise was that the level of damage on both sides following the strategic nuclear bombing phase would be limited enough to permit each to equip and sustain air, ground, and naval forces sufficiently large to carry on noteworthy military operations. These would, for one side or the other, be conducted at some distance from home, and would therefore require facilities such as ports and associated railway terminals which are generally found only in those larger coastal cities certain to be among the first targets hit in the nuclear phase! Surely these are dubious assumptions.

Another more practical reason for questioning the "broken-backed war" conception is that no one seems to know how to plan for such a war. At least, no one seems willing to do so. There are special psychological reasons why official war planners have always in times past found it impossibly difficult to predicate a war plan on the assumption of national disaster at the outset. In this case, even if the spirit were willing, the data and the imagination would be much too weak.

There are, of course, numerous examples in recent history of magnificent improvisation following upon disaster, or rather upon what used to be called disaster. In each of those

---

imagining not so much a "broken-backed" war as a war marked by an essentially one-way strategic air attack. One might well question, under such premises, the necessity for a full mobilization of the national resources!

cases the means of making war, including such vital intangibles as established governmental authority operating through accustomed channels of communication, remained intact. A few battleships sunk, a few armies defeated and lost, even large territories yielded, do not spell the kind of over-all disaster we have to think about for the future. There are limits to the burden that can be placed on improvisation. The improvisation which the survivors of thermonuclear attack may find it within their capacities to carry out will have to be largely occupied with restoring the bare means of life.

No one who has studied the German military, economic, and even social performance under World War II strategic bombing can fail to be impressed by it. But the German capacity to absorb the blows and to take compensatory measures for the damage received depended, among other things, on their having both the time and the incentive to organize those measures. When the main weight of our strategic bombing descended upon them in the spring of 1944, they had had at least three years of serious attacks, including the terrible warning of the Hamburg raids of July 1943. Even so, the campaign waxed only gradually to its climax, and never, even when the British-American strategic bombing forces were at the height of their power, were they able to inflict in six months or even a year of bombing the scale of destruction that would lie easily within the capability of the United States or the Soviet long-range bombing forces on Day One or even Hour One of a new war. The differences in circumstance that prevailed between the French resistance in 1914 and the collapse in 1940 were trivial compared with the differences between pre-atomic and present-day strategic bombing.

No one can specify how many nuclear bombs it would take to "knock out" (by which we presumably mean "render helpless") a country as large as the Soviet Union or the United States, since analytical studies of the problem can do little more than suggest broad limits to the reasonable range of figures. Such studies must depend on what are little more than educated guesses for various critical planning factors, including even those pertaining to the physical effects of bomb explosions. They must work with quite wide ranges of assumptions concerning such things as the size and the positioning of bombs delivered, the length of warning time, and so on. They cannot even touch the imponderables, such as popular panic and administrative disorganization, which might easily govern the end result. The people who do such analyses are as a rule interested in the results from the offensive or targeting point of view, and they therefore consider it a virtue to be conservative in their estimates of damage. One of the ways to be conservative is to dismiss imponderables as unmeasurable.

At the other end of the scale, methodologically speaking, is a judgment such as the following one by Marshal of the Royal Air Force Sir John Slessor:

I have the perhaps somewhat unenviable advantage of an experience, which fortunately has been denied to most people, of being in a city which was literally wiped out, with most of its inhabitants, in fifty-five seconds by the great earthquake in Baluchistan in 1935, a far more effective blitz than anything laid on by either side in the late war, except Hiroshima and Nagasaki. When people talk light-heartedly about that sort of thing on a widespread scale not being decisive, I have to tell them with respect that they do not know what they are talking about. No country could survive a month of Quetta earthquakes on all its main centres of population and remain capable of organized resistance.[13]

Sir John's conviction, which accords with the average layman's judgment, reflects a tacit assumption concerning defenses. In general, the assumption is that the prospects for the radical improvement of both active and passive defenses against nuclear weapons are not bright. We shall consider this question in detail in the following chapter, but when we recall the fantastic degree to which the coming of the A-bomb gave a lead to the offense over the defense, and consider also that subsequent developments in nuclear weapons have tended to further that advantage, the assumption referred to looks fairly invulnerable.

The Decisiveness of Strategic Bombardment

From all this one would seem justified in drawing the following conclusion: barring revolutionary and presently unforeseen advances in air defense, including extensive hardening of targets, an unrestricted strategic air campaign in a war in which the United States is engaged is bound to be decisive. It does not matter greatly whether the number of bombs-on-target required to guarantee decisiveness is a few score or several hundred, because we remain in realms of figures well within the capabilities of the United States and probably also the Soviet Union, the critical factor being delivery capability rather than size of the nuclear stockpile. If this capability is not in the hands of the Soviet Union at the particular date of this writing, it will be soon enough thereafter.

[13] Sir John Slessor, *Strategy for the West*, William Morrow, New York, 1954, p. 111.

It is barely conceivable that an enemy would have a capability only sufficient to destroy our Strategic Air Command (SAC), which it would then proceed to do by a sudden missile or bomber attack, but not enough to destroy or threaten our economy, especially if critical segments of the latter were hardened. In such a case strategic nuclear bombing could fail to be decisive. But this and various other conceivable contingencies tending to a like result are in the aggregate too improbable to be taken seriously.

When we say that strategic bombing will be decisive, we mean that if it occurs on the grand scale that existing forces make possible, other kinds of military operations are likely to prove both unfeasible and superfluous. The Red Army, if poised to spring, could perhaps have a certain brief career as an autonomous force even if its homeland were laid entirely waste behind it, though in such a case it would itself also be the target of nuclear weapons of all sizes. Anyway, such a career would be possible only for the Red Army, since it has the advantage, denied to the ground forces of Britain and the United States, of having its main potential spheres of operation in areas contiguous to its homeland.

If these views are rejected, the burden of proof rests on those who would show us how modern armies and navies can operate effectively and to a useful purpose when their home territories, and certainly the larger towns thereof, including all naval bases and ports, are masses of rubble and radioactive dust. Discussions in military journals of the operations of armies and navies, and even air forces, in a major war of the future almost always tacitly assume an intact home front, or at least one where the damage is so small as to be irrelevant to offensive plans.

From a sober appreciation of the possibilities in this field of dismal speculation, it seems safe to assume that the number of people and the kind and quantity of capital that may survive strategic attack will be important far more for determining the character and degree of national recovery *following* the hostilities than for controlling the subsequent course of those hostilities. The *minimum* destruction and disorganization that one should expect from an unrestricted thermonuclear attack in the future is likely to be too high to permit further meaningful mobilization of war-making capabilities over the short term.

We should also recognize once and for all that when it comes to predicting human casualties, we are talking about a catastrophe for which it is impossible to set upper limits very far short of the entire population of a nation. It is not only those in cities and in towns who will be exposed to risk, but, in view of the fallout effect, practically all. It is not true that the fallout effect, where the attacker is determined to amplify and exploit it, is something that is easily met and contained. The attacker, incidentally, has the option not only of selecting ground rather than air bursts but also, within wide limits, of altering the components of his bombs to get the kind of fallout he wants. Although the uninjured survivors of attack may indeed be many, it is all too easily conceivable that they may be relatively few. The latter contingency is the more likely one in the absence of large-scale protective measures, involving shelters, such as we have not yet shown ourselves prepared to take. But whether the survivors be many or few, in the midst of a land scarred and ruined beyond all present comprehension they should not be expected to show much concern for the further pursuit of political-military objectives.

The reader who was prepared to accept as obvious at the outset the conclusion we have labored these many pages to establish will wonder why all the bother. The answer is that in these respects there is a monumental ambiguity in public policy, which reflects in part the ambiguity in the public pronouncements of relevant officials of the highest rank. Even those who forecast catastrophic paralyzation following nuclear strategic bombing seem to find it impossibly difficult to grasp the full significance of what they predict. Sir John Slessor, whose trenchant comment on what to expect from nuclear strategic bombing we have already quoted, has furnished an outstanding example. A former Chief of Staff of the Royal Air Force, Sir John can also be abundantly quoted on the other side of the "decisiveness" question from the very same book, a book that has had a special importance as the most lucid and comprehensive presentation of the "massive retaliation" doctrine to be found in print.

Sir John urged, to be sure, that "it is very seldom wise to carry things to their logical conclusions, and the airmen can no doubt rely upon their comrades of the older services to assist them in resisting that temptation."[14] Nevertheless, this distinguished airman, who regarded it as "almost inconceivable" that a major war of the future fought with weapons of mass destruction (which he insisted *must* be used) could last "for any length of time,"[15] still considered it very important that navies be able to carry out their traditional functions of convoy protection,[16] which are defenses against attrition

[14] *Ibid.*, p. 76.
[15] *Ibid.*, pp. 107, 114.
[16] *Ibid.*, pp. 92, 99, 101. See also Field Marshal The Viscount Bernard Montgomery, "A Look Through a Window at World War III," *Journal of the Royal United Service Institution*, xcix (November 1954), 507ff.

warfare and therefore strategically meaningful only over a considerable span of time. One wonders also why he considered it necessary even in 1954 to profess disbelief in the thought "that air power by itself can defeat a first-class enemy."[17]

No doubt an answer is to be found in the only place in the book where Sir John portrayed his conception of the United Kingdom under nuclear attack:

When things are really bad the people's morale is greatly sustained by the knowledge that we are giving back as good as we are getting, and this engenders a sort of combatant pride, like that of the charlady in a government office who was asked during the London blitz where her husband was—"he's in the Middle East, the bloody coward!" We must ensure that defence, as adequate as we can reasonably make it, is afforded to those areas or installations which are really vital to our survival at the outset of a war, or to our ability to nourish our essential fighting strength. Much-Binding-in-the-Marsh and Littleville, Pa., are not in that category unless they happen to contain some utterly indispensable installation, and the inhabitants must steel themselves to risks and take what may come to them, knowing that thereby they are playing as essential a part in the country's defence as the pilot in the fighter or the man behind the gun.[18]

There is only one thing to be said about such language and imagery: it fits World War II, but it has nothing to do with thermonuclear bombs. Certainly it has no pertinence for the United Kingdom, which is both small in area and geographically close to the most likely enemy. One does not have to think in terms of modern missiles but only in terms of the V-1, the V-2, and the jet bomber to see Britain a shambles at the end of the first hour of nuclear attack.

[17] Slessor, op.cit., p. 106.
[18] Ibid., p. 120.

For countries such as the United States or the Soviet Union it might take a little longer. There was, however, no justification in 1954 for the kind of optimism expressed in the following sentence: "But when it is suggested . . . that the United States could be knocked out as the arsenal of the North Atlantic Alliance, then writing as one who has been concerned for a good many years with air bombardment planning, I beg leave to say that it is nonsense."[19]

It remains to be added that in an article published two years after the book in which he made these remarks, Sir John Slessor was seeing things in a quite different light.[20] Among the events that had intervened between the two publications was the release of a good deal of information about thermonuclear weapons and their effects, but one must also give due credit to Sir John for a flexibility of mind that is among his special distinctions. Perhaps there is also something about the experience of being the author of a book that brings one intimately into the rough-and-tumble of the marketplace so far as ideas are concerned. Anyway, the kind of drastic conversion in some of his fundamental beliefs that Sir John underwent within two years is not a common occurrence among his professional colleagues. As Sir John observes in the aforementioned article: "Not many people, even in the fighting services themselves, have really grasped the full tactical implications of an age in which nuclear power is the dominant strategic factor in war. There is a tendency almost subconsciously to shy away from those implications, which should not be ascribed merely to the influence of vested interest."

[19] *Ibid.*, p. 34.
[20] See his "The Great Deterrent and its Limitations," *Bulletin of the Atomic Scientists*, XII (May 1956), 140-146. It is the emphasis on the limitations of "the great deterrent," and the policy implications of those limitations, that mainly distinguishes this article from his earlier book.

The tendency to "shy away" to which Sir John refers is, to be sure, often overcome by the force of events. Such events are often not foreseen when they should be, but it is much harder to deny developments when they become present realities than it is when they are merely predictions. Even the acceptance of present realities may be reluctant enough to result in grave distortions, but it may nevertheless represent an ideological change of some consequence. In that connection, we should remember that Soviet ideas about the tactical and strategic consequences of nuclear weapons have also undergone some change. When the Soviets did not have the bombs they felt impelled (1) to acquire them as fast as they could, and (2) to depreciate their importance. Now that they have had them for more than a decade and had ample opportunity to test them and to reflect on what they imply, Soviet ideas on what can be accomplished, for example by surprise nuclear attack, seem to be developing along lines familiar in the United States.[21]

The sense of Emerson's remark about consistency being "the hobgoblin of little minds" has on the whole enjoyed remarkable verification in military history. Historical examples of prejudiced rejection of the novel need not detain us, except possibly to note that the catalog is long. More interesting for our purposes are the instances where eager acceptance of the new is coupled, not only within the same organizations but often within the same persons, with stubborn insistence upon retaining also much of the old. Such people have usually come off well when the scores were in. Their very inconsistency often provided them with a hedge against wrong predictions.

[21] See Herbert S. Dinerstein, *Nuclear Weapons and Soviet Policies*, Praeger, New York, 1959. See also his "Revolution in Soviet Strategic Thinking," *Foreign Affairs*, xxxvi (January 1958), 241-252.

The intensely conservative among the military are always proved wrong, because changes in armaments over the past century have been altogether too rapid and drastic to offer any cover to those who will not adjust. But, as we saw in our chapter on Douhet, the occasional brilliant seers who possess the analytical skill to recognize and expose inconsistency when they see it have often been tripped up by one or more critical assumptions which turned out to be in error. In such a case their consistency worked only to make their whole logical construction dangerously wrong.

No doubt a proper intuitive feeling for the hazards of prediction and for the terrible forfeits involved, in the military sphere, in finding oneself overcommitted to a wrong guess, is one of the reasons why military men as a group tend to put a rather modest value on analytical brilliance as an alternative to mature military judgment. Nevertheless, there is a limit to the amount of inconsistency that is reasonable, especially since in the world of nuclear armaments it may become, to say the least, exceedingly expensive. The kind of inconsistency which will permit some of our leaders to place a nearly exclusive dependence on thermonuclear weapons for the security of the country, and at the same time reject the most obvious consequences of the use of such weapons against us, is clearly beyond the limits that Emerson desired to indulge.

⊰6⊱

IS THERE A DEFENSE?

THE SIGNIFICANCE of nuclear weapons, as we observed in the preceding chapter, depends above all on the possibilities of defense against them in strategic attack. When we stress their utterly revolutionary and potentially annihilistic effects, in international politics as well as in strategy, we are implicitly assuming that the prognosis for defense is not good. On the other hand, very far-reaching claims have been vehemently asserted for certain defensive devices and strategies. Even the frequently-encountered supposition that total war is now impossible, because its mutually annihilistic or "suicidal" consequences must henceforth be obvious to all, is based on the implicit assumption that at least the retaliatory forces of each side are automatically defended, or anyway easily defensible.

It is necessary, therefore, to take a hard look at the facts concerning defense in so far as we can know those facts, for all our subsequent conclusions about strategies and national policies must be largely governed by our estimates of probabilities for the future of defense. Those estimates must affect also the policies we adopt concerning the defense effort itself. The questions of how much we will spend on defense and in what ways will presumably depend on what we expect to get out of our investment. On the other hand, we may find ourselves spending money uselessly simply because we despair of being able to spend it usefully, or because certain inherited biases compel us to do so, or perhaps because our policymakers cannot bring themselves to force disillusionment on the public.

The Influence of Doctrine

We have already seen that much of the historical discussion of strategic and tactical doctrine has revolved around the perennial question of offense *versus* defense. In dealing with issues relating to that question, military officers are trained not to be objective. They are trained to be biased in favor of the offensive, much as ordinary persons are trained to be biased in favor of virtue.

Aggressiveness in a commander is considered a great merit, and military history suggests that it should be. The dismal experiences of the Army of the Potomac under a succession of cautious or irresolute leaders prior to Grant proves how valuable and rare a thing it is. Among officers who are both intelligent and imaginative, bold commanders have usually been harder to find than cautious ones. The supreme commander in the field has always known that his decisions directly affected casualty rates and might also involve large risks for his nation. During battle he could see the hurt to his own forces, whose dangers he often shared, but could only guess at that to the enemy. Seeing the weariness in his own troops, he yet had to drive them to superhuman exertion and further exhaustion. If he was not to be merely brutal or insensible, he had to have strong doctrinal motivations for carrying the fight forward.[1]

[1]"Generals who become depressed when things are not going well, who lack the 'drive' to get things done, and who lack the resolution, the robust mentality and the moral courage to see their plan through to the end—are useless. They are, in fact, worse than useless—they are a menace—since any sign of wavering or hesitation has immediate repercussions down the scale when the issue hangs in the balance. No battle is ever lost till the general in command thinks it so. If I had not stood firm and insisted that my plan would be carried through, we would not have won at Alamein." From *The Memoirs of Field Marshal Montgomery*, World Publishing Co., New York, 1958, p. 125. The special incident referred to in the last

Just before and during World War I the offensive idea was pushed to grotesque extremes at the very time when technological conditions gave it the least support. As we saw in an earlier chapter, the British and French commanders of that time in their devotion to the offensive principle almost succeeded in discrediting it. Yet even in the era of the Maginot Line, French generals still insisted that the main function of the frontier defenses was to protect their mobilization, and that their over-all strategy remained offensive. They did not, however, act soon enough upon their convictions, and following their collapse in 1940 it was passivity that was again completely discredited.

The bias toward the offensive creates special problems in any technologically new situation where there is little or no relevant war experience to help one to reach a balanced judgment. Throughout the interwar period, and until a year after the United States entered World War II, the prevailing doctrine in the U.S. Navy concerning the amount of anti-aircraft armament to put aboard combat ships was: "Don't sacrifice offensive for defensive armament!" In practice this slogan resulted in extremely lean allotments of antiaircraft guns to major ships at the time of Pearl Harbor. Yet American battleships, old and new, were then carrying armor amounting to 35-40 per cent of their unloaded weight. The major part of it, incidentally, was vertical, above-water armor, useful against gun projectiles but not against bombs or torpedoes. The value of armor had been proved in naval engagements over the previous eighty years, especially at the

---

quoted sentence above is described at pp. 117f. It is described also by Montgomery's Chief of Staff in Sir Francis de Guingand's *Operation Victory*, Scribner's, New York, 1947, pp. 199f.

Battle of Jutland in World War I, but that of antiaircraft guns on ships had not been similarly demonstrated.

In considering the problem of strategic air defense, then, we must be prepared to find the military selling the defensive short. How much more likely is this in the atomic age, when offensive doctrine has a more rational basis than ever before. Today the supreme advantage of the initiative in launching an unrestricted thermonuclear war can hardly be contested, for the side possessing it can hope, reasonably under some circumstances, to obliterate the opponent's power to retaliate.

Nevertheless, Americans have to face the fact that if total war comes for any reason other than our deliberately choosing it in advance of special provocation (obviously an unlikely eventuality), the chances are high that we will receive rather than deliver the first blow. Moves calculated to assure to the United States the advantage of the first blow even in a total war springing from some sudden crisis must require such super-alertness and general aggressiveness of posture as are more likely to provoke than to prevent all-out war—and provoking the enemy to attack us diminishes the chances that the United States will actually have the initiative. The world has after all had some experience in these matters.

In any case, a fervent hope that American forces will move first rather than second must not be confused with a realistic estimate of their chances of doing so. So long as these chances are materially less than 100 per cent, as they clearly are, the United States must be profoundly interested in defensive devices. In other words, the rejection of a preventive war solution has committed us to a deterrence strategy, and we must now prove ourselves ready to pay the full price of such a strategy, including basic adjustment in military doctrine.

There is first the question of the security of the military forces, above all of the retaliatory arm itself. The very use of the term "retaliatory" to describe this force suggests the importance of retaining what has been called a "strike-second capability." The leaders of the Strategic Air Command, past and present, are keenly concerned with the security of their force. Generals Curtis E. LeMay and Thomas S. Power, despite their obvious offensive-mindedness, have repeatedly emphasized in public that national security depends on our maintaining a strong and *secure* retaliatory force. But choices must be made about the methods to be adopted for making SAC secure, as well as about the total level of expenditure considered tolerable for that purpose. Budgets are always limited, and costs have to be measured ultimately in terms of alternative capabilities that could be purchased for the same money. How much will or should SAC be willing to sacrifice of its strike-first offensive potential in order to buy itself more defense? What kind of defense should it buy? We may expect that even those who are converted in principle to the need for security, and in fact considerably aroused about it, may still show their bias in the defense systems which they consider compatible with an essentially offensive force.

The Special Value of the Offensive
in the Air Battle

In a previous chapter we gave Douhet good marks for detaching himself from what he called "the mystique of the offensive." Perhaps "detachment" is not the right word, because he not only separated himself from that mystique but railed against it. We noted that one of his basic views, that in ground war the defense would henceforth be much stronger than the offense, was proved by subsequent events to be wrong. But he was right when he insisted that in the air the situation is the exact opposite of what he presumed it to be on the ground, and that in the air the offensive is not simply the stronger but almost the only "valid" form of war.

Why should the situation in the air be so different from that on the ground? Let us first consider ground war. We know that an army has always moved somewhat ponderously, limited in speed until very recently by the marching capability of the foot soldier, and that its movements are canalized by various features of geography, especially the highway and railroad system. In the remoter past swift mounted couriers, and for the past hundred years the telegraph, have served to bring the defender days and even weeks of warning of a descent upon his vital areas, usually with much information about the direction and schedule of the enemy's movement and the magnitude of his power. Important strategic surprise might still be won by the attacker through deception or exceptional marching prowess, or through willful blindness on the part of the defender; but once a march proceeded into hostile territory the opponent was not likely to remain ignorant of its progress. Moreover, since the attacker was normally descending upon the heart of a country from its periphery, the defender had the advantage of interior lines. This advantage often made it feasible for him to redeploy to confront unexpected threats.

In 1914 the Germans were surprised by the speed of the Russian mobilization, which brought the Russian offensive into East Prussia earlier than had been expected; but once the Russian armies crossed the frontier their movements could be checked and clocked, and the arrangements for their decisive defeat at the Masurian Lakes could be thoroughly organized. Similarly, the French were surprised when the German armies poured into Belgium earlier and in much greater strength than predicted, and when the direction of their movement proved not to be in accord with French expectations. Nevertheless, following the collapse of their own ill-starred offensive in the east, the French were able entirely to redeploy their own and the British armies and to check decisively the German descent from the north at the first Battle of the Marne.

Their failure similarly to contain the German penetration in the Ardennes in May 1940—which also was a surprise in that the French expected the major weight of the German attack to fall elsewhere—was due not to any remarkable speed of movement on the part of the invaders, the bulk of whom were still moving on foot, but mostly to the fact that the French high command had no reserve "mass of maneuver" to throw against the gap. Eisenhower had such a reserve in 1944 and was able to contain the same kind of surprise breakthrough in the Battle of the Bulge.

On the tactical level, as a rule, few physical factors favor the attacker but many favor the defender. The defender usually has the advantage of cover. He characteristically fires from behind some form of shelter while his opponent crosses open ground, though in battle this advantage has often been qualified by the defender's usual practice of making local counterattacks where the opponent has temporarily gained an advantage.

For such reasons, even the most enthusiastic exponents of ground offensive doctrine in modern times have considered a decided local superiority of some kind to be essential to the launching of a tactical offensive. It has been considered the major advantage of the strategic initiative that it confers the choice of time and place for the battle and hence the opportunity to achieve a tactical superiority at that time and place, even when one's over-all superiority is not commanding and possibly even nonexistent. That is the theory anyway, and historically it has often worked. Of course it has usually worked better—certainly more continuously and smoothly—where the side that held the strategic initiative enjoyed also a considerable over-all superiority.

Air attack is intrinsically and radically different from ground attack. In form it consists not of a series of relocations of one's force, as is true of the advance of an army, but of a series of sorties or shots, each of which is complete in itself and marvelously swift in execution as compared with movements on land or sea. They could be called swift even in Douhet's time; today they involve supersonic aircraft and ballistic missiles. They are subject to no canalization by features of terrain. Aircraft have not only a wide latitude in choice of routes between base and target, within the limits of their range, but they also have a choice of altitudes, which can add tremendously to the bafflement of the defender. The invaders may have the capability to come in so high that the defender's interceptors either cannot reach their elevation at all or cannot maneuver there; or they may choose to come in so low that his radar detection and defensive missile systems fail. Ballistic missiles, of course, offer even greater, almost insuperable, problems to the defender.

Basic Forms of Defense: Active and Passive

Defense against hostile weapons in all forms of warfare, whether on land, sea, or in the air, has always basically consisted of a combination of two things: first, measures to reduce the number of enemy weapons dropped or thrown or to spoil their aim by hitting the enemy as he attacks, i.e., *active defenses*; and second, preparations to absorb those weapons that actually strike home, i.e., *passive defenses*.

A naval force under air attack during World War II sought to avoid being hit by dispersing and maneuvering its ships evasively, and relied on armor, compartmentation, and "damage control" activities in the individual units to minimize the damage of the hits received. These were its passive defenses. But all the while the naval force was shooting at the enemy planes attacking it, to their constant discomfort and frequent destruction. The fire power of its ships' guns and defensive aircraft were its active defenses, which served to reduce the number of bombs and torpedoes released against it and to spoil their aim. Naturally, the combination of active and passive devices sometimes has proved adequate and sometimes not, depending on circumstances and luck, but the chances for survival were usually better for having a defense which included both kinds.

The above example stresses the tactical situation, but the old dictum that "the best defense is a strong offense" emphasizes a strategic idea, namely that by taking the offensive a nation can forestall the enemy's blows and deprive him of the ability to hurl them. One may thereby also gain the advantage of hitting him at a time and in a manner for which he is least prepared. This is the idea of security-through-offense.

All these considerations apply in air as well as in land and naval warfare, with one major qualification. In ground warfare, force composition and tactics of fighting need not be and usually are not markedly affected by whether one is on the strategic offensive or defensive. The target in either case is the enemy *army*. In air war, the forces involved and the methods of fighting in offense are wholly different from those used in defense.[2] In strategic air war, defensive fighting is done with missiles fired from the ground or from defensive fighter planes operating on, over, or near home or friendly territories; offensive fighting, on the other hand, is done by bombers releasing bombs over targets in enemy territory, which may be on the other side of the world, and by long-range missiles directed against the same targets.

There are several important consequences of this difference between air and ground war, one of which affects the basic character of force organization. Since in ground warfare it is the same kind of army that assumes the defensive or goes over to the offensive, a commander's bias in favor of an offensive strategy may be only modestly reflected in the kind of field forces he asks for; but a comparable predisposition in the air commander affects fundamentally the forces that he requests.

[2] In naval warfare, which falls somewhere between air and ground war in these respects, the offensive takes the form of asserting command of the sea in a critical area, and of efforts both to expand the area of effective command and to increase the degree of naval control within that area. "Command of the sea" is best defined as ability to use the sea for one's own shipping and to deny it to the enemy. The instruments for asserting and exercising command on the one hand, and for disputing it on the other, do tend to differ. The former objective usually requires a heavy commitment, among other things, to escort vessels for the protection of one's shipping, and the latter usually makes much heavier demands on the use of raiding craft, especially submarines. Thus, naval war presents the paradox that the side that asserts command (i.e., the "offensive") appears to be engaged mostly in defensive activities against the opponent's raiding attacks. Such was certainly the character of the crucial Atlantic campaigns in both World Wars. The key to the paradox is that the fighting mostly concerns a value, that is, retention of ocean-going commerce, of which the inferior side has already been deprived. See Bernard Brodie, *Guide to Naval Strategy*, 4th ed., Princeton University Press, 1958, especially chs. I, IV, and V.

The commitment to the air offensive will obviously entail a predilection for large bombers and long-range missiles rather than interceptors and ground-to-air missiles, but it will also go far beyond the choice of vehicles. It might affect, for example, the character of the air-base structure. A complex of operating bases is very expensive to build, and it becomes more expensive as its designers attempt to provide protection against enemy attack, whether through surplus bases for dispersion of aircraft and missiles or through "hardening" bases by putting strong shelters around aircraft, missiles, and important facilities. The cost of such additional protection represents money which might otherwise be spent on more offensive vehicles. An alternative with more appeal to the offense-minded is to rely on measures which will presumably ensure getting off the ground on time, even if that must mean keeping a fair number of bombers in the air at all times. Fear of being charged with possessing a "Maginot Line mentality," with its connotation of decay and futility, fosters a preference for relying upon initiative rather than concrete.

In time of crisis, the offensive bias of the force structure will tend to force conformity with the ideas that molded it. There will be pressure upon the government to guarantee that its forces will hit before being hit, just as in 1914 all the European general staffs pressed their respective governments to guarantee the security of mobilization by getting it started soon enough. Such pressure, however, is likely to be resisted. A military planner ought not to rely for the security of his forces on governmental decisions and actions over which he has no real control. When it comes to exercising national military initiative in the thermonuclear age, it cannot be assumed for security purposes that one's own government will act other than deliberately and cautiously. It *may* do otherwise, but security should not rest on the premise that the government will move speedily and aggressively.

Let us now divide the air-defense problem into its separate components and consider each one in turn. We have seen that defensive devices or activities are of two kinds: the active defenses, which consist of shooting at enemy planes or missiles, and the passive defenses, which involve mainly hiding, shielding, or dispersing the targets. To these unequivocally defensive functions is added the security-through-offense mission of the strategic retaliatory forces, sometimes called the "blunting" mission, which seeks its targets on enemy ground in the form of grounded aircraft, airfield installations, missile launching sites, and nuclear stockpiles if accessible. The blunting mission is operationally almost indistinguishable from the other offensive missions of long-range vehicles. It differs from them mostly in the nature of the primary targets selected and *in the special value of speed in accomplishing their destruction.*

Before we look more closely at active and passive defense, we should take up a problem common to both, which also affects the blunting mission: that of getting some degree of warning of impending enemy attack.

The Problem of Warning

Warning is the key to the entire defense problem. Our expectations concerning the warning we shall get in the event of enemy attack largely determine the kinds of defenses we decide to spend our money on, and how much they are worth. If we could count *with high confidence* on having two or three hours' warning of an impending strategic attack, and if the enemy knew that we had that confidence and that it was justified, we should practically have eliminated the possibility that he would attack. Apart from the fact that we might counterattack with missiles before he struck us, that much time would suffice to get most of the aircraft of our Strategic Air Command off the ground and out of harm's way, and the enemy would have to reckon with a retaliation so powerful (assuming his own defenses were not genuinely impenetrable) as to be utterly unacceptable as the price of an attack on us. The expectation of retaliation would therefore surely restrain his hand, and "strategic deterrence" would be operating with nearly perfect efficiency and reliability.

This point highlights two basic principles about defense in general, and about warning in particular. First, whatever else it may be possible or desirable to defend, it is absolutely essential to defend our retaliatory force, or a substantial portion of it. *Known ability to defend our retaliatory force constitutes the only unilaterally attainable situation that provides potentially a perfect defense of our home land. Conversely, a conspicuous inability or unreadiness to defend our retaliatory force must tend to provoke the opponent to destroy it; in other words, it tempts him to an aggression he might not otherwise contemplate.* How can he permit our SAC to live and constantly threaten his existence, if he believes he can destroy it with impunity?[3]

Second, if there must be a choice, a *reliable and unequiv-*

---

[3] The fact that this principle need not be peculiarly one-sided in its application is attested to by the former existence in the United States of a "preventive war" school of thought. Beyond this, however, Dr. Nathan Leites has developed the thesis that in Bolshevik ideology there is a *special compulsion* to destroy the opponent's capability to destroy oneself, and whether or not this compulsion is acted out depends entirely on the prevalent estimate of feasibility. See his *A Study of Bolshevism*, Free Press, Glencoe, Ill., 1953, ch. xvii and *passim*.

ocal warning measured in hours, or even quarter-hours, is far more valuable than an equivocal indication received much earlier. The longer-term warning is what we tend to expect from secret or "strategic" intelligence. We cannot rely upon it to trigger offensive action when trouble is brewing unless we are ready to act on indicators that are fairly ambiguous and therefore likely to be misleading.

There is in these matters a stupendous difference between hindsight and foresight. The intelligence indicators of the Japanese attack at Pearl Harbor look almost unequivocal to the historian who studies them now, especially the information received through MAGIC, which involved the deciphering of Japanese coded messages. But they were not read as unequivocal warnings by the appropriate people at the time, and they did not then point the finger at Pearl Harbor rather than elsewhere. This was so for a number of reasons, most of them having to do with failings normal to human nature. The few persons—few because of extreme security precautions—who had the opportunity to read the decoded Japanese signals included men of outstanding intelligence and dedication. They were about as good a group as America is ever likely to have in comparable positions; but they were too harassed by other preoccupations, including the whole European war and the affairs of the Atlantic, to concentrate attention on the suggestive items of intelligence that were somewhat spasmodically brought to their attention.[4]

It is an old story that limiting vital information to a few highly-placed persons who do not have time to think about it can prove an excessive price to pay for security. The responsiveness of U.S. government agencies to war indicators

[4] For the definitive work on the subject, see Roberta M. Wohlstetter, *Signals and Decisions at Pearl Harbor*, a RAND Corporation study, to be published.

has no doubt been improved since Pearl Harbor by appropriate organizational changes. One should not forget, however, the powerful predisposition to believe that an existing peace will continue. Modern war is so hideous in its immediate effects, and so huge a gamble, that it is always difficult for any normal person to believe that someone or some group could be planning deliberately to start one *soon*. Even when the idea is accepted in the abstract, as it apparently was by some American leaders on the eve of Pearl Harbor, the tendency is to treat it merely as abstract knowledge rather than as a trigger to specific and vigorous action. To make an intellectual prediction of the likelihood of war is one thing, to project oneself imaginatively and seriously into an expected war situation is quite another.

Paradoxically, it is the very attachment of the military to the offensive spirit that creates in them a strong impulse to disregard the likelihood that the enemy may have comparable attachments and may therefore attempt to initiate hostile action. Too much worrying about what the enemy may do is by definition "defensive thinking," which is considered excusable in specialists with specific defense assignments but dubious in war planners or theater commanders. It is interesting that the precautions actually taken at Pearl Harbor before the attack were exclusively concerned with sabotage, a non-military form of hostile action.[5]

[5] The responsible commanders at the time did not know, as we know now, how unreal was the threat of sabotage from the large population of Japanese descent on Oahu. But it is characteristic of the perennial fear of sabotage that the threat is almost never quantified by those who express fear of or make preparations against it. For an interesting contrast between meager objective fact and grotesquely exaggerated British fancy concerning enemy espionage and sabotage during the German invasion crisis of 1940 following the fall of France, see Peter Fleming, *Operation Sea Lion*, Simon & Schuster, New York, 1957, Chapters 5 and 12.

The utility of long-range warning depends not alone on its reliability or degree of equivocality but also on what one wants to do with it. It is one thing to use it simply to intensify alertness and to take other elementary precautions of a strictly defensive nature; it is quite another thing to use it to trigger an attack that will anticipate and forestall the enemy's attack. The two reactions reflect different basic attitudes toward the nature of the problem. One school of thought has argued that the American system of defense must be based on the concept of anticipatory or "pre-emptive" attack, that is, an attack provoked by an imminent and certain enemy attack. One wag has described this as the principle of "I won't hit first unless you do." The pertinent question is: what is the probability that such fine calculations can be made to work in practice?

Unless a government is willing to be the aggressor—in which case it would surely do better to forget about warning and choose its own time to attack—the anticipatory attack implicitly requires that warning be unequivocal. Yet early warning is almost certain to be equivocal. Only if the enemy is very clumsy or stupid or both will he signal well in advance his intention to attack.

We should note also that the criteria of utility for short-term warning are different now from what they were in World War II. In that war, radar warning of enemy approach was useful primarily because of the assistance it gave to defending fighter groups. It permitted the bulk of interceptor aircraft to remain in advanced readiness on the ground, instead of wasting their limited flight endurance in "stooging" aloft; and it greatly assisted airborne fighters to make contact with the enemy. The British radar screen at the time of the Battle of Britain proved to be one of the important technological surprises of the war.

It mattered relatively little, however, if air-raid sirens sometimes did not sound until bombs were already falling. Few lives or aircraft were lost to those unannounced first bombs. Today the first bomb is likely to be the only one that a community or an air base will hear or feel. Although it is still a major objective of short-term warning to alert the active defenses, it is probably a greater objective to get targets covered or out of harm's way, especially the crews, aircraft, and missiles of the Strategic Air Command.

The United States and Canada are presently maintaining two radar lines in the north besides the "contiguous area" radar network which embraces the United States and southern Canada. One is the Mid-Canada Line, and in the arctic wastes, roughly between 68° and 70° north, is the DEW (Distant Early Warning) Line. The flanks of these lines continue out to sea through the use of picket ships, and airborne search radar carried in large, routinely-operated, military aircraft.[6]

Although the costs of erecting and operating this system have been substantial, even as national security budgets are now reckoned, the result is far from foolproof. We know that there are various devices, familiar since World War II, for confusing a radar screen (e.g., "chaff" or "window") and for obliterating radar information by jamming, and that new types of unmanned decoys have been developed to dilute defensive action. Moreover, the extensive commercial traffic in peacetime presents an enormous discrimination problem in some regions. Finally, existing radar screens may offer no useful warning at all against missiles launched from submarines, which may have ranges sufficient to penetrate 1,000 miles or

[6] See Charles Corddry, "Buying Time: The U.S. and Canadian Radar Warning Chains," *Interavia*, XII (June 1957), 566-568.

more inland, and they are likely to be of very limited utility against long-range ballistic missiles. They are likely also to prove inadequate against low-flying aircraft, unless much larger numbers of radar sets are provided than is necessary in screens contenting themselves with high-altitude search.

Not much more can be said descriptively about the longer-term warning system discussed previously, which depends on intelligence indicators. It is an area shrouded in close secrecy. Those who are not actually dealing with the relevant operations cannot judge whether there is much or little to be expected from them, but experience warns against optimism.

The problem of warning is not alone one of getting relevant information, whether from radar screens or secret operatives; it is also necessary to know what to do when the information comes. If a reaction system is to be sensitive enough to be promptly and reliably triggered when the real attack comes, it has to be sensitive enough to respond also to occasional false alarms. Occasional false alarms resulting in precautionary measures deserve to be not condemned but rather applauded for showing appropriate alertness. Yet if the response to each false alarm is elaborate enough to create considerable disturbance in the population, it might become politically intolerable for them to occur at all frequently. There is always the danger, too, of an action which is provocatory to the similarly fidgety opponent. The real attack will come only once, if it comes at all, and the problem of maintaining a fine balance between alertness and calm will, if we are lucky, prevail over many years. The permitted reaction time is meanwhile rapidly becoming less, and the long-range ballistic missiles promise to reduce it to a hard minimum so short as probably to allow no time for counteractions that are not largely automatic.

Active Defenses

By "active defenses" in air war we generally mean two major categories of instruments: the interceptor aircraft with the system of weapons it carries aloft; and the various latter-day derivatives of the antiaircraft gun, mainly ground-to-air self-propelled missiles. In the long-range, unmanned, expendable interceptor, such as the Bomarc missile, the two categories tend to merge. Both categories have undergone impressive technological development since World War II, but at the usual price of a complexity that involves greatly increasing unit costs. Steeply ascending costs make it in turn increasingly burdensome to provide the necessary numbers of weapons to assure good defense.

Although it appears that, in the net, active defenses have gained considerably and are continuing to gain, in their ability to cope with the conventional manned bomber as an invading aircraft, this gain has been far more than offset by the change in the weapons that the bomber carries—as well as by the advent of ballistic missiles. The problem of defense against bombers carrying nuclear bombs is simply not in the same category as that of defense against bombers carrying chemical explosives or incendiaries. The basic difference lies in the rate of bomber kills that the defender must regard as necessary, or the attacker as tolerable. From this difference, which is an extreme one, all sorts of other differences follow.

It is a common misconception that the problem of defense against manned bombers—as contrasted with that against ballistic missiles—is for all practical purposes solved. Lieutenant General James A. Gavin, among others, has in his writings popularized that idea.[7] The optimism for our own

[7] General Gavin also goes much further than most in his optimism

defenses which such an attitude generates is quite unwarranted. We know that a manned aircraft in flight can be reached by a variety of missiles and struck down, but that does not make defense against a well-planned bomber attack easy. There is still an important future for SAC bombers, and there is likely to be for some time to come a grave threat from enemy manned bombers. Aircraft are likely to remain in use for some years because they retain certain advantages over long-range ballistic missiles, especially in their greater payload (usable either in larger sizes or multiple numbers of nuclear weapons), their greater accuracy of aim, their ability to hunt for targets of which the location may not be exactly known (armed reconnaissance), and their adaptability to being launched when danger threatens subject to return if the alarm proves false. Although they will certainly be complemented and eventually outnumbered by missiles, they are not likely to be fully replaced by them until and unless active defenses against manned bombers prove much more effective than we presently suspect them to be. Let us consider why the capabilities of active defenses even against bombers are presently rated so modestly.

The Manned Bomber versus the Interceptor

The modern interceptor aircraft has an initial purchase price of about one million dollars per unit, and the price is rapidly going up. At higher altitudes it moves at speeds well above that of sound. In its "all-weather" form it carries aloft an AI (airborne intercept) radar, and all models use some form of radar or infra-red fire control. The armament used

---

about defense against ballistic missiles. See especially his "Why Limited War?" in *Ordnance* (March-April 1958), pp. 810-811.

is already vastly superior to the World War II kind, and is getting better. The new interceptor will fire guided missiles like Sidewinder and Falcon as well as rockets with small atomic warheads.[8] The fighter is also an impressive-looking object. Why then do experts usually attribute to it an effectiveness that to the layman seems astonishingly low?

Let us briefly imagine what can happen to a single squadron of twenty-five interceptors at the moment of enemy attack. At any one time during routine operations, a certain proportion of the planes will be undergoing a sufficiently extensive servicing to make them unavailable for action. Of the remainder, only a small proportion will be in an advanced state of readiness—that is with crews standing by and able to take off within five minutes—though increasing proportions will be available as the warning time is increased. Thus the availability factor will vary importantly with the warning time. The more advanced the position of the bases, however, the shorter the warning time is likely to be.

Of those planes that take off in time, a certain proportion will abort, either for mechanical reasons, usually involving electronics, or because of some gross pilot error. Even a plane properly vectored out to the location of the enemy bomber may fail to make its own AI detection. Or it may fail to convert a detection into a proper firing pass. Even if everything has gone well up to this point, the fire-control apparatus and the armament now have to show themselves to

---

[8] An unclassified survey of world aircraft armament in use and under development at the time of publication is contained in "Aircraft Armament," *Flight and Aircraft Engineer* (London), January 28, 1955, pp. 105-110, 114-122, 129. Two more recent articles on air-to-air missiles are: John A. Airey, "Fighter Defence Systems," *Interavia*, XIII (November 1958), 1170f.; and (anonymous) "American Air-To-Air Missile Development." *Loc.cit.*, pp. 1172ff.

be equal to the extremely severe requirements laid upon them.[9]

For these reasons we may find in the test that of our original twenty-five interceptors only a few have actually shot down enemy bombers. We may have no justifiable complaint about any part of their performance, though we should be entitled to be unhappy with the total result.

We have so far assumed that the interceptors will be properly designed for the task that awaits them. The enemy, however, may steal a technological march and use bombers that arrive at altitudes which most of our interceptors cannot even reach, let alone operate at effectively. If we design an interceptor for extremely high altitude performance, which may mean increasing the cost per unit and sacrificing lower-altitude performance, we may find that the enemy elects to come in "on the deck," that is, at very low altitudes, where he will be difficult to track and to hit.[10] Moreover, the attacker will surely be using all the electronic countermeasures (ECM) his scientists make available to him for confusing our search and airborne intercept radars and our defense-missile guidance.

The enemy can also avail himself of the ancient prerogative of the attacker to concentrate his forces in both space and time, and thus overwhelm the inevitably dispersed de-

[9] See "The Impact of High Speeds on Conventional Strategy," *Interavia*, XII (January 1957), 30-32.

[10] The attacker does not have altogether a free choice between high and low altitudes. All aircraft, and especially the jet-propelled varieties, have far better speed and range performance at high altitudes than at low, the optimum altitude varying with the type of aircraft. Because of the other protective benefits derived from flying at low altitude, the attacker would probably be quite willing to make the requisite sacrifice in speed, but he might find the range penalty too exacting. With nuclear-powered aircraft the range limitation problem would not arise at all, but even chemical-powered aircraft are potentially capable of dealing with it.

fenses. The interceptor does not represent "local defense" in quite the limited way that the antiaircraft gun does, but in terms of defending an area as large as the United States and Canada its legs are in most types pretty short. The requirements for very high performance and for a size modest enough to make quantity procurement possible limit the fighter's opportunity to extend its range. More to the point, the useful range of the interceptor may depend on the time available for tracking the enemy bomber by ground radar.

In World War II the defending fighters on both sides were effective enough at least to oblige the German and British air forces to do their bombing at night, when their bombing accuracy was very much impaired. The U.S. Air Force held to daylight bombing, but after a few disasters had to put long-range fighters in escort. The modern long-range bomber, with its almost complete reliance on radar navigation and bombing, is about as effective at night and in bad weather as at any other time. The influence which the interceptor might still have in forcing the invading bomber to elect night approaches would therefore bring it very little credit. The fighter can serve a useful function today only by actually shooting down the bomber before it reaches its target.

In fact, the interceptor is less likely in the future to force the bomber to choose nighttime as against daylight hours for its attack. For if the bomber is about as good at night as in daylight, so too is the all-weather fighter, which is almost the only kind the United States is currently buying. On the other hand, the Soviet Union seems still to have a very large number of day fighters. The all-weather fighter differs from the day fighter in that it carries airborne intercept (AI) radar, which, because it involves a good deal of weight and space, requires a larger aircraft.

The new Bomarc missile, the prototype of the unmanned interceptor, has several advantages over the manned variety. It can be faster and because it does not make a return journey or carry a man with his equipment, it can be much smaller than the manned interceptor and therefore much cheaper. It is free of the inhibitions on maneuverability that the frail human pilot imposes on the interceptor and can therefore alter its course more rapidly to compensate for the evasive action of the target aircraft. Also, it can approach more nearly more nearly than the interceptor to being in a condition of constant operational readiness, and being launched vertically it is free of dependence on air strips.

The Bomarc is dependent upon ground radar for its initial approach to the target bomber, but the interceptor is not much less so. The Bomarc simply exploits this dependence to do away with the agency of the pilot. Its range is over 400 miles in the Series B models, less than that of the interceptor, but surely capable of being increased. Anyway, the useful range in the Bomarc is limited by the same radar tracking limitations we noted with respect to interceptors, only more so. The Bomarc's characteristic of being only a one-shot weapon is a far lesser handicap than it would have been in World War II. Presumably one does not shoot off all one's Bomarcs against the first enemy attack, but in any case the total period of the enemy assault is bound to be short. The manned interceptor will also be limited to a very few sorties, and perhaps only one.[11]

[11] A good description of the Bomarc, with photographs, is contained in "Boeing Bomarc," *Interavia*, XIII (September 1958), 926-930. The same article also contains some description of the system called "semi-automatic ground environment" (SAGE) into which Bomarc was designed to be integrated.

Shorter-ranged Antiaircraft Defenses

The other kind of active-defense system comprises the modern derivatives of the old antiaircraft gun, in the form of ground-to-air missiles. The scorn in which Douhet, Mitchell, and their followers held the antiaircraft gun reflected an understandable inability to foresee the marvelous electronic fire-control devices that would be perfected in time for use in World War II. Before the end of that war we had gun directors that could fix on an aircraft target by radar, follow that target, and automatically compute the proper lead for the antiaircraft guns which were moving in complete synchronization with them. The guns of 5-inch caliber or larger fired shells armed with the proximity or "variable time" (VT) fuse, which was itself a miniature radar sending out impulses and responding to their echoes.

Progress since then has moved mainly in the direction of substituting guided, self-propelled missiles for the gun projectiles. The Army Nike, which is close to the prototype of this family of weapons, has enormously greater range (something well over 50 miles in Nike-Hercules) than any antiaircraft gun. It also has much greater killing power as a result of its larger warhead and its ability, under automatic command guidance, to adjust to evasive maneuvers of the target plane. It will no doubt develop further in range, and it has increased its lethal radius or killing power by adopting an atomic warhead.

On the other hand, the Nike-type missile has certain grave limitations. First, while it is of remarkably long range compared with a gun, it has very short range compared with interceptors or even the Bomarc. This means, among other things, that it is an inherently dispersed kind of weapon. The

Nike installation that defends a large city from the south is of much reduced help against planes approaching that same city from the north.

The site of a Nike battery is not easily concealed, and the locations of established ones are matters of public knowledge. Thus far there seems to have been little serious thought of hardening them. The invading bombers would know pretty well what it would take to saturate the Nike defenses of any given area. Manned bombers can also remain outside the range of local defense weapons while firing off air-to-surface missiles to destroy the target—or the Nike batteries.[12] The batteries, and for that matter grounded Bomarc and interceptor aircraft too, can also be destroyed by ICBMs or IRBMs, the latter launched perhaps from submarines, after which invading aircraft would have a free ride.

The Nike is further limited in its rate of fire. Each battery of launchers has but one radar-director system, which must remain fully occupied with one missile for the full time of its flight. If each missile in flight takes three to five minutes to get to its target, the number of missiles that one battery can fire at any one enemy formation cannot be large. Director systems and even whole batteries can be multiplied, of course, but they are not cheap.

Above all, any system that is heavily dependent upon radar (the Nike uses radar for search or "acquisition" of the target, for target tracking, and for missile tracking and guidance command) is inherently subject to confusion by appropriate measures. Atomic explosions themselves may conceivably make radar temporarily inoperable. The answer to enemy

[12] See the description of *Rascal* and *Hound Dog*, both air-to-surface missiles, in "A Longer Reach for SAC," *Interavia*, XII (August 1958), 840ff.

electronic countermeasures is counter-countermeasures; but the attacker has the initiative, and available learning time for the defender is going to be short or nonexistent. The radar and other limitations characteristic of Nike (and partly shared by Bomarc) are not necessarily inherent in all anti-aircraft self-propelled missiles. For example, a short-range missile with a built-in homing device (e.g., Hawk) is free at least of the rate-of-fire limitation to which Nike is subject.[13]

One must repeat, however, that the kinds of defenses mounted against high-level attack are not generally of much use against bombers that stay under roughly 1,500 feet during most of their approach to target. An additional low-level defense capability therefore has to be provided, which if done adequately involves great additional cost.

The Uses of Active Defenses

Our observations have so far tended to stress the limitations of active air-defense instruments. However, there are also a few observations to be made on the positive side. First, if the active defenses succeed only in obliging attacking bombers to concentrate in groups against individual targets, thus depriving them of the freedom to attack a separate target with a single aircraft, much has already been accomplished. In World War II, even where defenses could be disregarded, planes had to concentrate or converge upon large individual targets in vast armadas in order to drop enough bombs on those targets. With atomic and especially thermonuclear weapons, one bomber over target is usually quite enough. If

[13] For unclassified descriptions of the original Nike-Ajax and the later Nike-Hercules as well as the low-altitude Hawk, see Maj. Patrick W. Powers, U.S.A., "U.S. Army Tactical Surface To Air Weapons," *Interavia*, XIII (November 1958), 1183f.

it were not for active defenses, therefore, there would be nothing to keep an attacking bomber fleet of modest size from spreading out over the land to destroy every target on its list in one strike. The defenses may oblige it to assume tactics which greatly restrict its target list for the first strike. The extent to which this effect can be accomplished or is ultimately useful depends on a number of things, including the enemy's capability in long-range missiles.

The above argument, if sound, may be enough to justify a large expenditure on active air defenses against bombers. Their existence raises the requirements for the enemy's strategic bombing force and lowers his confidence in his ability to carry through a successful surprise attack with aircraft alone.

Of course, there is not much solace in raising the enemy's requirements if he is still able to meet them. And even if his first, inevitably devastating strike is significantly confined in its effects, we have to allow for subsequent strikes if we cannot meanwhile succeed in destroying his air force. Also, he will have missiles. These facts, incidentally, should remind us that defenses that are enough to worry the commander of an attacking force do not necessarily warrant comfort to the defender. The chief value of one's active defenses lies, as we have suggested, in what if anything they contribute to deterring an attacker

Large countries such as the United States or the Soviet Union can by dint of very great expenditures, much ingenuity, and constant alertness devise methods of active defense which, with luck, will exact fairly high attrition of attacking manned bombers. But the destructiveness of the nuclear weapons carried by the bombers that will nevertheless penetrate the defenses has grown to the point where "high attrition" does not carry much meaning unless it is very high indeed. There is also the question whether we can spend or have any intention of spending the amount of money necessary to promise us high attrition rates.

This question was hard enough to answer when there was no alternative offensive vehicle. Now, in addition, we have to take into account the ballistic missile, whether of the intercontinental or of the intermediate-range variety. We can say about active defense against ballistic missiles that it is theoretically feasible. Some say that Nike-Zeus already offers it, but we know that something that is technically feasible may have grave drawbacks on other grounds. It may, for example, be too expensive to be purchased in really adequate quantity. Or it may be subject to countermeasures of various kinds. An anti-missile missile would probably have to be largely automatic in its response and at the same time very sensitive. Since it would probably also have to carry a nuclear warhead, it might prove an objectionable instrument to have in a completely ready condition in peacetime.

The coming of the ballistic missile is enormously discouraging to the defense against strategic bombing, not only because it is so difficult to cope with itself but also because it calls further into question the usefulness of costly defenses against the bomber. Why spend billions for defenses against the manned bomber, only partial defenses at that, when ballistic missiles are bound to be available in large quantities? As suggested above, the enemy's missiles may also serve in part to knock out our active defenses against his bombers, or his subsequent missiles too for that matter. One might perhaps say that two billion dollars a year, or some comparable sum, is still a reasonable amount to spend on active defenses against enemy bombers, but would six to ten billion for that purpose alone also be reasonable? If we say "yes" to the former and "no" to the latter, we may find that we are left far below the critical sum necessary to buy a good defense even against bombers.

On the other hand, there is a rough rule-of-thumb principle that no enemy vehicle of attack must be permitted to have "a free ride." The enemy should not be relieved of uncertainty with respect to any avenue of attack which it is feasible for him to use. The main value of ballistic missiles over aircraft to the attacker is precisely their high probability of successful penetration per unit, at least under present techniques of defense. It would therefore be folly to make a gift to the potential attacker of the same high probability of successful penetration by his manned bombers as he already enjoys for his missiles, especially since the bomber does have, as we have seen, several intrinsic advantages in offensive potentiality.

We must say in conclusion that in considering active defenses, a realistic analysis does not first assume an offense and design a defense to counter it. In actuality the order is reversed. A defense is built, and the offense seeks to exploit its weak spots. And the history of the race thus far suggests that there is always a hole, an Achilles' heel.

Passive Defenses

While active defenses seek to reduce the number of enemy bombs dropped on target by downing the vehicles carrying them, passive defenses seek to minimize the effects of those bombs that actually penetrate to the target areas and explode there. It is the difference between deflecting the enemy blows and absorbing with as little harm as possible those that fall. There is no doubt that the former is preferable, but neither is there any doubt that one cannot depend upon it to achieve anything remotely like 100 per cent success. With ballistic missiles we presently have to think of something like zero probability of success for active defenses.

Just as local saturation through concentration is in theory the attacker's main answer to any kind of active defense, so the removal or concealment or sufficient hardening of the target is theoretically the defender's answer to any kind of attack. To be sure, many attractive targets do not lend themselves to protection by passive means, but others do. Once the special quality of passive defense is grasped—once, that is, the curse is taken off the term "passive"—it may be discovered that much can be accomplished by reasonable efforts.

Passive defenses fall into one or more of three different patterns: first, measures involving *concealment* of the target (including devices designed to deceive or confuse enemy missiles or bombers); second, measures involving some form of armoring or *hardening* of the target (e.g., provision of underground shelters); and third, measures involving *removal* or *dispersion* or *mobility* of targets. Perhaps one could add *stockpiling* of replacements for aircraft and other high priority military goods which are likely to be enemy targets, but replacements also have to be dispersed or otherwise protected if they are to survive. The same applies to any expansion of the active forces for the sake of providing extra "cushion" against enemy attack. The provision of such cushion over what might otherwise be regarded as "minimum" first-strike needs is obviously necessary, *if* it is intended to supplement other forms of protection and not to substitute for them.

There are several other generic differences between active and passive defenses. The former tend to be defenses of a locality rather than of an object. They comprise interceptors and antiaircraft armament and missiles, which, because they are detached from the targets they defend, can be relatively easily shifted on short notice.

Passive defenses, on the other hand, vary with the nature of the objects they protect, and are usually quite intimately integrated with those objects. An air raid shelter is fixed in a way that an interceptor aircraft is not; a shelter suitable for covering people is not suitable for protecting the equipment of an oil refinery plant. Thus, to provide meaningful passive defenses within tolerable limits of expenditure, governments have to decide well ahead of a crisis just what objects they are going to protect, against what kind of attack, and how thoroughly they will do so. Such decisions will not be easy to make, either conceptually or politically.

There is also an enormous difference in minimum cost. Active defenses, to be of any use at all, require a very considerable minimum expenditure, one measured in billions of dollars annually. Simply to provide a "no-holes" radar warning network, without which active defenses are essentially useless, is itself a considerable undertaking. In passive defense, on the other hand, much of value can be done at relatively little cost. The dissemination of advice to citizens telling them what to do in the event of attack, for example, might cost very little and yet be invaluable in a crisis—provided, of course, it is good advice. The major cost would be in carrying out the kind of research that would enable the appropriate officials to give good advice. Of course it is easy to think also of extremely expensive passive defense measures.

The things that one wants to protect through assorted measures of passive defense may be roughly grouped into three general categories: people, production capital, and military forces in being. These are obviously not mutually exclusive categories. People require a certain basic supply of consumer goods and, in the longer run, enough production capital to meet at least the continuing needs of bare subsistence. People also collectively represent cherished political and social institutions, which are imponderables and therefore defended only by defending people and their property. Similarly, extant military forces always comprise personnel in addition to material objects, and such nonmaterial elements as group integrity. Yet, despite overlapping, the rough threefold classification is a useful one for our purposes.

Despite remarks in earlier pages about the absolute necessity for protecting SAC, even if everything else must go undefended, it still remains true that of our three general categories only the first, people, represents an end value. People are individually as well as collectively precious, regardless of how many or how few survive. The other two categories are means to an end, that is, they provide for the welfare and protection of the people.

It is necessary to make this point because military officers of undoubted decency and humanity have often permitted their remarks on defense needs to reflect an apparent unconcern with the desirability of saving human lives for their own sake. Calculations which embrace the possibility of gigantic casualty lists tend to induce in the people who make them a callousness that, however superficial, may be operationally important in planning. On the other hand, civilians of established wisdom and temperateness have sometimes expressed impatience at a scale of priorities in defense which on the surface seems overwhelmingly to favor military forces.

A permanent and comprehensive dispersal of existing industries would, to a large degree, automatically entail a comparable dispersal of population. The result, in effect, would be dispersal of our cities. Insofar as such a program gave effective protection, its main advantages would be, first, that it would minimize dependence on the timely receipt of warning of enemy attack and, second, that production capital would be protected along with the people who service it. The decisive disadvantages of significant urban decentralization, however, are that it would be enormously costly and politically difficult to carry out and that the protection gained even by a high degree of dispersal would not be at all commensurate with the effort of achieving it.

Dispersion is undertaken for the purpose of either multiplying the number of widely separated targets which the enemy must hit to accomplish a given level of destruction or of reducing the density of valued objects in any one target location. The former is sometimes called "macroscopic dispersion" and the latter "microscopic dispersion." If the atomic bomb had remained of a power roughly comparable to the "nominal" weapon exploded at Nagasaki, a reasonably feasible kind of urban dispersal could have resulted in a situation where more bombs, perhaps very many more, would have had to be delivered to effect a given amount of injury. It is likely over the short term to be harder for the defender to increase the number of targets than for the attacker to increase proportionately the number of bombs delivered; but over the longer term, if weapons technology had remained at a standstill, the race would not have looked so bad for the defender. Even if there were no final limit to the number of bombs an enemy could produce, there would be a limit to the size of the delivery force he could maintain indefinitely during peacetime, especially if they involved only aircraft.

However, atomic bombs not only multiplied exuberantly, but also increased greatly in unit power, so that the attractiveness of permanent dispersion inevitably faded. With the coming of the thermonuclear bomb, potentially available in whatever numbers might be desired, and with the discovery of the radioactive fallout effect of large-yield ground-burst weapons, it became clear that costly dispersion could to a large extent be countered by the very cheap expedient of delivering a vastly more powerful bomb. The combination of increased numbers and enormously greater power per unit gives the nuclear weapon a completely dispiriting lead in such a race. If a metropolis as naturally dispersed as Los Angeles can be effectively destroyed by a single large weapon—or perhaps two or three to do a thorough job of it —we know that the forced dispersion of denser communities would have to proceed to much more drastic lengths than was previously thought necessary in order to be of any use at all. The ballistic missile only makes matters worse, for if it cannot for the time being carry as significantly powerful a weapon as the airplane, it can probably be maintained for any given budget in much larger numbers.

A modified dispersal plan that concerns itself only with the placement of new defense plants has for some years been actively pursued by the United States government, which holds a certain leverage of inducement in its methods of awarding defense contracts as well as in the provisions for amortization in the income tax laws. In a steadily expanding economy such as the American one, significant effects of such governmental action may eventually be discerned, especially in that part of it directly concerned with military production. But it is very easy to exaggerate both the cheapness and the benefits of such a program.

Thus far pressures for dispersal on the part of government agencies have not reflected any well-thought-out plan that seeks, among other things, to anticipate weapons developments or the enemy's future capabilities. The government, for example, has sought to break up the considerable concentration of plants producing military aircraft and missiles in a coastal section of southern California. These plants may indeed be vulnerable, but the attack that eliminated them would certainly not be an isolated one. It is doubtful whether plants situated *anywhere* in the United States could continue to build aircraft and missiles on a substantial scale after a major nuclear attack, unless far more drastic steps were taken to protect *all* industries related to their manufacture than have yet been contemplated. It is even more doubtful whether missiles and aircraft not yet manufactured and delivered would be of any use in a war involving such an attack. Meanwhile, forced dispersion could hurt not only the communities involved but the industries themselves (e.g., by causing the loss to research organizations of skilled engineers who would not wish to move), and could postpone the availability of new types of aircraft and missiles that are needed *before* any attack.

Nothing said above should be construed as expressing objection in principle to carefully planned, selective dispersion. On the contrary, certain limited segments of our polity and economy, particularly those concerned with the control of the armed services during wartime, seem to cry out for it.

On concealment as a form of passive defense, only a few general remarks can be made. There is an enormous disparity between the Iron Curtain countries on the one hand and the United States and its allies on the other in the degree to which each camp permits target information for strategic bombing to become available to the other. Except for a very few kinds of highly specialized military targets in the United States, the Soviet Union need employ no secret agents to get the information required to fill its target folders. It needs only a small staff to select target data from what is openly and abundantly reported to it in numerous unclassified publications, including highly detailed maps, or from what is plainly visible to visitors who have a free run of the land. Regardless of how good our own intelligence may be, the Soviets can probably always be more confident of the adequacy and accuracy of their target information than we can be about ours, at least until reconnaissance satellites mitigate the difference—and they are not going to do more than mitigate it for a long time.

To be sure, the disparity has clearly diminished as a result of the development of ever more powerful bombs. Even the Soviet Union can hardly hide the existence or location of its major cities, and, with thermonuclear bombs available, that information may be all we need to maintain a very considerable deterrent threat.[14] When it comes, however, to targets of the so-called "blunting" mission—mainly the opponent's long-range bomber and missile bases—one supposes that the Soviet Union must have an appreciable even if not a decisive advantage in target information. How critical is this disparity only a few intelligence officers can tell, if anyone can, and they may be deceived.

[14] With missiles there is a geodetic accuracy problem to compound the inherent inaccuracy of the steering mechanism. Conceivably, even cities might be hard to hit with intercontinental missiles if the two kinds of error proved substantial. See Maj. Kenneth A. Smith, "The Ballistic Missile and its Elusive Targets," *Air University Quarterly Review*, x (Spring 1958), 60-72. Some of the work of the International Geophysical Year of 1957-1958 was concerned with this problem.

There is another kind of concealment which depends on the use of decoys to confuse the attacking enemy. In World War II decoys were visual, often taking the form simply of fires lighted outside the enemy's target area to compete with fires lighted by his first wave of aircraft inside of it, but decoys against radar bombing are also feasible, as is radar jamming. This defensive use of decoys and jamming must not be confused with the attacker's use of flying decoys and of radar jamming. In the net, the use of electronic counter-measures (ECM) probably assists the attacker more than it does the defender.[15]

Hardening: Implications for Civil Defense

Finally we come to the kind of passive defense called "hardening," of which the typical air raid shelter is an example. It involves putting a shield between the objects to be protected, whether human or inanimate, and the bursting bomb. Against the usual bombs of World War II, the function of the shield was to stop the bomb itself, or its fragments, or material set in motion by the explosion such as flying fragments of masonry. Against nuclear weapons, however, the shield must protect also against blast (usually measured in pounds of "overpressure" per square inch, abbreviated "p.s.i."), ground shock, and, if the objects protected are persons or other living beings, against gamma rays emanating from the nuclear explosion. Anything sufficient to protect against blast and direct gamma rays will surely

[15] Descriptions of the U.S. airborne decoy missile *Green Quail* and of the ground-launched *Bull Goose* (the latter since cancelled) are given in the previously cited article, "A Longer Reach for SAC," *Interavia*, XIII (August 1958), 840ff. One would suspect on *a priori* grounds that the airborne decoy missile would be less critically affected than the ground-launched type by the confusion that would probably characterize a retaliatory strike.

suffice against thermal radiation. Thermal radiation, however, is with good visibility dangerous at much greater radii than are blast or gamma radiation, and radioactive fallout may cover enormous areas, so that some kind of shelter may be necessary even at very considerable distances from the point of bomb burst.

A thermonuclear weapon detonating on the ground will cause a large crater around the point of impact (in one of the Bikini tests the true crater, as contrasted with the apparent crater, was over 1½ miles in diameter[16]), and we probably should write off any but the very deepest kind of shelter in the area covered by such a crater. On the other hand, at very short distances beyond the edge, deep shelters would offer effective protection to people within them. With modest increases in distance, the amount of depth or thickness of shelter necessary to offer protection would fall off quite rapidly. Thus, on an over-all statistical basis, the chances for people in underground shelters to survive nuclear attack are sure to be very much greater than those of people in the same area who are not comparably protected. That will be true even in cities subject to attack, unless bombs become very much larger than ten to twenty megatons.

There remains much that we do not know about the relevant problems. One of the only two nuclear bombs thus far dropped on cities caused a firestorm (at Hiroshima), and that one was, as later revealed by Commissioner Willard F. Libby of the A.E.C., of a mere 15 KT yield. People in shelters may be preserved from destruction by blast or gamma rays and yet perish from suffocation, unless suitable provision be

[16] The apparent crater is the visible hole with lip; the true crater is the larger zone around in which significant shear has occurred. See *Effects of Nuclear Weapons*, pp. 196-198, 209-211.

made for providing oxygen for the duration of a firestorm. There is also the problem of the intense radioactive fallout in the near proximity of ground zero, which may prevent egress from the shelters for days or even weeks. These considerations qualify the value of shelters but do not negate them.

There is the further problem of seeing to it that people are inside the shelters when the bomb explodes. Inanimate objects of high strategic importance can be stored indefinitely in highly bomb-resistant shelters—as no doubt most of our stockpiled nuclear weapons already are—but people cannot be. This is a problem of warning, though the warning time necessary to get people into local shelters is obviously less than that required to conduct a successful evacuation of cities.

If the strategic bombing of cities at the onset of war were not a foregone conclusion (as, for example, in the case of a limited war), the government would probably want to persuade people to stay in the cities. Adequate shelters and a promise of adequate warning might well be a necessary part of the inducement. Moreover, having shelters available for the people might make the government better able to take the diplomatic initiative in a serious crisis. Such initiative might involve sending the people to shelters, thus solving for that occasion the problem of warning.

Nevertheless, funds for the elaborate shelters necessary in cities would have to be provided in the face of the ever-recurrent suspicion that they would probably be of no use. Basically, there has to be some kind of local warning if urban shelters are to be at all effective, and if there is such warning is not evacuation preferable? As we have said, much more warning time is necessary for successful evacuation than for resort to local shelters, but under what range of conditions will this difference in time be important? These are questions to which the answers have to be somewhat esoteric, and they are too dismal to encourage ready public discussion.

The case for the shelter against radioactive fallout in the country is much easier to make. For those who already live outside of urban target areas, warning is not necessary. Information that cities or other targets in the general area have already been attacked is all they need. Those who may have been evacuated from cities will also benefit. Such shelters are therefore much more clearly useful under a wider range of circumstances than deep urban shelters and they are much cheaper to build. If they are provided, half of the population or more may be assured of survival.[17]

However, the public apathy or skepticism which for years has effectively inhibited shelter programs of any kind would first have to be overcome. Part of that apathy in the city dweller unquestionably stems from the realization that though with heroic measures the statistical chances for his bare survival could be somewhat increased, the city with which his life is identified would inevitably be a charred and dismal waste after an attack. It would be hard to persuade him otherwise. But the apathy is also due to another fact: the typical citizen simply does not believe that there is any chance of a total nuclear war occurring. In that respect he is plainly wrong.

---

[17] In rural areas many ordinary dwellings, especially two-storey houses provided with cellars, can furnish considerable protection against radioactive fallout if suitably equipped for a siege with foods and other supplies, including the means of washing down roofs, and instruments for measuring intensity of radioactivity. However, these must be regarded as at best supplemental to specially-built shelters. For most of the eastern part of the United States, cities which might be targets are simply too numerous to permit an easy attitude towards the fallout problem.

Much has been made of the so-called "clean bomb," but such a bomb will have no effects upon our defense arrangements unless the enemy not only knows how to make one but also wants to confine himself to using such a bomb exclusively in his strategic bombing. Even then how could we know and depend upon it in advance that he would do so?

Actually, hope for civilians in a future massive war must depend to a large extent on the fact that there is no obvious military reason, except for pure deterrence threat, why anyone should want to destroy enemy refugee populations in addition to the cities from which they have been forced to flee. From the point of view of immediate military advantage, the attacker may have an interest in burdening the opposing government with masses of dispossessed and panic-stricken citizens rather than in killing them. Willingness to forego the destruction of enemy populations may in the future be fortified by written or unwritten understandings concerning reciprocity.

We must recognize that there is, unfortunately, a common tendency among strategic bombing analysts to regard every additional increment of injury inflicted upon the opponent, certainly including injury to population, a military advantage. The Soviet strategists are probably as much given as others to this view. Attitudes of this sort change slowly, but they can change. It is some help to know that the kind of destruction customarily regarded as "bonus" if it results from attacks against other objectives is not likely to be sought by either belligerent if it requires a large special effort—as it would if an enemy population had already succeeded in evacuating cities or had repaired to deep shelters within the cities. In other words, the next best thing to a positive attitude which wants to refrain from destroying populations is an attitude of indifference to population targets. But if a belligerent wants to destroy populations, and if he can seize the initiative in an unrestricted war with thermonuclear weapons while denying the opponent appreciable warning, the carnage available to him must be set at levels for which we know no certain limits short of the total population of the target state.

So far as the protection of industry is concerned, a program to accomplish it through a combination of hardening and dispersion would have to start on a highly selective basis. The traditional approach to the problem is to want to begin with industries manufacturing key military items. But one has to ask: what are the key items in this distinctly new kind of war? Are *any* military items not already manufactured and in the hands of the appropriate military organizations likely to be of use? One must not be dogmatic on this issue, but one observes how blandly assumptions are made and carried into national policy which seem to envisage a repetition in some future total war of the World War II type of wartime production![18] This ridiculous and reckless fantasy can be dismissed altogether for an unrestricted war. The duration of the decisive phases of such a war can hardly be more than a few days. It is hard to make a case for any kind of wartime production possessing even a modest degree of military utility.

Much more to the point is the preservation of the industrial basis for national recovery following the hostilities. This is the consideration that must govern selection of key indus-

[18] Fortunately for us, this tendency is at least as common in the Soviet Union as in the United States. See Raymond L. Garthoff, *Soviet Strategy in the Nuclear Age*, Praeger, New York, 1958; also Oleg Hoeffding, "Strategy and Economics: A Soviet Review," *World Politics*, xi (January 1959), 316-324.

tries. A program seeking to provide for such preservation would undoubtedly put permanently underground selected components of the nation's industry. Preliminary studies have pointed out that cheap underground space is already available in many abandoned mines and caves and that, even for new construction, underground facilities are far from being as hopelessly uncompetitive with those above-ground as one might assume. For warehousing, for example, underground space may actually be cheaper.[19]

The Special Case of SAC

SAC constitutes a relatively small segment of the national community in terms of the manpower and the materials it comprises. It has a special capability for defending itself in that the part of its strength comprised of aircraft can take to the air on short and even equivocal notice. However, after a defensive take-off, they would normally have to land to take on fuel and bombs before departing on their retaliatory mission, and sufficient facilities for these operations would also have to survive any surprise attack. This need not apply to aircraft kept at advanced readiness on the ground, ready to take off offensively on what is variously called the "fail-safe" or "positive control" plan. Neither does it apply to long-range missiles, which will occupy a major and increasing part of SAC strength within a few years.

In general, the strategic air arm must resort to some combination of dispersion, hardening of facilities, and provision of alert and airborne contingents. Just what the com-

[19] See *Report on a Study of Non-Military Defense*, The RAND Corporation, Report R-322-RC, July 1, 1958. This report is based on a study led and directed by Mr. Herman Kahn. Part IV is concerned with "Recuperation of the Economy," but other portions of the report deal with the protection of the population.

bination of measures should be has been the subject of intensive research. In this connection we must recall the observations made at the beginning of this chapter about the common military bias against "defense-mindedness," especially among western nations. Hardening, which depends on steel and concrete for protective purposes, is uncongenial to spirits nursed on the exaltation of the initiative. The United States Navy learned the hard way during World War II that, while it was all very well to refuse to sacrifice offensive for defensive armament, a warship had to remain afloat in order to have any offensive capability at all. That point had been quite clear to Grand Admiral Alfred von Tirpitz of the Imperial German Navy, who remarked once that a battleship had three functions: first, to stay afloat, second, to stay afloat, and third, to stay afloat. German battleships were built accordingly, and showed their exceptional powers of resistance at Jutland.

There can be no rule of thumb to determine how much the United States ought to spend to secure the protection of SAC. This force deserves and enjoys a first priority charge upon the defense budget, and to provide for its security is as important as to provide for its existence. Perhaps some rough guides may help determine whether or not the matter is being pursued seriously at any particular time. One elementary test, certainly, must be the absence of arguments to the effect that the security of SAC resides in its taking the initiative at the moment of crisis. Such a presumption, or hope, is a weak reed for the military to lean on in a country such as the United States, where they cannot control the decision for peace or war and should not wish to. It is also true that one of the glittering strategic prizes to be gained in making SAC reasonably secure is the freedom accorded

American leaders to decide whether or not they are going to use that force at any particular level of crisis. An insecure SAC would either *oblige* them to be trigger-happy or prevent them from facing up to a crisis.

Several kinds of missiles are being developed in a role competitive with and complementary to the long-range bomber aircraft as a means of delivering strategic air attack. The intercontinental ballistic missile (ICBM) of the Atlas, Titan, and Minuteman types and the Polaris type of inter-mediate-range missile (IRBM) designed to be launched from submarines, seem to be especially well adapted to the use of dispersion and hardening, or to the submarine equi-valent of hardening, for protection. Actually the ICBM is no more suitable for enclosing in an underground shelter than aircraft, but because it is new and obviously indefensible by protective fly-away tactics, there has been far less opposi-tion to the idea of encasing it in strong shelters than has been true of aircraft.

However, while the introduction of protected ICBM's and Polaris-type submarines into the retaliatory system will mitigate the vulnerability of the whole, the aircraft them-selves may still be left needlessly unprotected. As structures they happen to be exceptionally vulnerable, though no more so than missiles. When parked on the ground they are sub-ject to serious damage from blast overpressures of only one to two pounds per square inch and from displacement due to transient winds behind the shock wave ("drag loading" or "dynamic pressure"). An airburst thermonuclear bomb of only one megaton yield could seriously damage or destroy all parked aircraft within seven miles, which is about the radius to which 2 p.s.i. overpressure extends.[20] It is obvious

[20] The data for damage to parked transport-type aircraft (comparable

that long-range missiles would not have to be extraordinarily accurate for one to be able to destroy all the aircraft on a typical SAC base. If aircraft are worth maintaining at all—and the informed consensus is that they will be for a long time to come—they are worth putting in strong shelters. Such shelters could make it necessary for the enemy to send aircraft rather than missiles for the destruction of our bombers, because the former have the greater accuracy and the larger weapon charges, and to make his initial attack in such strength as to increase the chances that we will receive warning of it. More important, the chances for enemy success in a surprise attack upon our entire retaliatory system will be sufficiently downgraded to make his resort to it much less likely. The only comparable alternative is "airborne alert," which involves keeping some planes always in the air, but this system is too limited in effectiveness to be sufficient in itself and probably very expensive per unit thus protected.

While the utility of active defense systems and of tactical warning networks is enormously downgraded by the enemy's shifting from manned aircraft to ballistic missiles as his primary attack vehicles, the utility of shelters rises sharply, for shelters provide much greater protection against missiles than against aircraft. Therefore the relative value of hardening as compared with most alternative schemes for protection, such as dispersion, advanced-readiness standby dependent on warning, and advance provision of replacement vehi-

---

to bomber aircraft) is given in *The Effects of Nuclear Weapons*, U.S. Atomic Energy Commission, June 1957, pp. 173-175, 237f. Aircraft are damaged by blast overpressures as low as 1 to 2 p.s.i., and complete destruction may be expected at overpressures of 4 to 6 p.s.i. For retaliatory capability, it is damage rather than destruction levels that are significant, and anyway the radius for complete destruction of aircraft is only moderately less than the radius for significant damage.

cles, is greatly increased. The chances are, however, that any comprehensive system for protection would have to depend on a combination of several schemes or devices, though the least dispensable single one of these appears to be hardening.[21]

That at least will hold true until missiles become so accurate that a high percentage of direct hits (i.e., target falling within the cratering circle or fireball) become feasible at intercontinental ranges. When that time comes, and some think it may not be many years off, protection for the retaliatory forces may have to be sought in mobility, that is, in their being more or less continually moved about, whether on land, at sea, or in the air.

Recapitulation

From the facts reviewed above it is possible to make some tentative but important deductions about the possibilities of defense against strategic nuclear attack. First, the number of human casualties will vary greatly with the degree of surprise actually achieved by the attacker, with the types of targets he chooses and the kinds of bombs used, and with the extent and the wisdom of the precautions taken by the defender before the event. On the other hand, the *minimum* of expected fatalities in an enemy strategic bombing attack probably has to be reckoned in tens of millions. Much depends on how anxious the attacker is to destroy human life, as distinct from simply rendering the target state militarily impotent. The trend in weapons, with their ever-larger yields and greater potentialities for fallout, has certainly increased

[21] An analysis of the problem of selecting methods for the protection of SAC aircraft is contained in Albert J. Wohlstetter, "The Delicate Balance of Terror," *Foreign Affairs*, xxxvii (January 1959), 211-234.

the life-destroying capability of an aggressor who wishes to use it. The cities themselves, that is, the buildings and other physical equipment of urban life, and most of the industrial production associated therewith, are inevitably in jeopardy.

The old adage that every new offensive development inevitably provokes the development of a suitable defense is hard to justify historically, and it is certainly excessively optimistic for the nuclear era. One should hesitate especially to apply it to the ballistic missile. That is not to say that effective active defenses against the missile are technically impossible, or that their development should not be pursued; it is only to point out that one must have extraordinary faith in technology, or a despair of alternatives, to depend mainly on active defenses. The relevant problems are political and social as well as technological. With the very short flight times involved, a defense system that detects an enemy missile on the way has little room to permit human judgment and decision to intervene. A system with enough built-in sensitivity to react promptly to any real attack must be sensitive enough to respond also to false alarms or deliberate enemy "spoofing." Spoofing with missiles for the sake of tripping off defensive countermeasures is very easy, though somewhat venturesome, for they can be counted upon, unless specific provision is made against it, to burn themselves out upon reentering the atmosphere.

Whatever is done or not done to defend cities and populations—and much can be done at not unreasonable cost if we are only willing to face up to our dangers—there is no question that very considerable passive as well as active defenses should be put around our retaliatory air force. For that air force has the following characteristics: (1) it is absolutely sure to comprise the top-priority enemy target system if he attacks at all; (2) it is a naturally vulnerable target system in the absence of special and considerable defense provisions; and (3) it appears that its natural vulnerability can be critically if not decisively reduced by measures that seem to be of reasonable cost in relation not only to our entire defense budget but even to the cost of the strategic air arm itself.

It is also vital to remember that defense of a retaliatory force capability is defense of a *system*, one which comprises not only the bombardment vehicles but also the relevant decision-making authority—which begins with the commander-in-chief—as well as the communications system by which the decision is translated into action. Enemy planners are bound to be constantly searching for the weakest link in our retaliatory system, and ready to fix their attention upon it, as they did in the Pearl Harbor attack. A future aggressor, we may expect, will not want to take undue chances by leaving retaliatory vehicles intact while going after weaker links in the system, but the various factors which will bear on a "go" or "no-go" decision may very well be dominated by a developing conviction that it is possible to paralyze our response. It is necessary to do all we can to prevent such a conviction from taking hold in the enemy camp.

⟨7⟩

THE WISH FOR TOTAL SOLUTIONS:
PREVENTIVE WAR, PRE-EMPTIVE ATTACK,
AND MASSIVE RETALIATION

NOT so long ago it was possible for nations to enjoy a degree of security against foreign aggression which in some instances approached the absolute. Until the coming of the submarine the United Kingdom had such security because of her favorable geographical position and her ability to maintain a fleet superior to any that Europe might send against her; and it is not much more than a hundred years since she was able to maintain her primacy on the seas with an annual naval budget of as little as £4,000,000.

The United States from the War of 1812 to World War II had an even more complete security, so that we could dispense not only with an army but, for most of that period, with a navy as well. Although our country possessed in the first half of the nineteenth century a merchant marine and a shipbuilding industry that rivalled Britain's, we maintained during that time no substantial naval force. For unlike Britain, our national existence did not depend on the seas, and our strongest neighbors on land were the Canadians, the Mexicans, and the Indians. We managed to have a great war in the middle of the nineteenth century, but only by having it among ourselves.

Even on the continent of Europe nations could enjoy relative security, though the price was higher and the assurance of safety less. An efficient and powerful army was enough to give other nations pause—that is, to deter them—and if deterrence failed it might be enough to stop or destroy their armies. Smaller nations could also gain significant security by allying themselves with larger ones, by accepting neutrality under great power guarantees as Belgium did from 1839 to 1914, or by exploiting a natural advantage in terrain as Switzerland has always done.

Of course, the greater powers usually interpreted their requirements for security expansively, and the objects sought in its name often became in themselves the causes of conflict. What was security for one nation tended to become the insecurity of its neighbor, even as it is today. Nevertheless, when the place where one might be attacked was on a distant frontier (distant in days of travel rather than miles), or an island overseas, or the territory of a weaker ally, involvement in war could not be too frightening a prospect, especially since the methods of waging it were normally compatible with punctilious regard for the distinction between combatants and noncombatants.

That is not to say that nations went to war because they thought war was safe even in defeat. They went to war because they thought they would win. In this they were often mistaken. The perennial confidence of general staffs that victory will be theirs in the next war seems to thrive in the face of a quite poor record of verification for that kind of opinion. Nevertheless, in most cases the penalty for a wrong prediction was sufferable without too great anguish. In the event of defeat, national humiliation normally counted for more than casualties. One critical reason for this was that casualties and other material losses were bound in any case to be relatively light, certainly by present-day standards. What nation could have been more decisively defeated than France was in 1870-1871? Yet the price paid by the great majority of Frenchmen, especially those outside besieged Paris, was trivial. Whatever the Alsatians lost, it was not their lives, fortunes, or even appreciably their liberties. To the Germans the cost of victory was a very few lives lost out of a young and rapidly growing population, and the compensations appeared, perhaps deceptively, to be tremendous.

World War I shattered the pattern of intrinsically and mutually limited liability in war, and the atomic explosions that ended World War II seem to have eliminated it. Among the changes we have to cope with today, perhaps the most significant militarily is *the loss of the defensive function as an inherent capability of our major offensive forces.* Those forces no longer interpose themselves between enemy and homeland, as armies did and still do wherever the chief burden of fighting is theirs. The force or forces that today pose the main deterrent threat are those comprised in and exemplified by the Strategic Air Command, which does not become a shield if deterrence fails. Although the counter-air or blunting mission of SAC is intended to achieve such protection, the success of that mission depends essentially on our having the initiative, more specifically, on our hitting first. It is not the only requirement, but it is the basic one. It is also the one least likely to be met. That is an unpalatable fact which is too often hidden by incantations designed to glorify our power and to frighten the enemy.

The enormous destructiveness of each delivered nuclear weapon is what makes the ultimate prospects for the defense, especially for active defense, appear so hopeless. With multimegaton weapons, one on target is already appalling—assuming the target to be a large city—and the prospect of twenty or thirty on similar targets is horrendous. Yet the latter figure will surely be but a small fraction of the number hurled at the United States if an attack comes. If we knew how to erect a wall round our own country that would keep out all or almost all thermonuclear weapons, and if we could afford to build such a wall, we should still have to consider the existence of those weapons a matter of profound significance at least for our allies; but we should not then be obliged, as in fact we are today, to revise our basic conceptions about war and its role in our national fortunes.

The ultimate defeat of the defense must not be taken for granted. Research on defense, especially on passive defense, has not been popular, and has therefore been treated in niggardly fashion. For that and other reasons we may presume that we ought to allocate much larger funds than we have in the past to finding new ways of active and especially of passive defense. Nevertheless, it is necessary to consider American national policy in the light of the facts that (a) today the defense is in all its aspects immeasurably behind the offense in effectiveness;[1] (b) there is no present reason to suppose that future technological developments will, on balance, drastically favor the defense over the offense; and (c) the amount of damage that the United States must there-

---

[1] The British Defence White Paper of April 1957 (*Defense: Outline of Future Policy*, Cmnd. 124, 10 pp.) acknowledged, in Paragraph 12: "It must be frankly recognized that there is at present no means of providing adequate protection for the people of this country against the consequences of an attack with nuclear weapons. Though in the event of war, the fighter aircraft of the Royal Air Force would unquestionably be able to take a heavy toll of enemy bombers, a proportion would inevitably get through. Even if it were only a dozen, they could with megaton bombs inflict widespread devastation." This admission must be viewed in the perspective of such episodes as the highly successful defense of London against the *Luftwaffe* in 1940 and against V-1 bombs in 1944. Even the V-2 bombs, although they could not be stopped save by destroying the launching sites, could be absorbed. Obviously modern nuclear weapons, especially thermonuclear weapons, make the difference.

fore expect to receive from any Soviet nuclear strategic attack will be intolerably huge.

What do these facts mean for national security policy? They have meant different things to different people, and different things at various times to the same people. Some extraordinarily diverse convictions have been expressed among those persons, professional military officers as well as civilians, who have had primary responsibility for the defense of the country. There has indeed been general agreement on certain fundamentals—for example that any and all plans for the security of the United States must make provision for a strong strategic air power—and with the passage of time the area of basic agreement has tended to increase and the diversity to diminish.

Perhaps we should survey critically the major schools of thought on strategic policy that have had some influence in military circles since the beginning of the atomic era. We can dismiss those transitory views which obviously stemmed from smugness and poor information, like the view that the atomic bomb was "just another weapon" and that its influence on strategy was bound to be limited by its scarcity. We have not heard such opinions expressed for some time. On the other hand, it is not always true that views which have passed out of vogue deserve to be forgotten.

Preventive war[2] seems today no longer a live issue, though

[2] The term "preventive war" has been objected to by many on semantic grounds. However, the meaning of the term has generally been clear to those who used it, including those who wanted to reject it. Substitute phrases are usually euphemisms or circumlocutions. I am using the term to describe a premeditated attack by one country against another, which is unprovoked in the sense that it does not wait upon a specific aggression or other overt action by the target state, and in which the chief and most immediate objective is the destruction of the latter's over-all military power and especially its strategic air power. Naturally, success in such an action

it was that only a few years ago among a very small but earnest minority of American citizens. Pressures in favor of it diminished as the Soviets developed a nuclear capability, and especially as Americans became acclimated to living with those nuclear bombs that had provoked the idea in the first place. The ranks of the preventive war advocates appear now to be practically deserted. Indeed, it probably is true that, as Kissinger has put it, "there has always been an air of unreality about a program so contrary to the sense of the country and the constitutional limits within which American foreign policy must be conducted."[3]

Nevertheless, preventive war remains one of the alternatives theoretically available to us and would deserve a brief review for that reason alone. There are, however, at least three additional reasons why the case for and against it must be considered: (a) the issue might conceivably be revived at some critical point in the future, especially if some new technological development introduces another major turning point in our affairs; (b) the reasons for the decline in the support of the preventive war doctrine are not necessarily sound from the point of view of the internal logic of the doctrine; and (c) the idea of "massive retaliation," to which this country remains wedded in much of its defense policy, is in some of its aspects rather closely related to the preventive war principle. Many of the points raised in discussing the latter can be applied also to the former. A fourth reason worth mentioning is that consideration of preventive war as a conceivable, even if presently rejected, American policy

---

would enable the former power to wreak whatever further injury it desired or to exact almost any peace terms it wished.

[3] Henry A. Kissinger, "Military Policy and Defense of the 'Grey Areas,'" *Foreign Affairs*, xxxiii (April 1955), 416.

may help sensitize us to the factors that could cause it to become Soviet policy.

The Case for Preventive War

The usual arguments for preventive war have rarely if ever been committed to print in a systematic fashion. Those opposed to the idea have considered it too immoral or too utterly unfeasible to be worth discussing. Those in favor have had grounds for considering it impolitic to express their views too publicly, especially if they happened to be in the public service.[4]

The case for preventive war, almost overwhelming in its simplicity, has rested primarily on two presumptions: first, that in strategic air war with nuclear weapons, hitting first is certainly a crucial advantage and, with reasonably good planning, almost surely a decisive one; and second, that total war is inevitable. Additional arguments heard in the early years of the atomic era were that what was inevitable had better come early rather than late, because it would be less devastating that way, and that it was senseless to permit the Russians to develop a nuclear capability comparable to that of the United States.

The latter arguments were bound to lose their force after the American monopoly had been broken and bomb sizes and stockpile figures on both sides had risen to levels re-

[4] Dr. Hans Speier calls attention to a few persons who spoke publicly on the subject of preventive war during May 1954, one of them being Admiral Robert B. Carney, then Chief of Naval Operations. See Speier's *German Rearmament and Atomic War*, Row, Peterson, Evanston, Ill., 1957, p. 114n. Admiral Carney's remarks, restrained as they were, were nevertheless exceptional for a military officer. No doubt a chastening influence in this regard had been the dismissal of Major General Orvil Anderson as Commandant of the Air War College in September 1950, following his public remarks in favor of preventive war.

flected in terms like "abundance." However, neither of the first two presumptions stated above is necessarily invalidated by the fact that the putative enemy has also developed a nuclear capability. On the contrary, it is conceivable, and even probable, that our present strength is much more nearly adequate to the task of knocking out the Soviet Union quickly than it was when we enjoyed a monopoly of atomic weapons. Certainly the bombs in our possession today are very much bigger and more numerous than they were then, and Soviet defenses, as distinct from their counteroffensive capabilities, can hardly be proportionately better. This difference tends to offset the fact that formerly we did not have to fear receiving atomic bombs in return, while today we should have to be prepared to receive a few. To be able to attack with impunity is fine, but only if the attack can achieve its purpose. There is good reason to doubt whether in the days of our monopoly we had enough atomic strength to insure the defeat of the Soviet Union through surprise attack. It is, therefore, quite possible that the action urged by the preventive war advocates began to make some sense only when their urging of it lost vigor.

The old attitude that total war is inevitable has now given way in many quarters to the view that it is impossible. We shall comment on the earlier view in a moment, but we must assert right now that the later opinion is logically and historically indefensible. So long as there is a great advantage in striking first, and under existing conditions the advantage would be tremendous, we must realize that even rational men could start a total war, and irrational ones would need no such justification.

If we knew there was going to be an unrestricted war relatively soon, we should be incomparably better off by seizing the initiative than by letting the opponent do so. The side that hits first stands a good chance, assuming reasonably shrewd planning and preparation, either of destroying the opponent's retaliatory capability or of disorganizing and reducing it to such degree that the remnants could be easily handled, in an attempted counterattack, by the aggressor's active defenses. Thus the side initiating attack may be able to keep down the amount of damage it receives to a tolerable minimum while heaping militarily critical destruction on the enemy. Such an outcome spells total victory for the initial attacker.

This argument assumes, of course, that each side knows where to find the critical targets in the other's territory (mainly the bases for his long-range missiles and aircraft), that there are not too many such targets to hit, that the initiator could gain sufficient surprise to be able to catch a high proportion of the enemy long-range bombers and missiles on the ground, and that the protective measures discussed earlier have not been seriously adopted by either side. We know the Soviets have the information they need about the bases of the western allies. Whether the latter have similar information about the Soviet Union and how trustworthy it is are questions that depend on highly classified knowledge and discriminating judgment. The least that can be said is that our plan for offensive strategy, whatever it is, would have its best chances of being carried out if we struck first, and that those chances would be brought to a very low minimum if the enemy struck first. If we thought *only* about maximizing our chances of survival, the above circumstances might be considered reason enough for going ahead with preventive war.

The Case Against Preventive War

Apart from the questions of political feasibility and of morals, which we shall take up presently, the military case against preventive war must rest primarily on two principles: (a) the physical circumstances which appear to make it so tremendously advantageous today to strike first can be and to some extent are being altered to reduce that advantage markedly; and (b) it would be presumptuous and reckless in the extreme to base so cataclysmic an action on the thesis that total nuclear war is inevitable or nearly so. It may on the contrary have a very low probability for the term of years for which the present generation of political leaders can be construed to have responsibilities of decision, especially if we promote vigorously the steps alluded to under (a) above.

The previous chapter indicated the measures necessary to reduce sharply the enemy's chances to gain critical strategic advantage from attacking by surprise. Most important is the hardening of one's own retaliatory striking capability. Improving the timeliness and the reliability of warning is always desirable, but for the retaliatory arm itself it may be necessary in addition to make protection largely independent of warning. That will be especially necessary in the era of the long-range ballistic missile. Fulfilling this need requires mostly a combination of dispersion with very heavy shelters. Substantial additional funds will be necessary, but the amounts are not outlandish. In any case, the thing will be done for missiles, and should also be done for all aircraft not on airborne alert.

The Riddle of Estimating the Probability
of Total War

We now have to face the question of the probability of

total war between the two major power centers of the world. It is a difficult question to deal with reasonably, because we all know that the future remains inscrutable and that logic and reason may lead us to the kind of "correct" answer which has every merit except that of being confirmed by events. Even if we could prove, as we cannot, that total war is not inevitable or even very likely in the near future, it might still happen. It might still happen even if we knew the statistical chances of its occurring to be quite low; we are after all talking about a unique event, which by definition is almost bound to be an aberrant from any statistical indication of its probability. Since we cannot, in any satisfactorily objective way, prove that the chances are very high or very low or somewhere in between, it may be more meaningful, from the policy making point of view, simply to recognize that we have no guarantee either that it will happen or that it will not happen.

It helps also to remember that a speculation about the probability of war is a speculation not about what the gods will do but about what men will do. Perhaps this does not help very much, because the wisdom or unwisdom of mankind, especially as reflected in acts of governments, is something about which one easily becomes fatalistic. Nevertheless, it is important especially for the citizens of a great power like the United States to bear in mind that, within wide margins delimiting the choices available to us, what happens to us is largely affected by what we do. It is somewhat bizarre to argue that it would be wise to choose now an infinitely drastic and terrible course mostly because the problem that would allegedly be liquidated in that way is one which we or our heirs would be too stupid to handle properly later.

The recorded history of our civilization is now some five or six thousand years old. It is admittedly difficult to conceive of the human race going on for a comparable period in the future without once pulling the stops on the kind of destructive orgy which nuclear weapons now, and no doubt also other instruments in the future, will make possible. But for making operational decisions, even fifty years seems too far to look ahead. If we could defer total war that long, it would surely be worthwhile to do so even if we were only deferring the inevitable. Moreover, it is no longer clear (in 1959), as it was a few years ago, that postponement can only make worse any general war that ultimately breaks out. Against this we have to recognize that it is only by seizing the initiative now that we can make sure that it will be we and not they who seize it.

If we ask ourselves what the chances are of avoiding total war over a reasonably limited period like fifty years, even the pessimist ought to feel unsure about its inevitability. We cannot predict the changes in the world environment which will affect the chances. After all, the world of only fifty years ago was that remote one existing before World War I. The world of fifteen years ago was one in which nuclear weapons did not exist. These were profoundly different worlds from the one we know today, and different above all in their attitudes towards war.

It was Bismarck, certainly no pacifist, who said to his master: "I would . . . never advise your Majesty to declare war forthwith, simply because it appeared that our opponent would begin hostilities in the near future. One can never anticipate the ways of divine providence securely enough for that."[5] To be sure, the penalties for waiting too long were not the same then as now, but it is instructive also to note that

[5] Quoted by Gordon A. Craig, *The Politics of the Prussian Army, 1640-1945*, Oxford University Press, England, p. 255.

this admonition was made during the "war-in-sight crisis" of 1875, some thirty-nine years before the next war with France actually did break out, and that it was largely Germany's eagerness to seize the initiative which made it "unavoidable" in 1914.

Bismarck had in mind that there are always hazards as well as penalties in going to war, especially with a near-equal, as France then was, and that even success can be costly. He no doubt also had in mind that the threat which the Prussian generals wanted to liquidate would not remain liquidated for all time, or perhaps even for very long, by the action they advocated. That action would probably have provoked the development of comparable or greater threats from other quarters. All this is without reference to the moral issue, which seems not to have moved Bismarck any more than it has the modern advocate of preventive war.

Preventive War: The Moral Issue

Yet it is vain to suppose that the moral issue can be expunged from the argument, however much we confine ourselves to what we fondly regard as unemotional logic. We cannot possibly make a decision on any large issue of national policy, especially one like preventive war, without taking our bearings from a moral position, usually unstated. To deny the relevance of moral values is to plunge ourselves immediately into absurdities, for example the absurdity of holding that the lives of any number of foreigners are as nothing compared to the freedom-from-fear of a single American. We instinctively reject such a proposition on moral grounds, and no principle of logic suggests we are doing something foolish in rejecting it. Moral values are bound to be a part, and perhaps a major part, of that total complex of values which give direction and dynamism to our national policies. Without values and value judgments there simply can be no policies.

Sophisticated people nowadays become embarrassed at the intrusion of explicit reference to moral issues in debates on national policy, especially strategic policy. We are aware of a long history of conscious and unconscious hypocrisy concerning moral issues in war, and we have reacted strongly against that hypocrisy—which incidentally is a moral attitude in itself. We have also had to incorporate into our military methods certain new systems of war which raised new moral issues, and under stress we disposed of them either by pointing to comparable enemy behavior, though the enemy's immorality may have been an important reason for our going to war with him, or simply by demanding of ourselves that we further dull our sensibilities.

We are indeed accustomed to phrasing moral issues in terms which emphasize the propaganda aspects of a contemplated act. We ask: how will this act affect the opinion which others have of us? Due concern with the propaganda impact of an action is obviously good politics, on the international as well as the domestic level, but the very word "propaganda" connotes an object outside oneself, usually more or less distant. From the propaganda point of view we are always primarily interested in how a word or action influences others. We justify that interest on the grounds that the attitudes of others ultimately affect us, but the effect is indirect and is measurable in terms of advantage or disadvantage. Meanwhile we close our eyes to the fact that our own actions may affect us much more directly and intensely.

The phrase "preventive war" implies inevitably the unprovoked slaughter of millions of persons, mostly innocent of responsibility, on the inherently unprovable assumption that our safety requires it. Presumably also, when we visualize a U.S.-initiated preventive war, we are considering the action of a democracy in which both communications and dissenting opinions are still free. Only by adopting a rigid dictatorship within could American leaders shut out reports from abroad of the unimaginable horror of their own creation. It argues some want of imagination to assume—as many in fact once did assume—that the American people could acquiesce in such a deed and then go about their usual business of pursuing happiness, free of guilt as well as of fear. We are spared the necessity of speculating further about the consequences of such an attack, for in fact there now exists a powerful and rigid barrier, largely on moral grounds, to American planning of preventive war.

Preventive War: Who Decides?

We have still not reached the crux of what it means to say that a policy of preventive war has always been "unrealistic" in the American democracy. A decision for "timely action" (as one euphemism has it) would require an extraordinary, indeed almost boundless, degree of conviction and resolution on the part of the President. We cannot doubt that he has the power to decide and to execute such a policy. It was presidential action which committed us to the American Civil War, the "shooting neutrality" of the World War II era, the Korean War, and many lesser actions. What we are talking about now would be almost exclusively a SAC action, which the President can easily control. Since the normal cold-war-size SAC is quite big enough for the job, he need make no approaches to Congress for special appropriations.

237

Certainly no initiative or pressure from the general public is necessary. Yet the public attitude and temper are relevant and even vital in a number of ways. Prospective sympathy or aversion for the move which the President may be contemplating penetrates the lonely isolation in which he must make his decision and affects that decision. Many persons can remain impervious to public opinion, but special sensitivity to it is one of the main occupational requirements of politicians.

What is the mood of the public likely to be? It is clear historically that, prior to each of the three great wars in which this country has participated during the last century, the public aversion to the prospect of hostilities was unequivocal and pronounced. The neutrality periods of the two world wars are a matter of living memory, and for most of the years of crisis leading to the Civil War the abolitionists were almost as much reviled in the North as they were in the South, precisely for the reason that they seemed to be threatening trouble. In each case, to be sure, the aversion to war ultimately collapsed, but not without provocation of an extreme kind.

Whether the reasons for the public distaste for impending war were primarily noble or mean, foresighted or the reverse, is not at issue. It is clear that among these reasons fear and a dislike for personal sacrifice have played such a prominent part that we cannot reasonably expect the national mood to be more warlike in an age of nuclear weapons. The development of the Russian nuclear capability was decisive in quashing the school urging preventive war precisely because it reinforced the moral argument against preventive war with one founded on fear.

It is supposed to be a commonplace that the public temper

may force a government to a truculence toward the foreign opponent which in view of his ambitions and aspirations greatly enhances the likelihood of war; but historical instances of such a thing occurring are not as common, or as unequivocal when studied carefully, as is often supposed. At any rate, they have not been recent. The "critical level of exacerbation" between nations, as Professor Harold D. Lasswell has pointed out, has been steadily going up since 1914.

In short, war is generally unpopular, and the public mood inclines to support really bold action only in response to great anger or great fright. The fright must be something more dramatic than a sudden new rise in Soviet capability. The remarkable lack of public excitement in America when it was announced that the Soviets had exploded their first atomic bomb, and later their first thermonuclear weapon, is indicative. The Soviet-launched satellites seem to have had a more pronounced effect in the United States and elsewhere. They struck at our complacency by showing us for the first time that the Russians could lead us in a technological advance of great military significance. But the American response, while full of uneasiness, seemed to have no component of bellicosity. The event had amazingly little influence even on the national defense budget, though this diminished effect was largely a matter of the Administration's choice. If the American people should ever really become panicked at some development in Russian capabilities, experience suggests that their response is likely to take the form of demanding greater withdrawal from risk rather than the reverse.

However, as we have noted, the operational powers of the President are such that the attitudes of the public, and of the Congress too, can be disregarded for long enough to accomplish a commitment to war. In view of their training and the manner of their selection, the military chiefs are not likely to be insubordinate, especially when the decision is for bold action. It is the President's conviction, will, and decision which chiefly determine the issue of war or peace.

What kind of person is it likely to be upon whom the protagonists of "timely action" would place such dread responsibility? The personalities of the men who have held the office of the presidency have varied considerably, but certain characteristics seem to recur. In the first place, if the cards are not stacked against mediocrity, they are overwhelmingly against fanaticism, especially when it is concentrated on military security rather than welfare. It is a fact that, in almost every national election held during a time of threatening military troubles, the major contestants have striven to outdo each other in promising to keep the country out of war.[6]

Of the two American military leaders who achieved enough glamor and fame in World War II to be seriously thought of for the presidency, it was the humble and folksy one, the one whose talents were conspicuously in the field of human relations, who became the single serious contender. Not those virtues which might be called characteristically military but rather his apparent benignity and moral probity —and indeed his pacifism—were what his managers shrewdly chose to emphasize in his two election campaigns. By contrast, the imperious General Douglas MacArthur was not

[6] Lincoln, we may nostalgically recall, made no campaign speeches after his nomination in keeping with the custom of the day, but certainly the platform of his party and the speeches of his supporters were anything but bellicose. Lincoln himself had been chosen by his party as a more conciliatory offering than his chief rival, Seward, who was regarded as too outspokenly abolitionist.

even in the running. Well-established democracies seem to share a tradition against the man-on-horseback, even when they elect generals to high office, and the American democracy makes special demands for optimism and the homely touch in its presidential candidates.

Finally, and perhaps most important, we should remember that the kind of total preoccupation with the national danger from abroad which is the chief function of many military officers and some civilians is simply not permitted to the President. He is always obliged to concern himself deeply with a fantastically diverse array of political and domestic matters. To have a diversity of cares is to be spared excessive rumination about any one of them. This is an aspect of the presidency which the specialist in defense often finds it difficult to comprehend, let alone appreciate. The expert also knows the President to be, in a formal sense, fairly well informed on the relevant issues. He can hardly expect to convert him to a more excited attitude simply by bringing him some additional items of information. Moreover, the President is never a captive audience for any briefing; he hears only what he feels he has the time and inclination to hear.

Perhaps we have said enough to explain why preventive war has been so often dismissed simply as "unrealistic." As long as the United States remains the kind of democracy it is, and as long as there is not some overwhelming new fact like strong evidence of impending Soviet attack, the kind of "solution" we have been discussing would scarcely seem to be among the genuinely available policy alternatives.

Pre-emptive Attack

A few words are necessary about a variant of the preventive war idea which has on some occasions received serious discussion. It is more important in military planning than the relatively small amount of discussion concerning it would lead one to expect. The distinguishing characteristic of the idea, which has been called "pre-emptive attack," is that it envisages a strategic air attack by the United States upon the Soviet Union *only after* the latter has already set in motion its own strategic air attack, but *before* that attack is consummated and preferably before it gets well under way. A somewhat subordinate theme usually present is that the anticipatory counterattack will be carried out by relatively small forces and that the targets will be more or less confined to the enemy's strategic air force.

As we noted earlier, the idea has been somewhat unkindly referred to as the philosophy of "I won't strike first unless you do," though the phrase should no doubt be edited to read, "unless you attempt to." Anyway there is the insistence that, come what may, "I will strike first!"—though the "I" agrees to wait long enough so that any qualms on moral grounds are automatically resolved.

There is, naturally, a finite chance that we could in fact succeed in the nice anticipation of enemy action called for in the conception of pre-emptive attack. No doubt we ought to improve and refine our strategic warning or "indicator" techniques to maximize that chance, but whether the latter could ever be large enough to warrant any substantial reliance upon it is quite another question.

The idea has persisted that no nation can resort to war without first setting in train elaborate preparations such as are sure to be detected by a competent intelligence service.[7]

[7] The surprises of the Japanese attack at Pearl Harbor and of the German attack on the Soviet Union in June 1941, have been explained away on

One view has had it that the Soviet Union would not and could not make a strategic air attack upon the United States without first preparing its armies to move at the same time into the territories of our European allies.[8] Even those who are less inclined to regard a land invasion as an essential concomitant of an air offensive have felt that an attack upon us that limited itself, in the first instance, to air operations would nevertheless be "all out" in that category. The movements preparatory to a gigantic air offensive would no doubt be more difficult to detect than those leading to a comparable ground offensive, but there would nevertheless be plenty of activity to look for and possibly to see.

On the other hand, if we accept as sound the simple propositions (a) that the first order of business for the Soviet Union in opening total hostilities against us is the destruction of our retaliatory air capability, upon which everything else can wait for leisurely attention, and (b) that the most important and indeed the one indispensable ingredient for the success of such an attack is *surprise*, certain conclusions inevitably follow. One is that much in the way of military preparations can be sacrificed by the Russians, and probably would be sacrificed by them, in order to maximize the chance of achieving surprise. Another is that with surprise the force necessary to accomplish the desired result is probably small, so that it could be dispatched against its targets with very few telltale warning signs. There is time enough to dispatch

---

the grounds that in both cases the attacker was already at war with other countries, and therefore his home mobilization was not conspicuous.

[8] The official Soviet attitude expressed at the Geneva Technical Discussions on Safeguards Against Surprise Attack in December, 1958 was that preparation for ground attack would always attend preparations for surprise strategic air attack. It is by no means impossible that they believed it, at least at that time.

the rest when the first attacking wave is approaching its targets—assuming they are manned bombers—but in any case if that wave is successful in its mission the time permitted the Soviets for other military preparations is practically unlimited. All this, after all, reflects the basis on which we would probably be planning to make our own pre-emptive attack if provocation and opportunity afforded.

The indications which our strategic intelligence might bring us of impending enemy attack would always be of utmost value for the alerting of our own forces. However, whether those indications could ever be unequivocal enough to warrant an anticipatory attack by us is another matter. To be sure, it is a matter of policy to decide how unequivocal the indications must be before we respond with an offensive of our own; but we are assuming that since preventive war has been rejected, there is a great unwillingness to see a total nuclear war begin.

In the previous chapter attention was called to the difficulties during peacetime of grasping the import of war warnings which look after the event as though they must have been unequivocal. Roberta M. Wohlstetter's excellent study of the indications signalling the Pearl Harbor attack is useful and important partly because it is no doubt suggestive of ways of improving the handling and utilization of intelligence, but even more because it reminds us to be modest and skeptical in our expectations of what is likely to be accomplished even with exceptionally superior intelligence, at least where the event signalled involves a transition from peace to war.[9]

[9] See Roberta M. Wohlstetter, *Signals and Decisions at Pearl Harbor*, a RAND Corporation study, to be published. It is a peculiarity of the Pearl Harbor episode that while our leaders appeared to accept the idea that

One would conclude from all this that while a successful pre-emptive strike by the United States remains theoretically feasible, it would be foolish to rely upon it as though it were a good possibility, let alone a likely contingency. Yet that is what we presently appear in some ways to be doing, even if partly unconsciously. For example, it has become axiomatic in recent years that American strategic air power would be launched against the enemy only in response to overt enemy aggression. That aggression, according to accepted theory, might well take the form of strategic air attack upon us. Yet we do not seem to be taking any particularly heroic measures for the protection of our strategic air force apart from planning an airborne alert which, when in operation, can affect only a very small part of that force. Besides, preparations and concepts for the use of our retaliatory force seem always to be geared to the tacit assumption that that force will be essentially intact and unimpaired at the moment it goes into action. This situation can reflect nothing other than an abiding conviction that the enemy will not really succeed in surprising us—that it is we who will get the jump on him, and not the other way around.

Like members of other callings, the military people who design war plans have traditionally been subject to certain

war was imminent, they seemed oblivious to the fact that it might begin with an air attack on our fleet at that base. Yet we know that if war had begun in some other way, safeguards would have been established and made routine at Pearl Harbor which would have made much more difficult the kind of surprise actually achieved there by the Japanese on December 7, 1941. We know also that as early as 1931, studies made in the American armed forces considered the possibility of Japanese carrier-air attack upon the western coast of the United States, so that the idea of such attack was certainly not novel. The psychological barrier seems to be not so much in accepting the abstract probability that war may break out in the near future, as in projecting oneself imaginatively into the character of the war situation.

professionally-induced aversions. One is an aversion to basing any kind of plan on the assumption that the outbreak of hostilities will find us off our guard or otherwise discommoded. To consider the possibility of a disaster at the outset is of course out of the question. Another is an aversion to being charged with being "defensive minded," which in practice is construed as a frame of mind that seeks to take seriously into account the possibility that the enemy, rather than ourselves might seize and hold the initiative during the crucial early phases of the war.

Official planning studies may indeed start out by including among the stated assumptions one to the effect that the enemy has seized the initiative, at least to the extent of opening the hostilities. But since its implications are too unpleasant to be borne, the assumption itself is likely to be forgotten the moment the page on which it is announced is turned. The same fate is likely to overtake any declared assumptions to the effect that the enemy is shrewd and intelligent as well as aggressive, for if he has all these qualities and the initiative besides the outlook for us must be black indeed. The irrepressible tendency is to regard the enemy in the body of the study as rather dim-witted and passive, however respectful may have been the statements about him in the preface.

It is, incidentally, perhaps the greatest merit of the war-gaming technique that it, and it alone, overcomes these and like tendencies. It does not matter how simple or complex the particular game, so long as the enemy is represented by a player who is coequal with his opponent. He will see to it that an initiative accorded to him by the terms of the game will mean something in practice, and he will to the best of his abilities make the most of all the tokens he is given to play with. It is really remarkable what immunities the usual war-plans designer will take for granted as belonging of right to American forces, and how quickly his roseate fantasies collapse the moment he plays on paper a simple war game in which the enemy is given something like equal power and perhaps the initiative to boot. Another benefit of war games is that they force the players to consider the problem beyond the opening moves, which it is otherwise very difficult for a war planner to force himself to do. There are other advantages in war games—and also some disadvantages, chief among the latter being the tendency of the play, especially in the more complicated games, to induce in the players the illusion that they have really tested their initial hypotheses or presumptions in a conclusive manner.

Anyway, no war plan existing in 1941 could possibly have presupposed the kind of disaster we did in fact suffer at Pearl Harbor. Any study that had gone so far as to assume a Japanese attack on that place would have proceeded to spell out measures to avoid or minimize the damage—measures which were in fact completely available at the time—and would have assumed that those measures would in fact be taken. Tradition boggles at the thought of basing a study on the assumption that our people will at the critical moment be subject to the kind of errors which human beings are always heir to—subject, in other words, to normal human deficiencies in alertness and judgment.

Today, however, we tend to assume that our commanders will be entirely alert and wise in the event of surprise attack, and also that their alertness and wisdom will be of sufficient weight to win the day for us. In terms of the facilities provided or programmed at this writing, one wonders if there is any way in which that end could be accomplished except through successful pre-emptive attack.

Massive Retaliation

The descriptive term "massive retaliation" burst into notoriety as a result of a speech made by Secretary of State John Foster Dulles before the Council of Foreign Relations in New York on January 12, 1954.[10] The sentence from which this term is derived ran: "Local defenses must be reinforced by the further deterrent of massive retaliatory power." That sentence in itself was innocuous and truistic, but it gained special and pointed meaning from statements in the context making clear that henceforward *primary* reliance would be placed on that deterrent for coping with local aggression.

Observations elsewhere in the speech stressed the economic and military wastefulness of attempting to distribute military forces over the globe in order that local aggressions could be met in the places where they occurred. One key assertion was: "The way to deter aggression is for the free community to be willing and able to respond vigorously at places and with means of its own choosing."

Secretary Dulles also emphasized that the policy he was announcing was a distinctively new one, resulting from "some basic policy decisions" made by the National Security Council. "The basic decision," he repeated,

was to depend primarily upon a great capacity to retaliate, instantly, by means and at places of our own choosing. Now the Department of Defense and the Joint Chiefs of Staff can shape our military establishment to fit what is our policy, instead of having to try to be ready to meet the enemy's many choices. That permits of a selection of military means instead of a multiplica-

[10] Reproduced in *The New York Times* for January 13, 1954.

tion of means. As a result, it is now possible to get, and share, more basic security at less cost.

The warning was also made that if the Communists renewed their aggression in Korea, "the United Nations response would not necessarily be confined to Korea."

In response to the vigorous criticisms provoked by this speech,[11] Secretary Dulles and other members of the administration felt obliged, in subsequent "clarifying" statements, to backtrack considerably from the January 12 position. In sum, the clarifications and explanations made over the next several months by the Secretary and his associates amounted virtually to a retraction.[12] On the other hand, if one examines the course actually pursued by national defense policy and military programming over the next several years, it was the original speech which stood and not the retractions. The massive retaliation idea became, and to a major degree remains, the basic orientation of American defense policy.[13]

It is noteworthy that while the January 12 speech was a major policy declaration by a senior civilian member of the

[11] The public criticisms were in fact surprisingly slow in coming. One of the earliest comments appeared a few days later in a brief article by James Reston in *The New York Times* for January 17, 1954, in which he complained that the new strategy announced by Secretary Dulles, which he called "potentially graver than anything ever proposed by any United States Government," had thus far "not produced a single important comment on Capitol Hill." Within the next few weeks, however, trenchant criticisms were published in *The New York Times* and elsewhere, especially by Chester W. Bowles and Adlai Stevenson.

[12] One of the most important of these "clarifications" was the article published by Secretary Dulles in *Foreign Affairs*, xxxii (April 1954), 353-364, entitled: "Policy for Security and Peace." The writing of this article followed hard upon Secretary Dulles' participation in London in a conference with the foreign ministers of our European allies, and the views expressed in it seem to reflect that experience.

[13] See, in this connection, the book by Brig. Gen. Dale O. Smith, USAF, *U.S. Military Doctrine*, Duell, Sloan, & Pearce, New York, 1955.

government, the justifications it presented for the new doctrine appealed in the main to certain characteristically military ideas or doctrines. There was first the strong rejection, as bad military practice, of the dispersion of military forces over the globe—an appeal, in other words, to the idea familiar to military officers as the "principle of concentration." There was also strong emphasis on the virtues of seizing the initiative at the earliest moment and retaining it, and of making the enemy dance to our tune rather than our dancing to his. Finally, there was an implied rejection of limitation on means, that is, on weaponry. The emphasis was, to repeat, "upon a great capacity to retaliate, instantly, by means and at places of our own choosing."[14] It could not have been stated in more admirably concise military fashion.

To be sure, all this was going to have the additional merit of costing less money, but considering that the Secretary of State is the President's chief adviser and agent on international political affairs, the concentration on military considerations, to the near-exclusion of possibly countervailing non-military ones, was a little startling. The military ideas to which he gave expression are of undoubted merit, but one was obliged to wonder whether an important analytical component normally supplied by civilian statesmen had been missing from the policy deliberations he was reporting.

One notices also that this speech, presented only a half-year after the armistice which ended the Korean War, was a rejection, on tactical and strategic grounds, of our entire

[14] The word "instantly" in that statement suggests the personal intervention of the President. It is not quite the natural word for that context, and close readers of Dwight D. Eisenhower's *Crusade in Europe*, Doubleday, New York, 1948, will recall that "instantly" is a particularly favored word of his for describing responses, and recurs frequently through the book.

strategy in that war. The war had been limited with respect to weapons and geography, and as a limited war it had to be waged at a place determined by the enemy and peripheral to the sources of his power. Thus the Secretary fairly explicitly condemned the scope and methods of Korea as intolerably wasteful and unsatisfactory. This too reflected a characteristically military dissatisfaction, one made familiar previously in the MacArthur hearings.[15] In fact, the speech makes no sense *except* as a rejection of Korea, because otherwise its timing—four years after the first Soviet atomic bomb and some months after the Soviet Union had already exploded a thermonuclear weapon—is a little bizarre. The time seemed more suitable for an era of massive-retaliation philosophy to be drawing to its close, not to be having its dawn.

The latter point, to be sure, was somewhat concealed by the "point of no return" view current at the time, that is, the view that a clear-cut decision had to be made whether or not the United States was going to move in the direction of a whole-hearted embracing of nuclear weapons in all its strategic conceptions and planning. To put the question of choice sharply on an either-or basis was to elicit inevitably a decision favorable to atomic weapons. Since it made no sense to plan as though we were not going to use nuclear weapons, we moved in the direction of deciding that we would inevitably use them in all kinds of hostilities. And at that time the use of nuclear weapons tended to suggest in most people's minds an all-out rather than a limited war.

[15] See *Military Situation in the Far East*. Hearings before Committee on Armed Services and the Committee on Foreign Relations, U.S. Senate, 82nd Congress, 1st session, U.S. Government Printing Office, 1951. The same point of view is reflected also in the book by former Secretary of the Air Force Thomas K. Finletter, *Power and Policy*, Harcourt, Brace, New York, 1954.

No one has ever questioned the appropriateness of massive retaliation as a response to a direct attack upon ourselves. Let us also be clear that in the next most important and critical area of the world as far as our defense obligations are concerned, namely Europe, there has thus far been little alternative to massive retaliation as the basic organizing principle of a security system. The NATO powers were induced to make the precedent-shattering commitments of that alliance only upon our promise that the United States SAC stood ready at all times to implement it. The NATO alliance was the means by which our partners could avail themselves of that kind of support, and it was the only way in which the United States could bind them, if attacked, to defend themselves vigorously and in combination. It was also the only way in which the United States could get them to contribute the complementary forces which the entire defense scheme was deemed to require, as well as to provide the advance bases considered essential at the time for the appropriate wartime employment of SAC.

The prevailing conception of the functions of those complementary or local forces, tactical air as well as ground forces, has varied with time. In the beginning it was felt that a strategic air attack on the Soviet Union, however effective it might be in winning a war for the NATO powers, especially since no reply in kind had to be feared, would not be quick enough in its effects to prevent the Russian armies from invading and occupying western Europe. To stop them required also substantial ground forces. Later, as the inherent power of the strategic air threat grew on both sides, it became increasingly apparent (though not admitted by any government until the British Defence White Paper of 1957) that in the event total war broke out in Europe—or rather, over

Europe—the mutual strategic air strikes would so dominate events as to make rather unimportant and almost irrelevant the military events occurring locally.

Then the local ground forces began to be spoken of as having primarily a "trip-wire" or "plate-glass" function—that is, the function of signalling by their resistance, however brief, the fact that a major war had broken out, as well as of obliging the enemy to send enough troops to make the aggression unequivocal.[16] Certainly that is the function which the European governments have had consistently in mind in the importance they attached to having the few American divisions (presently five) in Europe.

There has recently been some discussion of the possibility of limiting war even in Europe. This material will be reviewed in the appropriate place, in the chapter on "Limited War." It is enough to point out here that the few military and civilian leaders of the NATO countries who have thus far revealed an interest in limited war strategies in Europe, including the Supreme Commander, General Lauris Norstad, have shown no great inclination to relinquish major reliance upon total intervention by the United States SAC in the event of Soviet attack.

The officials, especially in Europe, may have in the backs of their minds that there will be no important war in Europe at all, that the "Great Deterrent" will work because it must, and that the question of what happens in the event it does not is simply not to be considered. In any case, they have thus far appeared unready to entertain ideas that might

---

[16] The British Defence White Paper of 1957 says in this regard (Paragraph 20): "The possession of nuclear air power is not by itself a complete deterrent. The frontiers of the free world, particularly in Europe, must be firmly defended on the ground. *For only in this way can it be made clear that aggression will be resisted.*"

involve weakening the deterrent. As far as the United States government is concerned, in the Suez crisis of November 1956, and in the Turkish-Syrian disturbance of October 1957, it stated openly through its highest-placed servants that it was still ready to use SAC in the defense of its NATO allies, including Turkey.[17]

Perhaps our civilian leaders overestimated their own readiness to resort to this dread sanction if the moment for decision actually came. Perhaps they preferred not to probe their own hearts or minds too searchingly on the matter, as long as there seemed to be no clear and present danger of being called upon to deliver. Some of them may even have thought that as long as we freely threatened massive retaliation, and made ourselves behave as though we meant it, the enemy would avoid challenging us. Others undoubtedly really meant it. In any case, they were not conspicuously hunting for other solutions for the protection of the area.

Our readiness to defend even Europe by massive retaliation may be called into question sooner or later—by ourselves, by our European allies, by the enemy, or by all three simultaneously—but it is likely that the challenge will come sooner in areas beyond Europe. After all, the Dulles doctrine of January 1954 represented nothing new concerning the defense of our own country or Europe. The pronouncement was so startling because it seemed to reject the restraint sym-

[17] In the Suez crisis General Alfred M. Gruenther was selected to utter the warning to the Soviet Union, which he did in a news conference on November 13, 1956. The fact that he was still Supreme Allied Commander in Europe only slightly camouflaged his position as a spokesman for the United States. A year later it was Secretary Dulles who remarked, in a news conference on October 16, 1957, that the American response to a Russian attack on Turkey "would not mean a purely defensive operation by the United States, with the Soviet Union a privileged sanctuary from which to attack Turkey." See in each case *The New York Times* for the day following.

bolized by Korea for areas in which our interests, while lively, were obviously not vital.

Where our interests are not vital, how can a general threat of this kind be believed? It was not believed in 1950, when the general policy prevailed which the Dulles declaration was later supposed to reconfirm. The declaration itself implied a sliding scale of relevance for the massive retaliation principle, because it specifically stated that not all cases of aggression would be countered by so complete a reaction. One might say that the threat could be executed against the Soviet Union only if its leaders completely misjudged our response; for if they really believed we meant it, their choice would have to be either to refrain entirely from the intended aggression or to extend its scale by striking at us first.

However, let us assume that because of a misestimate of our response, an aggression has occurred in Asia. We now have to consider the principles of the Dulles declaration to be in operation. We can assume that it is in Korea again and that the North Koreans have violated the armistice by attacking southward with enough force to imperil the position of the South Korean Army, which would mean incidentally that the two American divisions presently on the spot would be in bad straits. Obviously, Communist China is again also involved, because the North Korean forces by themselves could not hope to challenge the strong and efficient forces established south of their frontier.

What would the massive retaliation principle call upon us to do at this point? Send some SAC planes at once to bomb the North Korean armies with thermonuclear weapons? Very likely, but surely it means more than that! In his famous speech Secretary Dulles did not limit himself, as he could easily have done, to saying that in the event aggression recurred in Korea, or elsewhere in Asia, we would not necessarily confine ourselves to non-nuclear weapons, as we did in 1950-1953. He said and implied much besides. He indicated clearly that we would not necessarily or even likely confine ourselves to a *local* response, that we would feel free to retaliate massively against the center of power of the major offending state. He seemed not to be talking about the use of nuclear weapons in a geographically-limited war, but to be tending rather to reject that kind of war altogether. He seemed to indicate that we might and probably would respond to such an attack by a full-fledged strategic nuclear bombing attack on China!

At this point we may ask ourselves whether or not our attack upon China, or indeed our use of nuclear weapons in North Korea itself, would be preceded by an ultimatum. There is no indication of the answer in the speech, but speeches which purport to be basic declarations of policy rarely go into details of that sort. We have to reason this out ourselves. If the decision were made to go ahead with the strategic bombing of China without further warning of our intentions, we should probably have to include the Soviet Union as well. Anything else would be almost unthinkable. It would be folly to destroy China and leave Russia intact—and at the same time desperately provoked—to destroy us.[18]

[18] This kind of image of massive retaliation is not the only one conceivable. Some have talked of hitting one city at a time until the Chinese government yielded. But this idea fantasies the survival of an American nuclear monopoly that actually ended in 1949, as well as a separation of China from Russia such as we have seen no hint of thus far. Incidentally, Mr. Nikita Khrushchev in a letter to President Eisenhower dated September 7, 1958 declared flatly: "An attack upon the People's Republic of China . . . is an attack upon the Soviet Union." Two weeks later, on September 19, he amplified this statement by threatening to use nuclear weapons

This, of course, is preventive war, save that we have waited for an excuse, a provocation. If we were really bent on preventive war, it would probably be better, at least much safer, to do it at a time entirely of our own choosing, if we could, so that our preparations could be perfected with a view to achieving the absolutely essential surprise. No doubt this country could not move without a grave provocation, but it is to say the least a gamble to put into enemy hands the whistle for signalling the beginning of one's preventive attack.

One may surmise, however, that Mr. Dulles would have been shocked at the suggestion that he had in mind our attacking without further warning, without first presenting an ultimatum. To be sure, presenting ultimata to major powers like Communist China or the Soviet Union is exceedingly dangerous in this age, unless one is *quite sure* that either or both will yield to an ultimatum. Otherwise the other party is merely being told that total war is imminent— and that he has the opportunity to hit first! If, however, we are sure the other side will yield, the threat of massive retaliation will have played its role admirably. A long, nasty involvement like that of 1950-1953 is avoided, and the enemy has suffered both humiliation and defeat. Our prestige is enhanced, and we have lost no blood.

Two questions need to be asked at this point. First, where would the government summon the courage—or brashness— for this kind of conduct? As one looks at the history of the Korean War itself, and of our handling of more recent crises such as those in Indochina and in Hungary, one develops a tempered view of our available fund of boldness. If our

---

against any country which employed nuclear weapons against communist China. See the *New York Times* for September 9 and September 20, 1958.

leaders and our allies cannot muster the courage to be bold locally, should we expect or desire them to have the stomach to be rash globally? They may indeed be rash while thinking they are playing it safe—which brings us to our second question: If we do manage to screw our courage to the sticking place, are we quite sure the Russians, or the Chinese, will yield before our ultimatum and halt their local aggressions? If so, we are basing the argument for massive retaliation not on the military needs of concentration and on the evils of dispersion, but on an optimistic forecast of Russian or Chinese behavior in face of our threats. Military knowledge helps us only marginally in making such a forecast. It helps somewhat more in telling us the price we shall pay if we are wrong.

We may theoretically prefer having one big war to fighting one or more little ones. There are few people who do not shudder inwardly when they let their thoughts range on what an unrestricted third world war would be like; but there are many persons, including some of considerable decision-making importance, who feel under compulsion to reject such unhappy thoughts. It is not that they are freer than others from emotional involvement; it is rather that they abhor other things more than the destruction of thermonuclear wars. They may abhor, for example, the idea of settling for anything other than a good, clean win in a fight, or the fact that menaces like the Soviet regime are permitted to continue unabated. An unqualified emphasis on winning goes naturally with impatience of any restrictions, as does also a passion for "cleaning house" in the presence of troublesome and disagreeable things. People of such emotional as well as intellectual orientation definitely believe that given an enemy aggression of whatever kind to cope with, the big strike is the preferred solution. They are not given to thinking about the price, but when it is forced upon their attention they often own to a willingness to see it paid. We must in fairness admit that among their primary considerations is usually found a lively appreciation of the advantages of hitting first when it comes to exchanging the big blows.

The fact is that if the enemy in his aggressions, especially those outside Europe, leaves to us the choice between fighting a total war or fighting a limited one, the chances are overwhelming that our government will opt for the limited one. We would, of course, always prefer to fight no war at all, but that choice may not be available except through local surrender. But no responsible government will opt for massive retaliation except where it conceives its stake in the matter at issue to be absolutely vital.

It is easy for persons who do not have the terrible responsibility of ultimate decision to call any prestige interest a vital one. Korea embraced primarily a prestige interest, by which we mean an interest in impressing the opponent and the rest of the world of our readiness and ability to oppose aggression, and as such it was deemed to be worth a considerable though still limited and local response. It could never reasonably have been called a vital American interest.[19] Recognition of that fact made for a kind of impatience with the demands of the war—in addition to the normal sorrow and regret—but did not stimulate among government leaders at the time any desire for more drastic action.

[19] The term "vital interest" is somewhat ambiguous in current usage. In traditional diplomacy the emphasis has been on subjective determination, that is, a nation's vital interests were what its government said they were, no more and no less, and the occasion for its saying so was usually an anticipation of some challenge. But it has also been increasingly used in a manner which implies an objective or at least a reasonable evaluation. It is in this latter sense that I am using it in the text above.

Good military planning should take into account the orders that the President is *likely* to give the military during a crisis, as distinct from those he may have promised in some general fashion to give. This is a very simple point to make, yet it is extremely difficult to get it accepted in practice. For one thing, military planners are characteristically bemused by what they think *ought* to be the orders, perhaps with the unconscious assumption that when it comes to a question of the use of military force, their views about degree and manner of application should and probably will prevail. One thing wrong with this expectation is the likelihood of disagreement among the services. At any rate, they find it difficult to face up to the fact that at the critical moment the civilian Commander-in-Chief may impose important restraints on their operations, including restraints on weapons, and he may do so despite what look like earlier explicit assurances to the contrary.

There, indeed, is the rub. What more authentic guidance can the military planner have than the official assurances of his own government concerning its intended behavior? From the point of view of legal authenticity, none. Yet it is clear that in the bureaucratic and political framework in which such assurances are normally developed, they are not likely to reflect real thoughtfulness about the future. The crises to which they are supposed to pertain have not yet arisen and may never occur. Why not then be bold, when it costs nothing in resolution or in hazard or even in thought?

The circumstances surrounding the Dulles declaration were in fact most unusual in that the publicity given the speech made for sharp and abundant criticisms in the press and appropriately qualified responses by the government. What about the more numerous cases where the official "guidance" is Top Secret and thus spared the kind of vigorous criticism which only a wide and informed public can guarantee? The argument has to be anticipated that important policy papers or ideas are always discussed and coordinated sufficiently within appropriate government agencies to ensure adequate criticism, especially since those who deal with them are normally the best informed people in the country on the subjects in question. There is, however, a vast difference between criticism available within the government structure and that available if a wider public is given access to the matter at issue. The reasons have to do with constraints imposed by habit, tradition, service and personal interest, and the hierarchy of authority within the corporate structure, all adding up to the absence of an indeterminate something called "freshness of outlook." Moreover, talent for asking pertinent and searching questions about anything is a relatively scarce commodity, not necessarily distributed among the same persons who have high executive ability.

In conclusion we may note that something like an epilogue to the 1954 speech was embodied in a new statement by Mr. Dulles less than four years later. In an article published in October 1957, he referred to the military strategy of the free world allies as having been "largely based upon our great capacity to retaliate should the Soviet Union launch a war of aggression." He then went on:

However, the United States has not been content to rely upon a peace which could be preserved only by a capacity to destroy vast segments of the human race. Such a concept is acceptable only as a last alternative. In recent years there has been no other. But the resourcefulness of those who serve our nation in the field of science and weapon engineering now shows that it is possible to alter the character of nuclear weapons. It seems now that their use need not involve vast destruction and widespread harm to humanity. Recent tests point to the possibility of possessing nuclear weapons the destructiveness and radiation effects of which can be confined substantially to predetermined targets.

In the future it may thus be feasible to place less reliance upon deterrence of vast retaliatory power. It may be possible to defend countries by nuclear weapons so mobile, or so placed, as to make military invasion with conventional forces a hazardous attempt. For example, terrain is often such that invasion routes can be decisively dominated by nuclear artillery.[20]

In other words, the massive retaliation idea is being "phased out," as it were, not because of the development of a Soviet strategic-nuclear capability, which of course we knew about in January 1954, but because of weapons developments that we presumably did not know about at that time. This is itself a remarkable statement. It was known long before 1954 that it was possible to make nuclear weapons of small yield, smaller, that is, than the already small-yield atomic bomb used at Hiroshima. We have always known, since we have had nuclear weapons, that they could be used tactically with great effect and that the problem of lingering radioactivity could be controlled to a reasonable degree by the manner in which the bombs were used. In the early years of atomic weapons there was a question of weapons scarcity, but by 1954 scarcity was no longer an issue. In any case, it must not be accepted as a foregone conclusion that we will always want to use nuclear weapons in local wars.

It would seem that Mr. Dulles came closer to the real reason for rejecting massive retaliation in the first two sentences of the statement quoted above—although it was less a question of what the United States was "content" to rely upon

[20] John Foster Dulles, "Challenge and Response in United States Policy," *Foreign Affairs*, xxxvi (October 1957), 31.

than what it was wise to rely upon in view of a sober examination of the facts. However, the question remains how the phasing out or attenuation of massive retaliation as a principle of policy is to be realized in future allocations of the national defense budget. If it is true that the ability to fight limited wars depends largely on the development of a special capability for the purpose—and this is likely to be true so long as tactical nuclear weapons are kept to very small size or interdicted altogether—then we have to concede that developments in our military force structure through 1958 and 1959 were in the direction of increased rather than lessened dependence on massive retaliation.[21]

[21] The above text was set in type before the final illness and death of John Foster Dulles. It may for that reason be appropriate to point out that the views expressed therein concern matters which were completely tangential to his stature as a statesman.

<8>

THE ANATOMY OF DETERRENCE

In an editorial published something over one hundred years ago, *The Economist* of London, in its issue for April 14, 1855, chose to take a sensible view of the state of affairs in the Crimea. Under the title "A Negotiated Peace?" the editors wrote as follows:

> We are not of those who regard the expedition to the Crimea as a mistake. We urged it early in the day. . . . As it is, however, we must admit that it has turned out unfortunately. From some cause or other our losses have been frightful and our profit has been microscopic. We have displayed marvellous valour in fight; marvellous patience in suffering—but we have made no way. We have lost 20,000 men, and we have not gained land enough to make them 20,000 graves. . . . These considerations may well make us reflect whether a reasonable though not a glorious peace may not be preferable to the continuance of such a disastrous and unadvancing war. May not negotiations which will bring us some profit, be better than hostilities which bring us nothing but gladiatorial renown? . . .

The mood is unhappy, but the spirit is commendable. Certainly rare is the gesture of admitting that the expedition which has gone so badly awry is one that the writers themselves originally favored and supported.

At that moment, however, winter was already giving way to spring, both at home and in the far-off theater of battle. The next few weeks brought better tidings. On June 16 of the same year, just two months after the above passage was published, a new editorial appeared in the same journal. Under the title of "War Aims," we find a rapturous outpouring:

The final and formal closing of the Vienna Conferences and the rapid progress of our arms before Sebastopol and the Sea of Azoff have wonderfully cleared our ideas and made plain the path of our policy before us. The character of the war enlarges in scope and dignity as its unavoidableness becomes more obvious, as it becomes clear that it must be ended by the sword and not the pen, and as its real, grand and sanctifying OBJECTS shake themselves free from the misty subtleties and wretched trivialities in which diplomacy has so long shrouded their actual majesty and worth. We are beginning to take in the conception that we are engaged in a contest which admits of no compromise; in which anything short of signal triumph would be virtual defeat; whose aim—if it have any worthy aim, whose justification—if it have any adequate justification, is the deliverance of Europe from a great peril, and the complete emancipation, once and for ever, of the cause of freedom, civilisation, and progress from their most irreconcilable and mightiest foe. . . .

The two editorials reflect a marvelous difference in climate. Apparently it is not hope but delirium that springs eternal in the human breast. At least it did in the nineteenth century. In the twentieth we expect our leaders of opinion to have better control of their romantic emotions. As it later turned out, the news was not really that good. Anyway, we get the lesson that while victory is undoubtedly sweet for its own sake, it seems to help not all in getting our ideas "cleared." On the contrary, as the earlier editorial suggests, a moderate dose of adversity seems to be the best specific for the purpose.

The hundred years that have passed since the Crimean War have not favored the romantic outlook on world affairs. In the twentieth century we have been at pains to deprive war of pretenses to glamor. We still admire the characteristically military virtues, such as physical courage and loyalty to duty and to comrades. We appreciate also the fact that war tends more than most peacetime pursuits to bring out these qualities in men who possess them. But that does not make the fighting itself glamorous. It has become too large-scale and mechanical for that, too menacing to all our hopes.

Yet the one great area in our public affairs in which romanticism survives is that of national defense policies. The word "romanticism" is semantically hazardous to use. It has been much corrupted in ordinary discourse, and it covers too broad a pattern of attitudes and moods. These attitudes and moods have, however, a common tendency to depart reality in favor of certain fantasies about ourselves and the world we live in. Romanticism exalts strong action over negotiation, boldness over caution, and feeling over reflection.[1] It exalts dedication to a cause, with minimum consideration for the utility of the cause. It also prompts us to imagine ourselves more courageous, alert, and idealistic than sober appraisals of our behavior would confirm.

The military officer is trained—and it is probably right that he should be so trained—to admire boldness and initia-

---

[1] War has usually reflected the triumph of feeling over reflection. Yet scholars in the field have paid amazingly little attention to the relevant findings of modern depth psychology. Much has been learned, for example, of the mechanism of displacement, whereby unconscious resentments or rages engendered in various of life's frustrations are turned upon the "safe" target, such as the rival nation abroad. The Soviet Union by its character and maneuvers lends itself ideally to becoming such a target. For useful though insufficient contributions on the subject, see Alix Strachey, *The Unconscious Motives of War*, especially Part II, International Universities Press, New York, 1957; T. H. Pear, ed., *Psychological Factors of Peace and War*, The Philosophical Library, New York, 1950; Harold D. Lasswell, *World Politics and Personal Insecurity*, The Free Press, Glencoe, Ill., 1950 (originally published in 1934); Edward Glover, *War, Sadism, and Pacifism*, London, 1933; R. E. Money-Kyrle, *Psychoanalysis and Politics*, Gerald Duckworth & Co., Ltd., London, 1951; and Maurice L. Farber, "Psychoanalytic Hypotheses in the Study of War," *Journal of Social Issues*, XI (1955), 29-35.

tive to the point of impetuosity. "Damn the torpedoes, full speed ahead" expresses a much lauded impulse in a great naval officer. It would certainly not do for a foreign secretary. The latter is indoctrinated to "consider all the angles" before moving. In theory there should be no antipathy between prudent statesmanship and the military approach, but in practice they do not lie easily together. These basic differences in outlook have nothing to do with how intelligent people are, but rather with how specialized they are in function and how complex in personality they can afford to be while still being effective in their chosen fields.

The theory of our form of government is that the civilian is supreme over the military officer in the topmost ranks of the hierarchy. Presumably, then, the caution, subtlety, and political sophistication that are supposed to be the hallmark of the statesman will be available not only to influence but actually to control the important strategic decisions of the military department. In practice it works out quite differently. For one thing, there are bound to be some civilians in high office who are not blessed with the talents for real statesmanship. Second, the interest of civilian leaders in strategic questions is likely to be strong in wartime but dormant in peacetime. Today, however, we are in a situation, essentially coeval with the A-bomb, where the basic decisions about wars and how to fight them have to be decided in time of peace; when war comes it is much too late. Third, at the higher levels of defense-policy decision-making where the civilians are supreme they are also dependent upon and somewhat overshadowed by the military, who have among other advantages the prestige of being the experts.

There is thus on the whole a much greater tendency for the military outlook to be adopted by associated civilians than the other way round. To be sure, one can easily exaggerate the original differences between civilian and military modes of thought, whether on matters of defense or on other issues. In educational background the differences between civilian and military leaders can often be quite small or insignificant. They become important only with respect to the institutional environment in which one lives and works, and especially in the relative degree of preoccupation with problems of war and national security. When civilians join the Department of Defense, the last-mentioned distinction tends to be erased. The result, in the net, is a kind of forfeiture or abandonment of values other than military at high decision-making levels, despite the apparent participation of political leaders.

All three approaches to the American security problem described in the previous chapter—preventive war, preemptive attack, and massive retaliation—reflect an idea congenial to modern military thinking, that of seizing the initiative and carrying the fight to the enemy. These approaches also reflect an abiding faith in the ritual of liquidation—the idea that some convulsive and fearfully costly act will justify itself through the elimination of the evil enemy and of the need to live in the same world with him. To secure that liquidation almost any price is worthwhile.

In this chapter and the next we shall be considering conceptions of national security which are fundamentally opposed to some of the ideas described above. Their justification is not to be found in traditional military axioms, to which they are in fact uncongenial. We shall be talking about the strategy of deterrence of general war, and about the complementary principle of limiting to tolerable proportions whatever conflicts become inevitable. These ideas spring from the conviction that total nuclear war is to be avoided at almost any cost. This follows from the assumption that such a war, even if we were extraordinarily lucky, would be too big, too all-consuming to permit the survival even of those final values, like personal freedom, for which alone one could think of waging it. It need not be certain that it would turn out so badly; it is enough that there is a large chance that it would.

The conceptions of deterrence and of limited war also take account of the fact that the United States is, and has long been, a status quo power. We are uninterested in acquiring new territories or areas of influence or in accepting great hazard in order to rescue or reform those areas of the world which now have political systems radically different from our own. On the other hand, as a status quo power, we are also determined to keep what we have, including existence in a world of which half or more is friendly, or at least not sharply and perennially hostile. In other words, our minimum security objectives include not only our own national independence but also that of many other countries, especially those which cherish democratic political institutions. Among the latter are those nations with which we have a special cultural affinity, that is, the countries of western Europe.

The policy which seeks to protect all we have has been called the policy or strategy of "containment." The conception of containment has been abused by those who would presumably do more rather than less, but the policy of doing more seems quite unable to generate any real dynamism behind it. The reason is that the moment something specific is suggested, one becomes aware of attendant risks and has to take account of them. Such awareness is pleasantly blanked out so long as talk about "liberation" or "rollback" remains general and abstract.[2]

The philosophy of deterrence takes account above all of the enormous American cultural resistances to our hitting first in a period of threatened total war. This is not to say it is out of the question that we should do so. It is even possible that we shall build so much automaticity and sensitivity into our retaliatory response that it could be triggered by an "indication of hostile intent" rather than a hostile act. Such a development would probably be attributable more to absent-mindedness on the part of our political leaders than to design, but such absent-mindedness is not uncommon in the area of strategic decision in peacetime. Also, we must not forget that there is likely to be a threshold of "intolerable provocation" short of direct attack upon us, even though we find it hard to determine before the event where that threshold is or ought to be.

Finally, we have and will probably continue to have obligations under treaties of alliance which require us to defend our partners with all the resources at our command from nuclear attack. For this and other reasons we need the capability to strike first, both in spirit and in military power. A "strike-first" capability must have as its primary mission the destruction of the enemy's retaliatory power. That, at least, is the bald way in which the requirement is usually put. Such a statement unfortunately does not tell us (a) whether a large-scale destruction of his retaliatory force will be feasible in view of the security measures he may take either on a permanent basis or as provoked by the special crisis, and (b) whether an enemy who saw us apparently

[2] The ideas alluded to in this paragraph have not been much heard since the national election campaign of 1952, when they were very prominent.

prepared to take so far-reaching a step for the defense of an ally would attack the latter without striking at us first. Only if he feared to strike at us first could our striking force deter the enemy from massive attack upon an ally.

At any rate, it remains unlikely that our government will ever deliberately initiate a total war for the sake of securing to ourselves the military advantage of the first blow, however considerable that advantage may be. The operational corollary of that point is that we must do what we can to reduce the advantage that will accrue to the enemy if he hits first. In other words, our rejection of that idea of "preventive war" has committed us completely and inevitably to the policy and strategy of deterrence. It is now up to us to pay the price to make it work. That price must include doctrinal adjustment, especially a certain de-emphasis of offensive principle as irrelevant, and a fairly heavy outlay of resources on measures to enhance the security of our retaliatory forces.

Deterrence Old and New

Deterrence as an element in national strategy or diplomacy is nothing new. Since the development of nuclear weapons, however, the term has acquired not only a special emphasis but also a distinctive connotation. It is usually the new and distinctive connotation that we have in mind when we speak nowadays of the "strategy of deterrence."

The threat of war, open or implied, has always been an instrument of diplomacy by which one state deterred another from doing something of a military or political nature which the former deemed undesirable. Frequently the threat was completely latent, the position of the monitoring state being so obvious and so strong that no one thought of challenging it. Governments, like individuals, were usually aware of hazard in provoking powerful neighbors and governed themselves accordingly. Because avoidance of wars and even of crises hardly makes good copy for historians, we may infer that the past successes of some nations in deterring unwanted action by others add up to much more than one might gather from a casual reading of history. Nevertheless the large number of wars that have occurred in modern times prove that the threat to use force, even what sometimes looked like superior force, has often failed to deter.

We should notice, however, the positive function played by the failures. The very frequency with which wars occurred contributed importantly to the credibility inherent in any threat. In diplomatic correspondence, the statement that a specified kind of conduct would be deemed "an unfriendly act" was regarded as tantamount to an ultimatum and to be taken without question as seriously intended.

Bluffing, in the sense of deliberately trying to sound more determined or bellicose than one actually felt, was by no means as common a phenomenon in diplomacy as latter-day journalistic interpretations of events would have one believe. In any case, it tended to be confined to the more implicit kinds of threat. In short, the operation of deterrence was dynamic; it acquired relevance and strength from its failures as well as its successes.

Today, however, the policy of deterrence in relation to all-out war is markedly different in several respects. For one thing, it uses a kind of threat which we feel must be absolutely effective, allowing for no breakdowns ever. The sanction is, to say the least, not designed for repeating action. One use of it will be fatally too many. Deterrence now means something as a strategic policy only when we are fairly confident that the retaliatory instrument upon which it relies will not be called upon to function at all. Nevertheless, that instrument has to be maintained at a high pitch of efficiency and readiness and constantly improved, which can be done only at high cost to the community and great dedication on the part of the personnel directly involved. In short, we expect the system to be always ready to spring while going permanently unused. Surely there is something almost unreal about all this.

The Problem of Credibility

The unreality is minimal when we are talking about what we shall henceforward call "basic deterrence," that is, deterrence of direct, strategic, nuclear attack upon targets within the home territories of the United States. In that instance there is little or no problem of credibility as concerns our reactions, for the enemy has little reason to doubt that if he strikes us we will try to hit back. But the great and terrible apparatus which we must set up to fulfill our needs for basic deterrence and the state of readiness at which we have to maintain it create a condition of almost embarrassing availability of huge power. The problem of linking this power to a reasonable conception of its utility has thus far proved a considerable strain. In the previous chapter we reviewed the doctrine of massive retaliation as a response to less than massive aggressions, and we concluded that one of the first things wrong with the doctrine is that in many instances the enemy may find it hard to believe that we mean it.[3]

[3] See William W. Kaufmann, "The Requirements of Deterrence," in the book edited by him under the title: *Military Policy and National Security*, Princeton University Press, 1956. See also Bernard Brodie, "Unlimited Weapons and Limited War," *The Reporter*, 11 (November 18, 1954), 16ff.

On the other hand, it would be tactically and factually wrong to assure the enemy in advance (as we tend to do by constantly assuring ourselves) that we would in no case move against him until we had already felt some bombs on our cities and airfields. We have, as we have seen, treaty obligations which forbid so far-reaching a commitment to restraint. It is also impossible for us to predict with absolute assurance our own behavior in extremely tense and provocative circumstances. If we make the wrong prediction about ourselves, we encourage the enemy also to make the wrong prediction about us. The outbreak of war in Korea in 1950 followed exactly that pattern. The wrong kind of prediction in this regard might precipitate that total nuclear war which too many persons have lightly concluded is now impossible.

Deterrence Strategy versus Win-the-War Strategies: The Sliding Scale of Deterrence

To return now to the simpler problem of basic deterrence. The capacity to deter is usually confused with the capacity to win a war. At present, capacity to win a total or unrestricted war requires either a decisive and *completely secure* superiority in strategic air power or success in seizing the initiative. Inasmuch as mere superiority in numbers of vehicles looks like a good thing to have anyway, the confusion between deterring and winning has method in it. But deterrence *per se* does not depend on superiority.

Prior to the nuclear age, a force which was clearly inferior to a rival's might or might not have some real deterrent value. One may surmise that if Stalin in late 1939 had had a better estimate of the capability of the Finns to defend themselves he would have been less eager to attack them. If we can deduce his incentive to attack from the peace terms he ultimately laid down, it seems not to have been a desire to conquer and absorb some extra territories, let alone the whole Finnish nation, but rather the wish to administer to them and to others a sharp diplomatic "lesson." That object was compromised by the successes of the Finnish resistance, despite their final defeat. What this example suggests is that deterrence was and remains relative, not absolute; its effectiveness must be measured not only according to the amount of power that it holds in check, but also according to the incentives to aggression which form the pressure behind that power.

Now that we are in a nuclear age, the potential deterrence value of an admittedly inferior force may be sharply greater than it has ever been before. Let us assume that a menaced small nation could threaten the Soviet Union with only a single thermonuclear bomb, which, however, it could and would certainly deliver on Moscow if attacked. This would be a retaliatory capability sufficient to give the Soviet government pause. Certainly they would not provoke the destruction of Moscow for trivial gains, even if warning enabled the people of the city to save themselves by evacuation or resort to shelters. Naturally, the effect is greater if warning can be ruled out.

Ten such missiles aimed at ten major cities would be even more effective, and fifty aimed at that number of different cities would no doubt work still greater deterrent effect, though of course the cities diminish in size as the number included goes up. However, even when we make allowance for the latter fact, it is a fair surmise that the increase in deterrent effect is less than proportional to the increase in magnitude of potential destruction. We make that surmise on the basis of our everyday experience with human beings and their responses to punishment or deprivation. The human imagination can encompass just so much pain, anguish, or horror. The intrusion of numbers by which to multiply given sums of such feelings is likely to have on the average human mind a rather dull effect—except insofar as the increase in the threatened amount of harm affects the individual's statistical expectation of himself being involved in it.

Governments, it may be suggested, do not think like ordinary human beings, and one has to concede that the *maximum possible deterrence* which can be attained by the threat of retaliatory damage must involve a power which guarantees not only vast losses but also utter defeat. On the other hand, governments, including communistic ones, also comprise human beings, whose departure from the mold of ordinary mortals is not markedly in the direction of greater intellectualism or detachment. It is therefore likely that considerably less retaliatory destruction than that conceived under "maximum possible deterrence" will buy only slightly less deterrence. If we wish to visualize the situation graphically, we will think of a curve of "deterrence effect" in which each unit of additional damage threatened brings progressively diminishing increments of deterrence. Obviously and unfortunately, we lack all the data which would enable us to fill in the values for such a curve and thus to draw it.

If our surmises are in general correct, we are underlining the sharp differences in character between a deterrence capability and strategy on the one hand, and a win-the-war strategy and capability on the other. We have to remember too that since the winning of a war presupposes certain limitations on the quantity of destruction to one's own country and especially to one's population, a win-the-war strategy could quite conceivably be an utter impossibility to a nation striking second, and is by no means guaranteed to a nation striking first. Too much depends on what the other fellow does—how accessible or inaccessible he makes his own retaliatory force and how he makes his attack if he decides to launch one. However much we dislike the thought, a win-the-war strategy may be impossible because of circumstances outside our control.

Lest we conclude from these remarks that we can be content with a modest retaliatory capability—what some have called "minimum deterrence"—we have to mention at once four qualifying considerations, which we shall amplify later: (a) it may require a large force in hand to guarantee even a modest retaliation; (b) deterrence must always be conceived as a relative thing, which is to say it must be adequate to the variable but generally high degree of motivation which the enemy feels for our destruction; (c) if deterrence fails we shall want enough forces to fight a total war effectively; and (d) our retaliatory force must also be capable of striking first, and if it does so its attack had better be, as nearly as possible, overwhelming to the enemy's retaliatory force. Finally, we have to bear in mind that in their responses to threat or menace, people (including heads of government) do not spontaneously act according to a scrupulous weighing of objective facts. Large forces look more impressive than small ones—for reasons which are by no means entirely irrational—and in some circumstances such impressiveness may be important to us. Human beings, differing widely as they do in temperamental and psychic make-up, nevertheless generally have in common the fact that they make their most momentous decisions by what is fundamentally intuition.

Besides, we have to bear in mind that, especially under a technology where each bomb can destroy a city, deterrence is affected also by the element of great *uncertainty* in the potential aggressor's mind concerning the number of bombs the retaliating enemy will succeed in delivering. It makes a very large difference whether he delivers ten or a hundred, though both may be very small numbers in comparison with his original capability. In this connection too, the fact that a nation has in the past undergone and successfully recovered from great injury does not mean that it will be blasé about a possible repetition of such a catastrophe. The Soviet leaders are not eager to see 1941-1942 repeated, let alone run the risk of having the damage and casualties of those years greatly exceeded.

All this is not to suggest that we have no interest in "win the war" capabilities and strategies. *So long as there is a finite chance of war, we have to be interested in outcomes; and although all outcomes would be bad, some would be very much worse than others.* Also, if we could imagine a conspicuous capability for winning wars which was able to survive even a surprise attack by the enemy, we should have the ultimate in deterrence. But we have to be ready to recognize that deterrence philosophies and win-the-war philosophies may diverge in important respects. We can say in advance that they are likely to diverge in terms of priority. The objective of erecting a high degree of deterrence takes a higher priority than the objective of assuring ourselves of a win-the-war capability, if for no other reason than the first is likely to be prerequisite to the second anyway. It is likely also to be a good deal more feasible to attain, especially for a country which has rejected preventive war. We are also likely to feel a divergence between the two philosophies when it comes to considering alternative military policies in terms of comparative degrees of provocativeness. For the sake of deterrence we want usually to choose the less provocative of two security policies, even where it might mean some sacrifice of efficiency. But if we were in fact interested primarily in winning and only secondarily in deterrence, we should be extremely loath to make any such sacrifices.

We must notice also that when we say that "maximum possible deterrence" probably depends on ability to win, we are implying, for the first time in the discussion, a *comparison* in the degree of damage likely to be suffered by each side. Prior to this point we were talking of deterrence as something resulting from a *unilateral* consideration of damage, that is, enemy estimate of damage likely to be suffered by himself. This is one of the issues that seems to provoke much confusion about deterrence. It is a truistic statement that by deterrence we mean obliging the opponent to consider, in an environment of great uncertainty, the probably high cost of attacking us against the expected gain thereof. It is only a shade less obvious that his cost has to be measured in terms of damage to himself. But what seems very difficult to grasp is that his gain cannot be measured simply in terms of damage to us, except insofar as that damage provokes an act or condition (i.e., surrender or military obliteration) which terminates the threat to him. Damage to us, however large, which fails to have such an effect may be no gain to him at all.

To be willing to accept enormous destruction only for the sake of inflicting greater destruction on the enemy (which may be all that some mean by "winning") argues a kind of desperation at the moment of decision which rules out reason. We have to expect that at certain extreme conditions of excitement, which may involve erroneous conviction that an enemy attack upon oneself is imminent, the deterrent posture will tend to collapse or be discarded without further regard to estimates of damage or gain to either side. All that means, however, is that the rationality upon which deterrence must be based is ultimately frangible—a conclusion of which history has already given us ample indication.

Another attitude that gets in the way of understanding deterrence is the one which alleges that Soviet leaders, when faced with issues of peace and war, would be indifferent to the loss of individual cities and certainly of the populations (as distinguished from the production capital) within those cities. The implication of this view is that a government or leadership imbued with that kind of indifference can be deterred not by considerations of loss in any graduated sense of the term, but only by the prospect of *losing a war*. This is hardly the place to attempt to weigh the evidence for and against such an attribution of indifference. But as this writer sees it, the view just described grossly distorts and exaggerates some undeniable and important differences between the Soviet system and our own.

Certainly insensibility to human suffering among subject populations, especially when it can be rationalized as a necessary price for alleged future benefits, is much more characteristic of the Soviet system than of our own. This fact probably affects significantly the dynamics of deterrence as described in the preceding paragraphs. But it is not enough to subvert those dynamics. The Soviet leaders might be appreciably less shocked and distressed than our own leaders would be in comparable circumstances by the loss through nuclear bombing of one or more of their large cities, but they certainly would not be indifferent to it—either on humanitarian or prestige grounds.

We have to remember, of course, that the Soviets have a very high incentive for destroying us, or at least our military power, if they can do so—the incentive of eliminating what is to them a great threat. As we emphasized earlier, the degree of incentive to aggression governs the magnitude of the deterrence problem. Under some circumstances the Soviet leaders might be willing to pay a very considerable price for that victory which our destruction would mean for them. But the price must be within their ultimate capacity to pay—i.e., fall well short of threatening the collapse of their own power, internally and externally—and they must have a *high degree of assurance* that (a) we will be destroyed, and (b) they will not be. Also, their incentives to destroy us, while always high, are probably not invariable. They are likely to change significantly with changes in the political and especially the military-technological environment.

The Problem of Guaranteeing Strong Retaliation

It should be obvious that what counts in basic deterrence is not so much the size and efficiency of one's striking force before it is hit as the size and condition to which the enemy thinks he can reduce it by a surprise attack—as well as his confidence in the correctness of his predictions. The degree to which the automaticity of our retaliation has been taken for granted by the public, unfortunately including most leaders of opinion and even military officers, is for those who have any knowledge of the facts both incredible and dangerous. The general idea is that if the enemy hits us, we will kill him.

A somewhat more modest view stresses the "mutual homicide" or "two scorpions in a bottle" analogy.

The number of bases on which our retaliatory forces are located and the proportion of them in advanced readiness or on "airborne alert" are data which are fairly certain to be well-known to the opponent. They tend to be usually unknown even among the best-informed of our own people, and the problems confronting a shrewd and aggressive enemy in surprising and penetrating our defenses are therefore usually exaggerated in the popular mind. If in this book we have frequently reiterated the importance of the *security* of the retaliatory force, it is because our ability to retaliate in great force to a direct Soviet attack is taken far too much for granted by almost everybody, including our highest national policy-makers.[4]

One of the reasons for such widespread ignorance is that many among those who are charged with defense planning, and who would otherwise enlighten the public or at least our political leaders concerning the dangers facing us, themselves unconsciously reject the concept of deterrence based on retaliation. The reasons for rejecting it may vary. Some are simply unused to thinking in terms of the enemy having the initiative, preferring always to think in terms of our having it. This is an age-old addiction of official war planners. Others, more sophisticated, apparently feel that a force that lets itself take the first blow will not be strong enough to win a war, regardless of what it has done to protect itself, and they are by training, tradition, and often temperament interested only in strategies that can win. They are preoccu-

---

[4] An incisive and well-informed discussion of this problem is presented by Albert J. Wohlstetter, "The Delicate Balance of Terror," *Foreign Affairs*, xxxvii (January 1959), 211-234.

pied with getting the offensive force launched against the enemy while it is still able to win, that is, *before* it is hit. They are either not interested in adjusting to a strategy of deterrence or they are convinced that a force not strong enough to win is not strong enough to deter. Underlying this view is also the conviction that money spent on protecting the retaliatory force might otherwise have been spent on expanding it.

This conviction is of course correct. As we noted in a previous chapter, the problem of how much it is worth paying in offensive capacity to design protection into an offensive force has been faced many times before, notably with respect to armor and later to antiaircraft guns in warships; but it seems always to require a *de novo* approach with each new category of weapons. Thermonuclear weapons have made it possible to reduce requirements for a strategic bombing campaign in number of bombs delivered, and at the same time have increased the vulnerability of the vehicles for delivering them. These considerations should dictate a shift of emphasis from buying more bombers and missiles to buying protection for existing bombers and missiles. In any case, the overriding considerations should be that *the nation is committed to a deterrence policy* and that such a commitment dictates primary concern with the survival of a retaliatory force of adequate size following enemy attack.

A force which fulfills that requirement is likely to be also a good strike-first force, because any force will be stronger in attacking first than in attacking second. To be sure, it will not be the best strike-first force that could be bought with the same money. Undoubtedly we could go too far in the direction of sacrificing first-strike capabilities for the sake of protection. However, we have not begun to as yet, and our tendencies are normally in the opposite direction.

Our deterrence-curve model suggests to us that it might possibly make sense to adopt a sliding scale of protection for different portions of our retaliatory force. A hard and not too small core of it must be extremely well protected, at almost any cost, against the worst (to us) kind of enemy attack it is possible for us to imagine. Other portions of it may perhaps do with somewhat less protection, on the ground that the worst imaginable contingency is fortunately not the only likely one and may not be even the most probable one. Against this view is the consideration that perhaps the best way to guarantee the survival of a hard-core force of sufficient size is to give a substantial degree of protection to the whole force. Certainly no part of it which is not substantially protected has much change of surviving enemy attack.

The principle of a sliding scale of protection, or a variant of that principle, is to some degree applied in practice by having at all times a few SAC planes on practice flights and by the device of keeping a small portion of the long-range bomber force at a very advanced state of readiness, prepared to take off immediately against enemy targets at first warning of impending enemy attack. The numbers of planes in flight and in advanced readiness status will undoubtedly increase with time, since the U.S. Air Force seems to lean towards this system as a preferred solution to the problem of vulnerability, but we have to note that the system is relatively expensive in its requirements for flying equipment, base facilities, and additional crew personnel, and, much more to the point, it can at best protect only a very small proportion of our SAC. It has been popularly assumed that the proportion of SAC bombers always in the air and presumably combat-ready has been something like one-third; actually, data publicly available in the Symington Committee Hearings of 1956 indicated that it then *averaged* only 4 per cent, and that the Air Force hoped with an increase in the ratio of crewmen-to-aircraft to drive it up in a couple of years to about 6 per cent.[5] These figures gain added significance when we remember that a small force would have far greater difficulties in penetrating alerted enemy defenses than a large one.

How many of the planes in the air are fit at any one time to start on an offensive mission is still another matter. We do not know how much fuel they have, or the condition of crew fatigue, even if we may assume they have bombs aboard.

So far as concerns "advanced readiness" on the ground, it too is expensive in crew and maintenance personnel, and while it has considerable value against manned aircraft attacks, it has little or none against missile attacks—especially short- or intermediate-range missiles such as might be hurled from submarines. Other and supplementary devices may therefore have to be adopted in the future, probably including very heavy shelters for individual aircraft as well as for long-range missiles.

The fact that it makes good sense to pay disproportionately for a guaranteed first installment of retaliatory bombs on target induces one to look with more indulgence than one otherwise might on high-cost techniques of protection or delivery for limited numbers of weapons, provided they can be pretty sure of penetrating enemy defenses. There is likely also to be an added value in diversification of the hard-core survival forces, even if each of the several ways chosen is relatively costly. If the enemy is obliged to think of not one

[5] See Wohlstetter, *op.cit.*, p. 218.

but two or more kinds of hard-core forces which he would have to eliminate in a surprise attack, his uncertainty of success is disproportionately enhanced.

For example, the use of nuclear-powered submarines as a means of hurling nuclear missiles against strategic targets would seem to be a desirable supplement to a well-protected, land-based force, even if it proved to be (which is by no means presently established) a costlier method in relation to effects achieved. The submarine is free of that main defect which characterizes the aircraft carrier and which denies the latter any real future as an adjunct to the strategic deterrence force: its relatively easy detectability by air-borne radar, combined with high vulnerability to atomic attack.

Deterrence and the Choice of Bombing Vehicles: Missiles Versus Aircraft

We have emphasized that for deterrence purposes a retaliatory force must be able to survive surprise attack. But the surviving force must also appear to have a good chance of penetrating fully-alerted enemy defenses even if launched in relatively small numbers. This requirement affects the choice of vehicles for the hard deterrence core of the retaliatory striking force. It upgrades, for example, the value of the long-range ballistic missile as compared with the manned aircraft.

If the ballistic missile is compared with the manned aircraft on grounds other than penetration capability, the latter appears able to hold its own for some time in the future. There is no doubt that the airplane can carry heavier and therefore, for the present, more powerful thermonuclear weapons (or several at a time among the less powerful varieties) and that it can deliver them more accurately than the missile. The airplane has a severe range liability, especially if its sortie plan requires it to return to base. The present American system of advanced SAC bases abroad has been molded largely by the range limitations of the B-47. Nevertheless, we have learned to live with the range problem and are coping with it by (a) building planes of longer range, (b) perfecting a system for in-flight refueling with tankers which are compatible in performance characteristics with the planes they service, and (c) providing staging bases for possible post-strike refueling.[6]

The airplane is not much more difficult to protect on the ground through the use of a heavy shelter than the missile, and it has in addition the special factor of "recallability," which in the opinion of many Air Force officers gives it a decisive advantage over the missile. The fact that it can be recalled makes the airplane capable of being sent out with inconclusive warning of enemy attack—thus getting it off the ground into the safer air—subject to returning on a "fail-safe" basis (i.e., the absence of positive orders to proceed) within a given period of time if the alarm turns out to be false.[7] The capacity for early take-off, subject to being recalled, is especially valuable to the advanced-readiness force as a protective device. There is, incidentally, no inherent incompatibility between being in advanced readiness and

[6] See Townsend Hoopes, "Overseas Bases in American Strategy," *Foreign Affairs*, xxxvii (October 1958), 69-82.

[7] The "fail-safe" or "positive control" feature is achieved by stipulating that bombers are not to proceed beyond a certain line unless they receive positive, confirmed instructions to do so. A failure of communications thus results in the return of the bombers. This arrangement contrasts with the obvious alternative, which would be to have the bombers return only if positively recalled. The danger of the "fail-safe" plan is that bombers may return because enemy attack has interfered with radio transmissions; but it is undoubtedly preferable to having a war begin because of a failure of such transmissions.

being in shelters, because the latter can be designed for quick emission.

We do not yet know how reliable the long-range missile will become over the next decade or so, how accurate, or how much its readiness factor will be improved by the use of solid fuels and other developments. We expect, however, that for some time to come the airplane will be more effective for special targets where accurate aiming is required, like hardened missiles or planes, and useful also for "armed reconnaissance," which is simply the hunt for targets either because they have been missed by other weapons or because their location may not be accurately enough known for missile attack.

The conclusion is unavoidable that for some time in the future the ideal strategic bombing force will be a mixed missile and manned-aircraft force. However, because the problem of penetrating enemy defenses is for aircraft much more difficult in counterattack—which is bound to be against fully alerted defenses—than in surprise initial attack, and because the problem increases disproportionately in difficulty as the number of counterattacking vehicles is reduced through losses to the initial enemy attack, one would expect that the missile would be favored over the aircraft for the hard core or "guaranteed" retaliatory capability. We must notice, incidentally, that with aircraft the counterattack problem is almost the opposite of that of initial attack, because against non-alerted defenses small numbers of attacking aircraft may have a better chance than large numbers for achieving surprise against the enemy's retaliatory forces. In other words, against alerted defenses the indicated tactic is saturation; against non-alerted defenses it could be, for a small force, evasion. Thus, in his use of aircraft, the dilemma of the counter-attacker is that he has the greatest need for numbers, and for good organization in executing his attack plan, just when he is suffering heavily in both respects from the enemy's initial blows. With missiles, on the other hand, the problem is much more nearly confined to that of surviving enemy attack.

The Problem of Target Choice in Retaliation

Among the items of information with which the U.S. Air Force has thoroughly acquainted the public, one is that our individual SAC crews are thoroughly briefed on specific primary and alternative targets for their initial D-day strike. Another, emphasized especially since the Soviet Union achieved a nuclear bombing capability, is that while the ultimate strategic target remains the enemy "war economy" (whatever that may mean under thermonuclear conditions, where the conventional materials of warfare are almost certainly meaningless), top-priority in time and perhaps also in weight of bombs has to be given to their strategic bombardment force.

We pointed out in an earlier chapter that a thorough attack on enemy air and missile base facilities is likely to involve also cities,[8] but it is obvious that the attacker has much latitude in determining whether that involvement is to be large or relatively restrained. If he considers damage to cities a "bonus," he will seek to maximize it, which he can do by targetting more airfields near cities, by using bigger bombs than he otherwise would, and by pushing his target centers towards those cities which are near the target airfields. If he considers destruction to cities an evil to be avoided, at least at the outset, he will use smaller and cleaner

[8] See above, pp. 155f.

bombs and shift his target points in the opposite direction. In either case the attack is primarily on the airfields and missile bases. But, depending on the total number, size, and character of bombs dropped in the counter-air campaign, the chances are that the net difference in city destruction deriving from the opposed kinds of orientation would be considerable.

The above observations apply only to an attack in which we hit first. All the major conditions governing target selection are changed, however, if the enemy strikes us first and ours is a retaliatory mission. In the first place, our retaliatory force is smaller by some unknown factor than the original offensive force. This smaller force, no doubt much disorganized, will now have to attempt to penetrate fully alerted defenses. The enemy strategic bombardment force, including missiles, is no longer at rest at its bases, ready to be struck by us to maximum effect. Its attractiveness as a strategic target began to decline sharply from the moment its own attack got underway. Moreover, according to the degree of surprise it has achieved, it has already done a good part of its total work, certainly the major part as far as one's own air force is concerned.

Many of the enemy's missiles and aircraft will no doubt be held in reserve for the purpose of exercising further pressure upon our survivors, to force accession to his demands, and it would be most desirable to hit these remaining ones if we could. But we would have to know exactly where they were, and to have the ability to destroy at least the major portion of them—requirements which are going to be difficult if not impossible to meet. In theory we can always limit further damage to ourselves by throwing our surviving bombardment power against the strategic striking power he has not yet expended, but under disaster circumstances this kind of damage-limitation is going to be marginal at best.

What then happens to the priority of the counter-air mission? The enemy's air force has ceased to be anything like so profitable a target as it was prior to hostilities, and at the same time our capabilities for hitting it have been reduced markedly. They may have been reduced to the critical limits within which we can no longer injure his surviving air power appreciably. Perhaps we can prevent some of his planes from flying second and third missions even if we have been too late to stop the first, and that opportunity is not to be dismissed lightly. Perhaps, too, he has been much slower in getting his missiles and initial-wave aircraft off the ground than he should have been. But if we cannot be sure of these things in advance when the planning must be done, we have to call into question the utility of combining the "strike second" contingency with a counter-air strategy.

What then? Perhaps we will have succeeded in putting enough target flexibility into our system so that surviving units do not simply go charging off against originally assigned targets. Even if it were a rational decision not to change the identity of the top-priority target *system*, a substantial loss of planes, and hence a reduction in the number making the counterattack, certainly argues that individual targets must be reassigned to avoid serious lacunae. But of course we also have to reconsider the whole system.

If we consider the problem strictly from the point of view of achieving the maximum deterrent effect from our retaliatory force *before* hostilities, the answer is apparently simple. We assign the hard-core elements in our retaliatory force to the enemy's major cities, provide for the maximum automaticity as well as certainty of response, and lose no opportunity to let the enemy know that we have done these things. The enemy therefore has reason to calculate that even a very great success against our air and missile force in a surprise attack, as long as it is short of 100 per cent and as long as the surviving force can penetrate his defenses, will result in his losing a number of his largest cities. Certainly he cares more for those cities intrinsically than he does for a few airfields, especially after the latter have done most of their work.

Such an arrangement must surely maximize the deterrent effect of our retaliatory force. We assure the enemy, by assuring ourselves (long-term security about our intentions being very undependable), that we will not reconsider the matter in the event he attacks us. We will hit back with all our surviving power at his cities and, especially if that power contains a fair number of missiles, he can count on losing those cities. It should not be difficult, if we make the appropriate effort beforehand, to assure him that, come what may, he will lose thirty, fifty, or more of his largest cities. This prospect should give him grave pause.

The rub comes from the fact that what looks like the most rational *deterrence* policy involves commitment to a strategy of response which, if we ever had to execute it, might then look very foolish. The strategy of deterrence ought always to envisage the possibility of deterrence failing.

Suppose, for example, the enemy attacked our retaliatory forces with great power but took scrupulous care to avoid major injury to our cities, a form of attack that has already been publicly proposed as a strategy we might adopt ourselves if we ever initiated the attack.[9] He might indeed under-

---

[9] See especially Col. Richard S. Leghorn, "No Need to Bomb Cities to Win War," *U.S. News and World Report*, January 28, 1955, pp. 79-94.

stand that, in a thermonuclear war, the mere ability to destroy cities may well confer more military advantage than the actual destruction of them. If his attack is successful to any serious degree, we should be left with a severely truncated retaliatory force while his remained relatively intact. These hardly seem propitious circumstances for us to *initiate* an exchange of city destruction, which would quickly use up our remaining power, otherwise useful for bargaining, in an act of suicidal vindictiveness. Our hitting at enemy cities would simply force the destruction of our own, and in substantially greater degree.

Thus it is easy to imagine a situation where it would be of little use to hit the enemy's airfields and disastrous as well as futile to attack his cities. No doubt in our rage and recklessness we would strike at something, and no doubt also the enemy's anticipation of such "irrational" behavior would help deter him from precipitating such a situation. One view might be that for the sake of maximizing deterrence it is wise deliberately to reject the Napoleonic maxim, *"on s'engage; puis on voit"* (one engages; then one sees), which after all applied to a state of affairs where one had far greater control of events after engaging than would be possible in modern total war. For the sake of deterrence before hostilities, the enemy must expect us to be vindictive and irrational if he attacks us. We must give him every reason to feel that that portion of our retaliatory force which survives his attack will surely be directed against his major centers of population.

A reasonable opposing view, however, is that no matter how difficult it may be to retain control of events in nuclear total war, one should never deliberately abandon control. If so, how should we cope with an enemy offensive which exercised the kind of discriminating restraint described above? With abundant examples from history to suggest how unrealistic prewar conceptions of impending hostilities can be, it would appear supremely sensible to want to preserve the capacity to make new decisions when the shooting begins. But one of the implications of that statement are that wartime decisions may be very different from those we presently like to imagine ourselves making. To retain control of decisions is to make oneself accessible to coercion concerning those decisions. If that is the course we choose, we should be all the more determined to reduce our general vulnerability, so that we may retain the stance for making strong decisions.

Choice of Weapons for Maximum Deterrence

The first underwater shot of a nuclear weapon, the Baker test at Bikini in 1946, revealed the appalling extent of radioactive debris which results from the explosion of a nuclear weapon, even one which by present standards was quite small, wherever soil or water is permitted to capture that debris. For a while it was possible to ignore this result because succeeding shots were set off, as a rule, atop towers more than 200 feet high. However, the Bravo shot in the CASTLE series on March 1, 1954 involved a large thermonuclear device set off at ground level, and the enormous reach of the fallout on that occasion confirmed the existence of a tremendous lethal by-product from low-level detonations. Putting so powerful a device atop the usual tower would have made little difference because of the size of the fireball.

The military would have been happy to do without this radioactive by-product. Not only is it impossible to control its distribution in the general region of the target, but in wartime some of it is likely to fall on neutral or friendly countries and even to drift back to the territories of the users of the bomb. That is especially true of the long-lived, insidious soil contaminant, strontium 90.

For this reason a great deal of research has gone into producing a so-called "clean" bomb, that is, a thermonuclear weapon which will produce only a slight amount of radio-active fallout in relation to its blast and thermal effects. The opposite course has also been known to be feasible; by adding various chemicals one could produce a weapon which released a much greater amount of radioactive fallout for its size than the already quite dirty thermonuclear weapon of the CASTLE-Bravo type. Development of such super-dirty weapons was bound to be retarded by the conviction that they could not be justified militarily, let alone morally.

When, however, we consider the special requirements of deterrence, with its emphasis on the punitive aspect of retaliation, we may find a need even for super-dirty bombs. Since the emphasis must be on making certain that the enemy will fear even the smallest number of bombs that might be sent in retaliation, one wants these bombs to be, and thus to appear before the event, as horrendous as possible. This grim objective is advanced by making the bomb very large and also intensively contaminating. It may also prove feasible by the appropriate selection of chemicals to augment close-in fallout without increasing the output of those radioactive isotopes which are characteristically carried to a considerable distance.

Deterrence and Civil Defense

We have noted that what we called basic deterrence, which concerns retaliation only in direct reply to attack upon ourselves, involves little strain on credibility. The enemy knows that if he hits our cities we will hit back, if we can. The question is one of feasibility, not intention. We suspect also that this statement holds good without regard to the state of our civil defenses at the time.

However, we have already noticed one case where, even in the event of direct attack upon our own territories, the character and spontaneity of our response become slightly more doubtful. This is the case where the enemy hits us hard at our air and missile bases but takes care to minimize injury to our cities. It is plausible to argue that in that moment of catastrophe we will be too insensitive to whatever discrimination he is practicing to let our responses be affected by it, but at present we cannot be sure of that. This uncertainty allows the consideration to intrude that perhaps our response will be affected by whether or not we have some shelters for our people.

The moment we think of deterrence to safeguard territories beyond our shores, the issue of whether or not we have provided reasonable protection to our population may become critical. We may be quite sure we will hit back if hit directly ourselves, regardless of the state of our civil defenses, but will we do so if the United Kingdom is hit? Or if it is threatened with being hit? Of course we are legally committed to respond with all our power, and our leaders may presently be convinced that if occasion arose they would honor that commitment. But surely they would on such an occasion be much affected by the consideration—assuming no radical change from the present situation—that our people are hopelessly exposed to enemy counterattack.

We cannot predict for any hypothetical instance that having the appropriate shelters will make a great difference in our behavior. We could be supine with shelters and brave, even reckless, without them; but surely if they existed at the moment of crisis, they would tend to sustain and fortify an attitude in favor of courageous decision. It would, of course, help if the allies we were protecting also had shelters.

We should note that in the kind of crisis situation we are hypothetically posing, the question of whether or not we have enough warning to get people to the shelters in time does not greatly disturb us; we are assuming that it is our government that sends them there as a result not of enemy attack but of its own resolution to act. If we have to assume that we shall certainly be hit first in a surprise attack, and that all important population centers will be included as targets in the first wave of the enemy attack, then there is clearly little use for shelters in those areas. That is certainly one possible contingency, but fortunately it is not the only one that we are obliged to consider.

It has been pointed out also that an adequate civil defense program may prove an indispensable factor in keeping wars limited. The maintenance by the enemy of limitations acceptable to us depends on our willingness to retaliate in kind and in greater degree in the event of gross enemy violation —going as far as the full use of SAC if need be. The enemy must also believe that we are ready to do so. Surely it would be easier to develop in ourselves the requisite willingness, and in the enemy the necessary credence, if we had meanwhile provided some cover for our populations.

We are describing a kind of crisis and decision which may seem to be utterly improbable. Most of the billions we are spending on the total-war aspect of national defense cover situations which are, we hope, at least equally improbable. All our efforts are in fact directed—at least we intend for them to be directed—towards making such situations still more improbable. That is what national defense is all about in the thermonuclear age.

Naturally one does not accord to civil defense the same level of priority that one accords to measures for the defense of SAC. We have already noted that a *secure* retaliatory force is not only the *sine qua non* of deterrence and of national defense generally but the one instrument which could conceivably make all other instruments designed for total war unnecessary. Prudence tells us, however, that we need some backstops even to a relatively secure SAC, and a well-designed shelter program for civil defense appears to fill such a need.

One school of thought holds that it is necessary and feasible to protect not only our people but also the tools and materials required for national economic recovery within a reasonable period after the war. This view suggests that a nuclear war is not necessarily the end of the world for us, let alone all humanity, and that we need not settle for anything less than the capacity to protect and preserve under attack the economic basis for our position of world leadership. The sums required to purchase this capacity over a five to ten year period are, allegedly, not outlandishly huge. It is possible to purchase relatively cheaply, in caves and unused mines, a great deal of floor space for the storage or actual operation of essential production capital. Some of this space is held to be already competitive, on an economic basis, with comparable space above ground.

Whether or not this apparently optimistic appraisal is true cannot be determined without a careful and detailed technical survey, which at this writing has not yet been done. But we can say that at the very least protection of population must be seriously provided for, and that such protection can be reasonably justified on political and strategic as well as on humanitarian grounds. We are currently spending about five billion dollars annually on active defenses which are inadequate to save our cities, and less than one per cent of that amount on civil defense. On *a priori* grounds, that is not likely to represent a wise allocation of our defense funds.

Some persons may in fact reject this kind of concern. They may feel they had rather take their chances with a hazardous future than see shelters dug into the ground around them to provide, at best, a marginal kind of safety. The usual observation on the subject includes some reference to the general undesirability of life anyway following a thermonuclear war. Individuals are entitled to adopt such attitudes for themselves, and just conceivably for their children as well, though they may be deceiving themselves about their feelings in a future crisis. Governments, on the other hand, have no moral right whatever to adopt cavalier attitudes about the value of individual survival.[10]

Deterrence and Armaments Control

We come finally to the question of the political environment favoring the functioning of a deterrence strategy, especially with respect to the much abused and belabored subject of international control of armaments. There is a long and dismal history of confusion and frustration on this subject. Those who have been most passionate in urging disarmament have often refused to look unpleasant facts in the face; on the other hand, the government officials responsible

[10] For this entire section see *Report on a Study of Non-Military Defense*, The RAND Corporation, Report R-322-RC, July 1, 1958. This study was prepared under the leadership and direction of Mr. Herman Kahn. See also above, pp. 210-216.

for actual negotiations have usually been extremely rigid in their attitudes, tending to become more preoccupied with winning marginal and ephemeral advantages from the negotiations than in making real progress toward the presumed objective. There has also been confusion concerning both the objective and the degree of risk warranted by that objective.

Here we can take up only the last point. One must first ask what degree of arms control is a reasonable or sensible objective. It seems by now abundantly clear that total nuclear disarmament is not a reasonable objective. Violation would be too easy for the Communists, and the risks to the non-violator would be enormous. But it should also be obvious that the kind of bitter, relentless race in nuclear weapons and missiles that has been going on since the end of World War II has its own intrinsic dangers. We could not view it with equanimity even if Sputnik I and its successors had not shaken our confidence in our ability to keep ahead in military weaponry for an indefinite period. Inasmuch as this race itself imposes the gravest risks, we ought not to look askance at measures for slowing or otherwise alleviating it simply because those measures themselves involve certain finite risks. In each case the risk has to be measured and weighed against the gain. In a world abundantly supplied with multi-megaton weapons and therefore destined henceforward to be living always on the edge of total disaster, military thinking has to move beyond its traditional fixation on immediate advantage.

The kind of measures in which we ought to be especially interested are those which could seriously reduce on all sides the dangers of surprise attack. Such a policy would be entirely compatible with our basic national commitment to a strategy of deterrence. The best way to reduce the danger of surprise attack is to reduce on all sides the incentives to such attack, an end which is furthered by promoting measures that enhance deterrent rather than aggressive posture—where the two can be distinguished, which, if one is looking for the chance to do so, is probably pretty often. It also helps greatly to reduce the danger of accidental outbreak of total war if each side takes it upon itself to do the opposite of "keeping the enemy guessing" concerning its pacific intentions. This is accomplished not through reiterated declaration of pacific intent, which is for this purpose a worn and useless tactic, but through finding procedures where each side can assure the other through the latter's own eyes that deliberate attack is not being prepared against him.

Professor Thomas C. Schelling, whose analysis of this problem is one of the most incisive contributions to the literature of disarmament, quotes General Leslie R. Groves as follows: "If Russia knows we won't attack first, the Kremlin will be very much less apt to attack us. . . . Our reluctance to strike first is a military disadvantage to us; but it is also, paradoxically, a factor in preventing a world conflict today." As Schelling adds, " 'Self Defense' becomes peculiarly compounded if we have to worry about his striking us to keep us from striking him to keep him from striking us. . . ."[11] Inasmuch as the chief if not the only reason why either side might want to hazard a deliberately planned war against the other would be to remove a menace which had become subjectively intolerable, we can add that the

---

[11] Professor Schelling's paper, "Surprise Attack and Disarmament," is scheduled for publication in 1959 by Princeton University Press, in a symposium volume to be entitled *N.A.T.O. and American Security*, edited by Professor Klaus Knorr.

measures which reduce the probability of accidental out-break of war also reduce the probability of planned or "pre-ventive" war.

Our over-riding interest, for the enhancement of our deter-rence posture, is of course in the security of our own retalia-tory force. But that does not mean that we especially desire the other side's retaliatory force to be insecure. If the oppo-nent feels insecure, we suffer the hazard of his being more trigger-happy. There may be, as Schelling says, ". . . not only secrets we prefer not to keep, but military capabilities we prefer not to have." To be sure, our massive-retaliation threat against some kinds of Soviet aggression is rendered less effective as the security of their retaliatory force improves, and that may conceivably be a serious price to pay for the purpose of improving the stability of the strategic situation. It may, on the other hand, be a largely fictitious price, and in any case we have no way of stopping the opponent from making his force more secure.

But why attempt to do bilaterally by negotiation what it is to each side's advantage to do anyway? One answer is that the *methods* of seeking security of the retaliatory force, even if that is all one seeks, may, as we have pointed out, vary widely in degree and certainly in appearance of aggressive-ness. They are therefore always a matter of concern to the other side. In that connection, there seems to be a widespread conviction that for purposes of deterrence speed of retaliation is as important as certainty of retaliation. This conviction tends to influence such decisions as, for example, whether the normal stations of our future Polaris submarines should be off Soviet shores or our own. Surely the Soviet Union will have strong feelings on the matter, as will we with respect to comparable Soviet submarines. Speed of retaliation must no doubt have some value in deterrence, but how much has never been thoroughly examined. It surely cannot compare in importance with certainty of retaliation, and therefore there must be some room for negotiating with respect to schemes that trade off speed in retaliation for less provocative deterrence postures.

In any case, in our national security considerations on both the domestic and the international levels, the factor to be emphasized always is not the symmetry or asymmetry of offensive power between the two sides, which is of largely fictitious importance when striking first matters so much, but the *stability* of the balance between them. To quote Schelling again: "The situation is symmetrical but not stable when either side, by striking first, can destroy the other's power to strike back; the situation is stable when neither side can destroy the other whether it strikes first or second—that is, when *neither* in striking first can destroy the other's ability to strike back." The latter situation removes both the temptation to strike first and the "need to react quickly to what might prove to be a false alarm." It would be rather difficult so to stabilize the strategic relationships between the powers that there would be no strategic advantage in striking first—and the task undoubtedly gets more difficult as nuclear bombs get larger—but such an ideal situation is not at all necessary.

Stability is achieved when each nation believes that the strategic advantage of striking first is overshadowed by the tremendous cost of doing so. If, for example, retaliatory weapons are in the future so well protected that it takes more than one missile to destroy an enemy missile, the chances for stability become quite good. Under such circumstances striking first brings no advantage unless one has enormous numerical superiority. But such a situation is the very opposite of the more familiar one where both sides rely wholly or predominately on unprotected aircraft.

Technological progress could, however, push us rapidly towards a position of almost intolerable mutual menace. Unless something is done politically to alter the environment, each side before many years will have thousands of missiles accurately pointed at targets in the other's territory ready to be fired at a moment's notice. Whether or not we call it "push-button" war is a matter of our taste in phraseology, but there is no use in telling ourselves that the time for it is remote. Well before that time arrives, aircraft depending for their safety on being in the air in time will be operating according to so-called "air-borne alert" and "fail-safe" patterns. Nothing which has any promise of obviating or alleviating the tensions of such situations should be overlooked.

‹9›

LIMITED WAR

IN THE PREVIOUS CHAPTER we sought to establish that the inescapable alternative to preventive war is the policy of "deterrence" in its special modern sense and with its special modern requirements. The first function of deterrence is to make strategic air attack, whether preventive, pre-emptive, or purely aggressive, look completely unattractive to the other side. The only way to do so is to make certain that an attack by the other side will be met in kind, not necessarily to the same degree but at least to a substantial one. The error in popular judgment is to assume that this certainty of retaliation comes as a matter of course, without considerable special effort. On the contrary, a great effort is required to accomplish it. Now we must examine the implications of this fact in terms of a concept that is, like deterrence, both old and new—the concept of "limited war."

The coming of the modern thermonuclear bomb was bound to give a great new impetus to an idea that had already suggested itself to some with the coming of the first atomic bombs: the prospect of a large-scale mutual exchange of nuclear weapons on cities reduces war to a suicidal absurdity. It is difficult to imagine a set of positive national objectives that could be realized in such a war by the side that was "victorious" (the word is put in quotation marks only to remind ourselves that it has lost its former meaning and needs redefining). Certain objectives can be spoken of as though they make sense even under the new conditions, but these usually have to be presented negatively, that is, as the preservation of values the loss of which would presumably be worse than death. Put more honestly, there are some things which we want very much (for example, national integrity and independence) and which we do not know how to defend against external menace except by threatening certain actions which do risk national suicide. We justify or rationalize this posture on the ground that our threats will suffice to hold the menace in check and will not be challenged.

In the long history of warfare we have become accustomed to a good deal of posturing on the subject of things "worse than death." Threats of carrying on "to the last man" have long been a debased currency in causes good, bad, and misdirected. Less than a hundred years ago patriots speaking for some millions of Americans were threatening to fight to the last man rather than let themselves be subject to the "tyranny" of the Federal Government. War as an institution has thrived on the assumption that the whole national community can partake of its hatred and excitement, but that only a small proportion at worst will pay with their lives. Now that we are talking of a war which could kill half the national population and reduce gravely the health, happiness, and welfare of the rest, we have to interpret much more carefully, and certainly more restrictively, the categories of things to which war-to-the-death is preferable.

However, the view just expressed seems to offer little upon which we can erect a national policy. Armed aggression by one nation against another is an old story, and there is not much reason to suppose that we have seen the last of it. We have thus far found no way to control it except by the threat or the action of opposing it with sufficient force.

From an historical position of exaggerated indifference

to aggression occurring outside the Western Hemisphere, the United States has progressed in little more than one generation to an attitude favoring almost automatic involvement against aggression wherever it may occur in the world. Perhaps we shall interpret this obligation somewhat more modestly in the future; nevertheless there must remain important places in the world where communist aggression is clearly conceivable and where we have a real interest and even an obligation to intervene. What then?

Following World War I it became axiomatic that modern war means total war. This attitude seemed to be confirmed and reinforced by World War II, despite the appearance of nuclear weapons. During the period of American monopoly of these weapons, there was no great incentive for Americans to think otherwise. The principle that was later to be described as "massive retaliation" was taken utterly for granted and, as we pointed out earlier, it was only because our Korean War strategy seemed to disturb that principle that our national leaders saw fit to reassert it, with minor modifications. It involved, especially in its pre-1950 form, essentially an "all or nothing" attitude to the use of force: one either did not fight at all, or one fought with all one had or could lay hands on. The experience of two world wars argues that it was not a nonsensical view. It implicitly took account of the fact that war always deeply involves the emotions and that the collapse of inhibitions in the transition from peace to war does not augur well for the containment of the succeeding violence. It is significant, nevertheless, that the total-war idea, which seemed so overwhelming in its logical simplicity, was a fairly novel one historically.

During and following the Korean War, however, certain ideas became possible which would have appeared hopelessly aberrant without that experience. The Korean War proved anew that great-power rivals occasionally prefer to test each other's strength and resolution with limited rather than unlimited commitments to violence, and it demonstrated also some of the major constraints necessary to keep a war limited. Most important among these was a willingness to settle for goals representing a considerable degree of compromise with the enemy, and thus readiness to keep contact and to enter into and maintain negotiations with him.

We were, however, ideologically unprepared for such an experience, and this is probably the chief reason we did not accomplish a great deal more with the strength we committed to the enterprise. If our behavior was in general correct, it is a credit to our intelligence even in confusion and not to our foresight. Nevertheless, thoughtful people learned much about modern war from Korea, which enabled them also to view in a new light such earlier experiences as the Berlin airlift, our involvement in the Greek civil war, and the Spanish civil war of 1936-1939.

The attractiveness of limited war as an alternative to total war starts from the fact that as a matter of national policy we have conclusively forsworn preventive war. At the same time we have some confidence that preventive war will not, or at least need not, look very much more attractive to the other side. The advent of the thermonuclear bomb seems to have had a decisive influence in this respect by making it highly probable that even a relatively small amount of retaliation would do a very large amount of damage. This stabilizing factor is, however, at least partly offset by the fact that extremely destructive surprise attack upon the opponent's retaliatory force is more feasible with thermonuclear weapons than with the ordinary fission variety.

At any rate, if we assume reasonably secure retaliatory forces, unrestricted thermonuclear war seems to be at once much too destructive and too unpredictable to be invoked in any but the most dire straits. It is unpredictable because not only industrial superiority but even superiority in mobilized forces will probably count for less than in the past, being much overshadowed by questions like who strikes first, and in what way. Such questions can be answered with reasonable satisfaction only if one is completely willing to accept the role of aggressor. These reasons are perhaps sufficient to explain why serious thinking about limited war had to await the coming of the large thermonuclear bomb—besides the obvious reason that basic patterns of thinking, and certainly of political and diplomatic behavior, always change slowly.[1]

The Meaning of Limited War

What distinguishes limited war from total war? The answer is that limited war involves an important kind and degree of restraint—deliberate restraint. As a rule we do not apply the term "limited war" to conflicts which are limited naturally by the fact that one or both sides lack the capability to make them total (for example, the colonial war in Algeria). We generally use it to refer to wars in which the United States on the one side and the Soviet Union or Communist China on the other may be involved, perhaps directly

[1] A survey of the more important and original literature on modern limited war is contained in my review article "More About Limited War," *World Politics*, x (October 1957), 112-122. My own contributions to this subject began, on a classified basis, at the beginning of 1952, and were later published in the following articles: "Nuclear Weapons: Strategic or Tactical," *Foreign Affairs*, xxxii (January 1954), 217-229; and especially "Unlimited Weapons and Limited War," *The Reporter*, November 18, 1954, pp. 16ff.

but usually through proxies on one or both sides. In such wars the possibility of total or unrestricted conflict is always present as an obvious and immediately available alternative to limited operations. That is why we must emphasize the factor of deliberate restraint.

The restraint must also be massive. One basic restraint always has to be present if the term "limited war" is to have any meaning at all: strategic bombing of cities with nuclear weapons must be avoided. The minimum restraint is thus already a very great one, particularly in view of the existing traditions of air strategic doctrine with their great emphasis on strategic bombing.

Limited war might conceivably include strategic bombing carried on in a selective or otherwise limited manner, for example bombing with nuclear weapons on selected targets such as airfields while being as careful as possible not to hit cities. It is certainly conceivable that strategic bombing could be carried on in a restrained and discriminatory fashion; one could argue it *ought* to be, for strategic as well as moral reasons, if carried on at all! But usage has already crystallized enough to indicate that such strategies are not generally included in the meaning of the term "limited war." By now it practically always connotes a war in which there is *no strategic bombing between the United States and the Soviet Union*. Logically there must be other restraints as well, but that one at least is always included. One reason, perhaps, is that a situation which admitted of some strategic bombing with nuclear weapons would be simply too near the blow-out point where restraints of any kind are abandoned. It would be, in other words, inherently an extremely unstable situation.

When we describe limited war today as requiring deliberate non-use of a gigantically powerful military instrument, one that remains ready at hand to be used, we are differentiating modern limited war from anything that has happend in the past. We are talking about something quite new. If wars were limited in ages past, the reasons why they were so have little relevance for us today. Apart from the existence of moral, religious, and dynastic scruples, and the fact that anything as basic as national existence or even the survival of a dynasty was rarely at stake, wars were kept limited by the small margin of the national economic resources available for mobilization and by the small capability for destruction that could be purchased with that narrow margin. Today, on the contrary, we speak of limited war in a sense that connotes a deliberate hobbling of a tremendous power that is already mobilized and that must in any case be maintained at a very high pitch of effectiveness for the sake only of inducing the enemy to hobble himself to like degree.

No conduct like this has ever been known before. Nations and princes have often refrained from mobilizing their full potential strength while engaged in war, usually from lack of incentive. But to limit one's effort is not the same as to restrain one's available military power. *The chief problem of limited war today is the problem of finding sanctions for keeping out of action, on a stable basis, just those existing instruments which from a strictly military point of view are far the most efficient—and which tend to be dangerously vulnerable to attack while on the ground.*

We can think of some wars between major powers in the last century that seemed to be limited through the choice of locales for the fighting—like the Crimean War of 1854-1856, the Spanish-American War of 1898, and the Russo-Japanese War of 1904-1905. In these cases the main geographical centers of the opposing powers were far removed from each other, and the belligerents came to grips with the maximum strength they could bring to bear at points of contact. Perhaps the effort in each of these cases could have been more heroic in magnitude than it actually was, but judgment in these matters must take into account the traditions of the time. At any rate, these were not colonial wars, or wars that were deliberately confined to remote regions. At the time of the Fashoda crisis between France and Great Britain in 1898, there was no doubt in anyone's mind that if war broke out between the two countries it would not be confined to the Nile. It is hard to find instances since the sixteenth century when wars were confined locally through common tacit agreement, except when they were fought through proxies.

Objectives in Limited War

Limited war has sometimes been defined as "a war fought to achieve a limited objective."[2] This definition refers to the necessary relationship between limited war and limited objectives, the recognition of which was originally an important insight, but it distorts importantly the character of that relationship. It diverts attention from the crucial fact that the restraint necessary to keep wars limited is primarily a restraint on means, not ends. It provokes the notion that we will be willing to accept restraint only when the end we are

[2] The full definition from which the above quotation is taken was printed in the official program of a "Seminar on Capabilities and Techniques of American Armament for Limited War," held under the auspices of the American Ordnance Association in New York, December 4, 1957. It reads as follows: "A limited war is a war fought to achieve a limited objective. In the achievement of this objective a nation may be expected to plan to expend a limited amount of its national resources; and in carrying out the war it may be expected to plan to hold the war to a limited geographical area."

pursuing is not very important to us. It suggests also that in any instance we will look very critically at the restraints proposed and accept only those which are convenient to us.

Unfortunately, however, even in peripheral areas limited war is not going to be as easy to arrange as that. We shall have to work very hard to keep it limited. We should be willing to limit objectives *because* we want to keep the war limited, and not the other way round. And we want to keep the war limited simply because total war as it would be fought today and in the future against a well-armed enemy is simply too unthinkable, too irrational to be borne.

World War I was a war fought for limited objectives, amazingly limited objectives in view of the efforts involved and the costs sustained on both sides, but it was certainly not a limited war. It was a far less terrible war than the kind we should have today if we let ourselves go in a comparable fashion, but none of the major belligerents practiced notable restraint. World War II was also, though somewhat less clearly, a war of limited objectives. Against both Germany and Japan we insisted on the right, together with our allies, to dictate the peace; but when that prerogative was won the dictation was remarkably restrained. On the other hand, the objectives of the Korean War were by no means as limited as they appeared on the surface, because the main objectives were psychological and lay outside Korea.

It is of course true and important that we cannot have limited war without settling for limited objectives, which in practice is likely to mean a negotiated peace based on compromise. Clausewitz's classic definition, that the object of war is to impose one's will on the enemy, must be modified, at least for any opponent who has a substantial nuclear capability behind him. Against such an opponent one's terms must be modest enough to permit him to accept them, without his being pushed by desperation into rejecting both those terms and the limitations on the fighting. This principle, if consistently pursued, should dispose of the hackneyed argument that limited war is impossible because the losing side will always be constrained to reject limitations rather than accept defeat. We have already admitted that keeping war limited will be difficult. We must be clear, however, that the curtailing of our taste for unequivocal victory is one of the prices we pay to keep the physical violence, and thus the costs and penalties, from going beyond the level of the tolerable. It is not the other way round.

The reasons for stressing this point are several, but one of them concerns the question: How much and what kind of restraint must we practice? It has been suggested above only what the minimum restraint has to be—avoidance of strategic bombing of the major enemy—but no doubt other restraints also have to be imposed if we are to make sure of maintaining the basic and indispensable one. We cannot deal reasonably with this and like questions unless we are constantly clear in our minds what it is we are after. *We want to discourage and curb the enemy's aggressions while avoiding total war.*

Resistance to Limited War Thinking

All of us assume almost without question that peace is better than war, but it is curious and interesting that we do not have the same consensus that limited war is preferable to total war. One reason is that some people apparently still entertain fantasies of total war which have the United States doing all the hitting while receiving few if any nuclear bombs in return. How these fantasies can exist is a matter of wonder inasmuch as we have rejected preventive war. There are, however, other reasons too.

In an earlier chapter we considered briefly some of the psychological reasons why responsible persons may prefer total war to limited war, even when they expect fairly heavy punishment from the former.[3] A fuller account would have to tap some of the findings of modern psychology concerning the repressed rages harbored in so many breasts, but we shall not pause for that here. There are important institutional reasons as well, more pertinent to our inquiry.

General Douglas MacArthur's remark following his dismissal—"There is no substitute for victory"—reflects an attitude endemic in all the armed services, one which works strongly against any restraint upon the use of force during wartime. Clausewitz, ambivalent in this as in many other respects, can be and has often been quoted out of context to demonstrate his vehement rejection of restraint in war.[4] However, while this and similar attitudes are shared by all the military services, they are not always shared in equal degree.

Many American army officers have discerned that their own service might have no function at all to perform in a total war other than servicing part of an air-defense system and perhaps the distasteful duty of maintaining public order. Naval officers too have begun to see that in a total war the Navy would be without its traditional function, which is to

[3] See above, pp. 258f.

[4] Clausewitz, *On War* (Modern Library ed., 1943), bk. 1, ch. I, pp. 3-18. In this opening chapter, Clausewitz states almost on the first page that the "use of force is theoretically without limits," and uses some pungent language to push the point home. Within a few pages, however, he begins to insist that "the probabilities of real life take the place of the extreme and absolute demanded by theory." The first group of statements has been quoted very frequently by military writers, the latter group very rarely. See also above, pp. 37f.

win and exercise command of the sea, though it might participate in strategic bombing through it missile-launching submarines. Airmen, however, have always felt, with special justice since the atomic bomb arrived, that a total war would be primarily theirs to fight. A limited war, on the contrary, seems to throw the Air Force back into the unpalatable role of providing support to the ground forces.

Officers of the Air Force have been reared on the doctrine of the predominance of strategic bombing. This was a fighting doctrine, a basis for contest and controversy with the other services. At the end of World War II that philosophy received a tremendous boost from the atomic bomb, which to any unbiased observer appeared to quell all remaining arguments concerning the ineffectiveness of strategic bombing. Strategic air doctrine was riding high, when suddenly it began to be bruited about that perhaps atomic and especially large thermonuclear weapons made strategic bombing *too* effective, too tremendously destructive to be released under any but the ultimate challenge. The idea could hardly be congenial to the service that had but lately won not only its separateness and its right to an independent mission but also the most favored position in the allocation of the defense budget. Let it be said, too, that in an era when peacetime defense budgets amount to forty billions of dollars or more, the argument that the thermonuclear bomb can do everything, and that no significant military action is likely to be or should be carried on without it, carries a tremendous political appeal in the name of economy!

Adverse Results of the Korean War

It is necessary also to recall the adverse effects of the Korean War on limited-war thinking. We said some pages earlier that the Korean experience made it possible to think of limited war in its peculiarly modern form, and on something other than a trivial scale. However, this possibility could be realized only from searching reflection upon the event. During the affair and for some time afterward, the spontaneous national reaction to it was generally one of distaste and rejection. It had been a costly and painful business and in its defeats a humbling one. Many Americans high and low indulged themselves in rueful thoughts about how our handling of the affair had erred in the direction of too much restraint. The long hearings before Congress on the Mac-Arthur dismissal were full of such ruminations. The most conspicuous result of the war in the field of American diplomacy was the Dulles "Massive Retaliation" speech of January 1954, described in an earlier chapter.

Admittedly, our handling of the Korean War does not stand as a model for shrewd limited-war strategies. Our strategy, diplomatic as well as military, was vastly affected by the conviction of both the Truman and the Eisenhower Administrations that it was, in General Omar Bradley's words, "the wrong war, at the wrong place, at the wrong time, and with the wrong enemy." Those words were used concerning the possible extension of the war against China, but by implication they applied to the whole affair.[5]

For much of the first year of that war it was the dominant conception in the Pentagon that the Korean aggression was a ruse by the Soviet Union with the sole object of causing us to commit our forces to the wrong theater while they made ready their major attack in Europe. Even when that idea

[5] *Military Situation in the Far East*, Hearings before the Comm. on Armed Services and the Comm. on Foreign Relations, U.S. Senate, 82nd Cong., 1st sess., U.S. Govt. Printing Office, Washington, D.C., p. 732.

faded, another view prevailed, this time more among the politicians than the military, that the Russians and the Chinese could be all too easily provoked into making total the limited war in which they were engaged. The fact that the Chinese were obviously already committed to the full limits of their capabilities seemed not to affect that anxiety. There was also the fear that the Soviets might start several additional "Koreas" along the periphery of the U.S.S.R. Since these basic assumptions were almost certainly wrong, it is remarkable how appropriate and effective our strategy actually was.

No doubt the cardinal error as we see it today was the halting of our offensive at the moment when the Communists first indicated an interest in opening armistice negotiations. This error, attributable to our political rather than our military leadership, had nothing to do with our desire to keep the war limited. Interrogation of prisoners revealed that the Communist Chinese army facing us had been in a truly desperate condition, undergoing large-scale defections, when a few words by Jakob Malik in the United Nations headquarters in New York caused us to relax our pressure.[6] Although there were some limited U N offensives afterward, the pressure was never fully reapplied. We paid bitterly for that error in the great prolongation of negotiations, in the unsatisfactory terms of settlement, and above all in the disillusionment and distaste which the American people developed as the main emotional residue of their experience with limited war.

[6] Here I am indebted to Dr. Herbert Goldhamer of The RAND Corporation, whose important work with POW interrogation in Korea and especially with the U N delegation that negotiated the armistice has been recorded in some unpublished papers which I have been privileged to read.

Non-Use of Nuclear Weapons in Korea

The non-use of nuclear weapons in the Korean War has also been criticized. This criticism, which is harder to justify, bears on an exceedingly important issue for the future. It is therefore worth recalling why, at a time when we enjoyed practically a monopoly of nuclear weapons, we refrained from using them. If this was a wise decision when measured by its consequences, as the present writer believes it was, then, like so many other right decisions of that war, it was blundered into for the wrong reasons.

There seem to have been three main reasons why we did not use atomic bombs in Korea. First, because our Chiefs of Staff felt that the war in Korea was basically a Soviet feint or diversion, there was a strong motivation for saving for the main show our then relatively limited nuclear stockpile. Second, local commanders kept reporting the opinion that the Korean conflict presented no suitable targets for nuclear weapons. This view of course reflected an uninformed attitude about the uses of nuclear weapons. It was generally thought, for example, that atomic bombs were of little use against bridges.[7] These weapons were still new and the officers in Korea were too busy fighting to have much opportunity to read reports from the testing grounds on nuclear weapons effects. Third, our allies, especially the British, were strongly and emotionally opposed to our using nuclear weapons. This opposition merely strengthened our own

---

[7] This odd idea probably resulted from a mis-reading of the results at Hiroshima and Nagasaki. Some bridges were indeed badly damaged at those places and some were not, but for the latter it was generally forgotten that a bridge only 270 feet from ground zero at Hiroshima was actually 2,100 feet from the point of explosion, and also that it received its blast effect from above rather than from the side. See *The Effects of Nuclear Weapons*, A.E.C., 1957, pp. 94f., 165ff.

deeply-felt anxieties about reintroducing into war those still new and terrible instruments. A subsidiary reason was that while we were still enjoying a quasi-monopoly advantage in nuclear weapons, we had to credit the Soviet Union with having at least a few, and even one on Pusan or on one of our Japanese bases could have been very embarrassing to us. It is doubtful, however, whether this last-mentioned reason played a conscious part in the relevant decisions.

The first thing to notice about the three most important reasons is that none of them is likely to obtain, at least not nearly to the same degree, in some comparable event of the future. Whether or not that event is regarded as a ruse, there will be no significant limitations of stockpile to worry about. On the contrary, the liberal and almost indiscriminate use of nuclear weapons in limited wars is now urged *because* they are themselves almost a free good, militarily speaking—that is, are likely to be in far more abundant supply than aircraft and especially bombers—and because intervention is therefore construed to be much cheaper with their use than without. Second, military officers are now in no doubt that not only a bridge but even a tank or a platoon of men may be a good target for a nuclear weapon of appropriate size. Third, although a considerable residue of anathema and horror for the use of nuclear weapons remains in the world today, it has been considerably eroded by repeated insistence, emanating mostly from the United States, that the use of nuclear weapons must be regarded as absolutely normal, natural, and right. Whether it was really in the American interest to attack the emotional resistances to using nuclear weapons was never soberly examined. The question was acted upon as though the answer were unequivocal. One of the things that makes it equivocal may be listed as the fourth major difference between the Korean War and one occurring any time henceforward: nothing resembling an American monopoly of nuclear weapons remains.

Current Insistence on the Use of Nuclear Weapons

Nevertheless, many Americans, including high civilian officials as well as military officers, insist that if our response to an aggression has to be limited geographically, at least it must be atomic.[8] The reasons usually given are, first, that it is much cheaper to prepare for and fight limited wars this way—we could perhaps even do it with just a small part of our SAC—and second, that otherwise we might lose.

Of course the use of nuclear weapons makes an air or ground force more effective than it would be without them. Even the smaller nuclear weapons can enormously enhance fire power with a great saving in logistics. But we cannot assume, as we seem to be doing, that American use of them will be unilateral. The moment we start visualizing them as being used reciprocally, their use ceases to look overwhelmingly advantageous to us. They do not make intervention cheaper, or the prospect of winning surer. They seem to be at least as useful to the offense as to the defense. The exception would be the case where the enemy was invading a country with masses of ground troops and we and the allies we were defending had few or none in the area—in short a situation

[8] One noteworthy author who has committed himself to the use of nuclear weapons in limited war (though not necessarily in "brushfires") is Henry A. Kissinger, in his *Nuclear Weapons and Foreign Policy*, Harper, New York, 1957. Another is Edward Teller, in numerous speeches and articles. For criticisms of this view, see James E. King's long (two-installment) review of the Kissinger book in *The New Republic* for July 1, 1957, and July 15, 1957; and the review by William W. Kaufmann, "The Crisis in Military Affairs," *World Politics*, x (July 1958), 579-603.

where the opponent was presenting all the targets. Even then he could retaliate against friendly towns and villages.

It is probably true, as some have written, that readiness to use atomic weapons against limited aggression would have a great deterrent effect, but only if the prospect of fighting in a nuclear environment did not reduce our willingness to intervene. For it would seem that our willingness to intervene is more important as a deterrent than the choice of weapons. Since presumably we are no longer thinking of unilateral use (if we are, we should make clear the circumstances under which we would expect to get away with it), it is not at all clear that we will be as ready or readier to intervene if we expect nuclear weapons to be used as we would with a contrary expectation.

If we are going to use nuclear weapons in limited wars—and of course we have to be prepared for their use in any case—several questions immediately arise. How big should the tactical weapons be? How many should be used, and on what targets? How do we fix and preserve the limitations called for by our answers to the above questions? How can we reach the needed understanding with the enemy on the rules governing the use of nuclear weapons—an understanding, incidentally, that will almost certainly have to be tacit rather than explicit—and what are the available sanctions for enforcing those rules?[9] One answer might be that so long

[9] Soviet commentary on the limited-war thinking emanating from the West has thus far been uniformly hostile and derisive. Especially derided has been the thought that wars might remain limited while being fought with atomic weapons. See for example the article (called to my attention and translated by my colleague, Leon Gouré) by Colonel V. Mochalov and Major V. Dashichev, "The Smoke Screen of the American Imperialists," *Red Star*, December 17, 1957. This attitude may not be conclusive in establishing the impossibility of arriving at a formal agreement with the Soviet Union setting down some rules for fighting limited wars,

as geographical limitations are observed, there need be no limitations on types and numbers of nuclear weapons used. If so, what will that philosophy mean for the areas involved?

The use of any kind of nuclear weapons probably increases markedly the difficulties in the way of maintaining limitations on war. For one thing, it is much easier to distinguish between use and non-use of nuclear weapons than between the use of a nuclear weapon below some arbitrary limit of size and one well above that limit. This discontinuity in effects and in identification coincides with a moral feeling on the subject.

Many, including the President of the United States, have made public assertions to the effect that a man killed by a nuclear weapon is no more dead than one killed by a bullet and that, war itself being immoral, there is no sense in attempting to discriminate between more or less moral ways of fighting it. Some of these people point to the remarkable gradation in size of nuclear weapons, which in the smallest categories are scarcely more powerful than the largest H.E. weapons and which therefore form a continuum with the latter. These "practical" and "logical" attitudes are belied in part by our own national behavior both in World War II and in the Korean War, when we not only refrained from using gas or bacterial agents despite some temptation to use at least the former but also protested vehemently and bitterly the calumnies of our enemies when they falsely accused us

---

but it seems a very unlikely occurrence on other grounds as well. This means that agreement will have to be tacit rather than explicit. For research on how tacit agreements are reached, see Thomas C. Schelling, "Bargaining, Communication, and Limited War," *Conflict Resolution*, I (March 1957), 19-36; also the same author's "The Strategy of Conflict," *Conflict Resolution*, II (September 1958), pp. 203-264.

of doing so. And what is gas in heinousness, or bacterial warfare for that matter, compared to nuclear weapons?

It should be a familiar idea, hardly in need of restatement, that men's opinions have an importance apart from the facts that may or may not support them. Our civilization, like any other, is formed of a tissue of customs and beliefs, many of them so nonrational as legitimately to be called "myths." By the term "myth" we mean not an idea which is false but one founded on legend or tradition, including legal tradition, rather than on the kind of objective, verifiable facts with which scientists deal. In this sense the term covers most of the basic attitudes for which we are ready to go to war and undergo untold pain and cost. We often make, for example, extremely important distinctions between an American national and a person of other nationality, and especially between American territory and foreign territory: yet we know that in the former case there is no physiological difference between the two and often not even a linguistic one, and that in the latter case the distinction has to do not with soil but with the historico-legal interpretation of imaginary lines called boundaries. For comparable reasons the existence of possibly nonrational feelings sharply differentiating the use of nuclear from that of non-nuclear weapons, which despite the erosion noted above remain conspicuous and strong, ought not be blandly waved aside as unimportant.

In terms of narrower diplomatic interest, one must take into account also the preferences of those non-American peoples whom we shall presumably be defending against aggression. However peripheral a war may be in relation to the areas we regard as of central importance, the places we find ourselves fighting over will not usually be uninhabited. A people "saved" by us through our free use of nuclear weapons over their territories would probably be the last that would ever ask us to help them. We might have to insist on rescuing future victims of aggression even against their own will, but it will not be a good diplomatic position to be in. One solution, *if* the appropriate rules could be established and maintained, would be to use nuclear weapons only on relatively uninhabited areas within the theater of action, as for example mountain passes. But the "if" is a big one.

It is necessary to clarify one fact that seems to be confused not only among laymen but also among many scientists and even professional military officers. One frequently meets references to "tactical" nuclear weapons as distinct from "strategic" ones with the implication that there are marked intrinsic differences between them or the factors governing their use. The most common belief is that the former are necessarily of small yield and the latter of large. These ideas are completely erroneous.

The first A-bombs were tactical bombs as much as they were strategic; more so, in fact, since their yields were of a size now regarded as falling entirely inside the tactical range. But there is no *military* reason why tactical weapons should have to be of small yield. Usually, where a small weapon is good, a larger one is better; and the delivery of the latter is likely to be about as feasible and not much more expensive. Various modern multi-megaton thermonuclear weapons can be handled and delivered by the smaller types of combat aircraft, and smaller than that "tactical" weapons do not have to be. They could still be used tactically even if they required large bomber aircraft, but usually they do not.

There is also little inherent reason why the larger weapons cannot be as accurately aimed. The degree of hazard to one's own troops on the ground, if any are in the vicinity, is controlled by warning, and by the distance of the bomb burst from their front lines. It is obvious that big bombs cannot be permitted to fall as close to one's own troops as small ones can, but that fact will limit the use of large bombs only in special cases. It may indeed be useful also to have small nuclear weapons, but no reason is to be found in economics or military science why tactical weapons must be predominantly of the smaller varieties, let alone exclusively so.

Those, therefore, who insist that they want to use only the very smallest atomic bombs tactically should be clear that they are talking about a restriction which will have to be arbitrarily imposed and not one for which the users will have an automatic preference.[10] Besides, the argument that we *must* use nuclear weapons tactically but that only the smallest nuclear weapons should be so used seems to be somewhat wanting in consistency. If they must be very small, why not none at all? If they must be used, why not use large ones? The answer to the first question is that even small nuclear weapons are likely to be more efficient than H.E. bombs, but large bombs are certainly more efficient than small ones, both in military effort and in the use of fissionable material.

Talk about "quality" weapons and about "efficient" versus "inefficient" weapons is rather beside the point. By settling for limited war, which by definition excludes strategic bombing, we are agreeing not to use against our enemies the most efficient instrument of all, at least not in the most efficient way. If we limit the size of the nuclear weapons used tactically to the smaller categories, we are accepting further large

[10] The AEC's *The Effects of Nuclear Weapons* (1957), pp. 340-389, shows that the gamma rays and fast neutrons released in nuclear explosions scale differently from thermal and blast effects. Thus, in very small bombs (*e.g.*, 2 KT or less) immediate nuclear radiation may exceed other effects in military importance.

sacrifices of efficiency. Naturally, this argument must not be pushed to extremes, because once we find a suitable category of weapons we will want to pursue maximum efficiency within it. But between the use and non-use of atomic weapons there is a vast watershed of difference and distinction, one that ought not be cavalierly thrown away, as we appear to be throwing it away, if we are serious about trying to limit war.

The President's Decision

In the previous chapter we noted that in a crisis, questions concerning the use of weapons may be decided by the President in a way that is neither desired nor expected by the military.[11] It is remarkable how often relevant experience is ignored. Before Korea, it would have been rash to predict that the United States would fight for as long and hard as it did, suffering some bitter humiliations in the process, without resorting to nuclear weapons. The same is true of the Egyptian crisis of November 1956, where the British and French forces were not only denied use of any kind of nuclear weapon, which the British Government certainly possessed, but were even ordered not to use their heavier naval guns! No shells larger than six-inch caliber were fired by British or French warships, although heavy cruisers and at least one battleship were present! These restrictions, imposed at the last minute by the governments on their respective military forces, were nowhere condemned as unwise or unreasonable.[12] American forces standing by in the Mediter-

[11] See above, p. 260.

[12] In his speech before the House of Commons on November 7, 1956, in which he described his note of the same date to Soviet Premier Bulganin, Prime Minister Sir Anthony Eden talked about the British-French attacks having been conducted "with the most scrupulous care in order to cause the least possible loss of life." He spoke also of the convoys ap-

ranean would no doubt have been subjected to comparable orders if their intervention had finally proved necessary. The American troops later landed in Lebanon labored under broad restrictions imposed at the highest executive level.

The Concept of Sanctuary and Nuclear Weapons

Another of the ideas that arose out of the Korean War is that of "sanctuary." Each side seems to have practiced certain area restraints which were presumably influenced by considerations other than capability. A conspicuous example was the scrupulous UN avoidance of bombing in the Chinese territory north of the central channel of the Yalu River, despite the existence there, in full view from the air above the river, of bases from which enemy tactical aircraft were operating. This is the sharpest example in that war of deliberate area restraint, exercised despite an unquestioned capability on the part of the side practicing it to pursue a different course. It is also the only clear-cut example.

Some of our commanders in the field, however, were convinced that the Communist neglect to bomb our airfields in South Korea, or U N warships off the peninsula, or the port facilities of Pusan represented comparable restraint. Possibly it did. It is also possible that the North Korean and Chinese Communists did not feel able to bomb U N bases or ships without undue losses to themselves, quite apart from the danger of thereby inciting us to drop our own restraints. However, if we give the adherents of the sanctuary thesis the benefit of each doubt, we acknowledge some impressive instances of sanctuary observance in the Korean experience.

---

proaching the coast "under orders to cause the minimum possible casualties and damage consistent with the safety of our troops." At the latter statement *Hansard* records "Ministerial cheers."

As a result, the concept of sanctuary has played an important part in speculations on limited war as well as in certain war games. We ought therefore to consider how the issues would have been affected if both sides had used nuclear weapons. After all, we spared the Communist bases north of the Yalu largely because the tactical aircraft operating from them were not seriously hurting us. On the contrary, they were mostly presenting targets to our own fighter aircraft and being shot down at a ratio of twelve to fourteen of theirs to one of ours. If, however, those enemy planes had dropped some nuclear weapons on our airfields, would we have continued to observe rigidly the line of the Yalu? And if we had dropped nuclear weapons from aircraft operating from our own South Korean air bases, would those bases have been immune to any nuclear counterattack within the enemy's capability? The answer to either question cannot now be determined, but it is a safe guess that it would in each case be negative.

Although sanctuary is intriguing as an idea, it has little historical backing apart from the old rules applying to "open cities," which required always that those cities not be used for military purposes, and none at all if we are assuming a nuclear war. Limited war of necessity implies the existence of a great sanctuary area in the rear of each major contestant. Keeping the war limited may depend on not using that sanctuary area as a base for attacking the other with nuclear weapons. And it is unlikely that any satellite sanctuary will be respected as a sanctuary if it is used for such attack.

Conclusions on Nuclear Weapons in Limited War

We have no basis for arguing that the use of nuclear weapons in limited wars is clearly mistaken. One must add, however, that it is far from being unequivocally right. It is certainly wrong to conclude they must be used in *all* limited wars except possibly the very smallest. Perhaps they will have to be used in some situations, but one would expect that the situation which required their use would be spelled out in terms that could not be stultified the moment we consider *reciprocal* use. The conclusion that nuclear weapons *must* be used in limited wars has been reached by too many people, too quickly, on the basis of far too little analysis of the problem. Decisions of great moment have stemmed and continue to stem from that conclusion, decisions which work to deprive us of a capability for fighting even a small war without nuclear weapons. Once we are in that position, the original proposition, however mistaken to begin with, appears to be proved right, for the fact that we cannot fight without nuclear weapons argues cogently that we should not attempt to do so.

Because of our complete lack of experience with the problem, we simply do not know whether it would prove both sound and feasible to use nuclear weapons in wars that otherwise have a chance of being kept limited. By "sound" use we mean one where nuclear weapons would work for rather than against realization of the political objectives of the war. By "feasible" we mean, first, that use of nuclear weapons will not make it critically more likely that a limited war will erupt into total war; and second, that the decision whether or not we intervene is not affected adversely by the fact that we are committed to fight with nuclear weapons. If we were so committed, that fact might press us to avoid involvement, that is, to abandon the local issue. The American decision against intervening at the time of the Dien Bien Phu crisis in Indochina in the spring of 1954 seems to have reflected such a dilemma. We can let our thinking be paralyzed by the conception of masses of Soviet divisions, but the only direction in which the major part of the Russian ground forces could be deployed is westward into Europe. In other regions on the periphery of Communist power the terrain and logistic facilities simply would not permit it. Europe is a special case which we shall consider presently.

It is true, no doubt, that the outlook would be very different if we lived in a world in which there was very little incentive on either side, or at least on the Soviet side, for surprise strategic attack. Then we should have much less reason to fear the quick spiraling upward of the level of violence. Some means of controlling that level for the local area would still have to be found, but the problem would nevertheless be of much more moderate dimensions than the one we face now, when the "balance of terror" is far from stable.

The Question of a Separate Capability

A school of thought, mentioned above, holds that our obligations in a limited war occurring anywhere on the globe could be easily handled by dispatching a portion of SAC. This view is naturally congenial to the national Administration because of its money-saving implications. As Sir John Slessor has put it for the United Kingdom: "The dog we keep to deal with the cat will be able to deal with the kittens."

If this view is sound, it can be so only on a basis which permits the forces involved to use large nuclear weapons. Assuming a situation similar to that in Korea in 1950, if American strategic bombers or missiles were permitted to drop thermonuclear weapons on the aggressor's invading ground forces, and if the aggressor did not reply in kind, it would be unnecessary in most cases for the United States to contribute also ground forces to support the native defense forces already in the area. If the aggressor did reply in kind, however, we should probably be most loath to send in our ground forces, but for reasons other than confidence in the sufficiency of our nuclear-bombing intervention. It is curious, incidentally, that many army officers who insist on the primacy of ground forces in limited-war operations apparently want also to use nuclear weapons liberally. The fact is we do not even know yet whether armies can fight in a nuclear environment. One of several major unsolved problems is the likelihood of heavy casualties being suffered simply from the blinding effects of enemy nuclear weapons, especially when used at night. There is no comparable inconsistency among those officers in another service who want to be free to use large nuclear weapons in limited wars but who would also like to avoid the use of ground troops.

Whether or not large ground forces must be provided for limited war operations in addition to those we already support depends partly on the functions for which existing ground forces are planned. If the idea were accepted that ground combat forces *per se* (that is, not counting those absorbed in what are essentially air defense operations, like manning Nike batteries) can have little or no offensive utility in an unrestricted nuclear war, we could reorganize existing American ground forces primarily for the limited-war function. This kind of perception requires the final abandonment of anything resembling the "broken-backed war" philosophy described in an earlier chapter.[13] Ground troops might indeed be useful as occupying forces following a strategic bombing exchange which was overwhelmingly one-sided in our favor, but if such an improbable thing occurred we could reverse Sir John's phrase and say that the

[13] See above, pp. 160-166.

dog we keep to deal with the kittens is quite enough to deal with the nearly dead cat.

On the other hand, if additional combat units of all kinds, together with their supporting facilities, are necessary in order that the United States should have a substantial capability for fighting limited wars on a non-nuclear basis, then they must be provided. How much to provide is a question we cannot settle here, but it is likely to be far more than the term "brushfire" seems to suggest to the people who use it. The Lebanon crisis of 1958 may have been a "brushfire," but the Korean War of 1950-1953 was definitely more than that. It is very likely, in short, that a serious view of the necessity for our being able to fight non-nuclear limited wars would require quite considerable funds beyond those already provided. This proposition reverses the argument usually heard, namely, that because we cannot afford such a fighting capability financially, we must use nuclear weapons.

The question of the economic capacity of the United States to bear a larger defense burden than it already carries will be the subject of the next chapter. For the present it is enough to say that tender concern for what "the economy can stand" is often expressed by persons who have no competence for making such a judgment. Very few if any economists would support the proposition that the United States could not safely spend more than 10 per cent of its gross national product on defense, which is about the going rate at this writing.

One seems to be flying directly in the face of "progress" in arguing for the old and certainly less effective weapon systems over the new and tremendously powerful ones. Yet it is not progress to forget the political objectives towards which any and all military interventions abroad are presumably directed, and the fact that the manner of our intervention may defeat those objectives even if we are for the moment "victorious." Nor is it progress to forget that we no longer have a monopoly of nuclear weapons, and that the enemy's use of them in response to ours may embarrass or defeat us even in a limited war. Above all, it is not progress to forget that the chief problem in any limited war will be, not how to fight it conveniently, perhaps not even to assure ourselves a decisive local victory, but rather how to make sure that it stays limited—more particularly, how to make sure that it does not erupt into that total war which starts disastrously with our receiving the first blow.

There is also the technical argument that decisions have been made—presumably they had to be made—which either have deprived us already or are bound to deprive us soon of the ability to fight effectively without nuclear weapons. For example, ground-to-ground missiles, into which so much development effort has been poured, are too expensive and too inaccurate to permit their being used profitably with anything but nuclear warheads. Such statements are true as far as they go, but they allude to errors of omission rather than of commission. If we are willing to budget for it, we can simultaneously develop a new technology also for non-nuclear war. The same or a similar technology, incidentally, would also be suitable for the family of miniature nuclear weapons, which some regard as the appropriate weapon for limited wars.

It takes only one to start a total war, but it takes two to keep a war limited. All the statements above refer to what the United States should do as long as the decision remains in our hands. An enemy can force us to use nuclear weapons by himself using them, though even then our object might conceivably (though improbably) be to force him to desist from further use of them. But if hostilities open without his using them, our government ought to be prepared to think twice about forcing the pace into the wide-open realm of nuclears. In these matters it is always much easier to shift upward in level of violence than down.

A limited war, especially one fought with non-nuclear weapons, would permit the expansion and mobilization of our industrial war potential in the style of the Korean War. The major question is: How large can a war get and still remain limited? This terribly important question is one to which there is no present way of finding an answer, though we have already reviewed some of the circumstances that will affect the answer. It is obvious that the larger the conflict, the more pressure there must be for abandoning limitations.

The Special Case of Europe

The problem of keeping wars within limited dimensions of destruction looks difficult enough even for the so-called "peripheral areas" in southeast Asia or the Near East. Could a war fought for the defense of western Europe against the Soviet Union be kept limited in any important respect? When the question is put in that way, we think of a war which has the sharp outlines and the magnitude of either of the two world wars. It is difficult at present to imagine our attempting to fight such a war without resort to nuclear weapons tactically, even if strategic bombing could somehow be avoided. It is almost equally difficult to imagine both sides applying to the uses of nuclear weapons such controls as would prevent the complete devastation of the Continent.

Yet Europe has been the cradle of many wars. It is reckless to assume that this important area can be held permanently stable by a simple threat of massive retaliation. Those who insist on its being an "all-or-nothing" area, as did the authors of the British Defence White Paper for 1958, must consider what such insistence could mean at a critical moment in the future. If Europe is to be defended against attack from the Soviet Union, it must be by the joint action of a group of states comparable to the present NATO. The strain on joint action becomes extreme when each member realizes that the action required of it will likely mean a rain on itself of multi-megaton weapons. The United States itself may not forever be willing to incur such a penalty in order to defend the nations of western Europe. It is therefore time we began to think of some alternatives to total war as a means of defending them.[14]

Moreover, it should not be taken for granted that Soviet aggression is likely to come in the form of a clear-cut violation of some clearly established boundary. The diplomatic initiative which resulted in the formation of NATO was provoked by the Soviet rape of Czechoslovakia early in 1948 and by the Berlin blockade which began in the same year. The former action was carried out not by a military invasion but by a nearly bloodless revolution; the latter event, too, after dragging out its long course, was finally resolved with practically no exchange of shots.

Instances of Soviet military violence in Europe since that

[14] George F. Kennan would deal with this problem by de-emphasizing it. He argues: "We must get over this obsession that the Russians are yearning to attack and occupy Western Europe, and that this is the principal danger." He suggests, therefore, that a withdrawal of American, British, and Russian forces from the "heart of the Continent" and reliance in the NATO countries upon paramilitary forces on the Swiss example to prevent communist-inspired *internal* eruption are the best guarantee of their security. See his *Russia, the Atom, and the West*, Harper, New York, 1958, pp. 56-65.

time have been pretty much confined to suppressing the up-rising in East Germany in 1953 and the Hungarian revolt in 1956. For none of these events would the basic NATO military strategy, as it has been publicly described, have had any relevance. If we bear in mind that conflicts in Europe are most likely to arise over issues which are comparably fuzzy, if we want to be effective in those conflicts, and if we wish to be able to take a strong position without precipitating total war, then we ought to be interested in developing a real NATO limited war capability.

The first official break in the NATO "all or nothing" philosophy was signalled by General Lauris Norstad's speech of November 12, 1957 in Cincinnati, Ohio, which bore the title: "NATO: Deterrent and Shield." In this speech General Norstad reiterated the two previously accepted functions of the NATO ground forces—that of providing a trip-wire to signal massive Soviet aggression, and that of resisting the advance of the Soviet Army while the U.S. SAC was doing its work—and he mentioned also a third function, which he described as providing us "with an option more useful than the simple choice between all or nothing." He added: "If . . . we have means to meet less-than-ultimate threats with a decisive, but less-than-ultimate response, the very possession of this ability would discourage the threat, and would thereby provide us with essential political and military manoeuver-ability."[15]

[15] Published in *The New York Times* for November 13, 1957. I am, however, indebted for the passages quoted and for several of the ideas in this and the following sections to my RAND colleague, Dr. Malcolm W. Hoag, whose paper, "The Place of Limited War in NATO Strategy," is scheduled for publication in 1959 by Princeton University Press in a symposium volume entitled *NATO and American Security*, edited by Professor Klaus Knorr. See also Hoag's "NATO: Deterrent or Shield?", *Foreign Affairs*, xxxvi (January 1958), 1-15.

One of the older functions which General Norstad still attributed to NATO ground forces, that of stopping the Soviet Army while our SAC is destroying its home base, is now subject to very grave doubts. It made sense in the early days of NATO because we had at the time too few atomic bombs to carry out a brusquely decisive strategic bombing program, let alone also a ground-force retardation attack of any consequence.[16] However, the NATO powers hardly provided nearly enough troops to carry out that function. With the tremendous thermonuclear capabilities obviously existing on both sides from about 1955 onward, however, the idea that ground operations in Europe could form an important component in a war marked by unrestricted nuclear-strategic attacks between the Soviet Union and the United States became almost preposterous. If the Soviet Union lost such an exchange, its army almost certainly could not move—and actually would have very little purpose in moving.[17] If the

[16] The three classic missions for a strategic bombing campaign have been known as "Bravo," for the blunting or counter-air mission; "Delta," for the attack on the enemy economy; and "Romeo," for the "retardation" of his ground forces through direct attack upon bridges, marshalling yards, and the like. A very powerful strategic attack should make a strong retardation program less necessary; yet if the means existed for the former they would probably be available also for the latter. In the early days of NATO we could carry out neither mission in anything like overwhelming strength.

[17] At the beginning of the NATO era, a popular criticism of the strategy of defending Europe through the threat of the strategic bombing of the Soviet Union was that "the Soviet Army cannot be cornered." One of the ideas behind this criticism was that the Soviet Army by moving westward could take over the intact economy of western Europe and that this would more than recompense the Russians for the destruction of their economy. I criticized this view in my "Strategic Implications of the North Atlantic Pact," *Yale Review*, xxxix (Winter 1950), 193-208. Since that time the development of the Soviet economy has made such an exchange, even if it were feasible, appear a poor one from a Soviet viewpoint; but, more important, the great proliferation of nuclear and thermonuclear

Soviet Union won the exchange, it would be useless and senseless to try to stop the Red Army. Moreover, nothing that could happen as a *result* of ground operations would affect the strategic-nuclear exchange. Whether or not the missile and aircraft bases in western Europe survived the opening phase of a total war would depend not on the Red Army but on Soviet missiles and aircraft. General Norstad's inclusion of this outmoded idea was probably in the main a gesture of deference to a view which his predecessors had advocated and which was therefore still "official."

Concerning the other traditional function, that of providing the trip-wire to signal premeditated Soviet aggression, we have to concede that the activation of such a mechanism could result only from incredible Soviet recklessness or stupidity. If the Soviet leaders feel that there is a fair chance that the United States Government means what it says about defending Europe by massive retaliation, they can reasonably choose one of only two courses. Either they must be dissuaded from an aggression in western Europe sufficiently clear-cut to be identified as such, or they must launch it not by a massive land attack westward but by striking at the United States directly through the air. Presumably, encouragement to the Soviet leaders to choose the former course is what justifies the entire NATO strategy, but we should be clear that this arrangement *presupposes a powerful Soviet reluctance to start World War III even with the benefit of the first strike.* The NATO system does not contribute to that reluctance in any important way; it merely relies upon it. Indeed,

---

weapons guarantees that if the Soviet Union lost the strategic air battle then (1) the Soviet Army could not move, and (2) no important installations which it managed to seize would be permitted to remain intact.

the NATO system actually burdens that reluctance, and may conceivably strain it.

It is true that we have to count on a strong Soviet antipathy against initiating general or total war. Otherwise World War III would become not merely possible but virtually certain, and the only sensible policy for the United States under those circumstances would be not a NATO-type strategy but preventive war. But we must not suppose that the Soviet leaders dislike total war simply because we do. If they dislike it, they do so for reasons of their own which we must continually analyze, measure, and if possible refortify.

General Norstad's announcement of our readiness to consider limited war strategies in Europe symbolizes a certain relaxation in the previously rigid massive retaliation policy. Naturally, it could be construed as betraying a weakening of resolve on our part, but the possibility that the enemy can make propaganda capital out of major changes in our policy should rarely be in itself a sufficient reason for refraining from such changes. As General Norstad pointed out in his speech, the readiness to apply less-than-ultimate responses to less-than-ultimate threats tends to discourage such threats. Thus the element of resolve, far from being impaired thereby, becomes more realistically oriented and therefore more dependable.

If one of the traditional functions for the NATO forces is obsolete and the other can be circumvented, we must conclude that the only operational purpose which they can serve is that of providing the limited-war capability which General Norstad listed as his third and newest function. This conclusion does not touch upon the question whether or not that force should be substantially larger than it is. Obviously it has not yet been organized and trained primarily for its limited-war function. Moreover, the General's excellent statement of the new function is compromised by his explicit identification of that function with the use of nuclear weapons. He made clear that this is what he meant by a "decisive" though limited response.

It is obvious that the handful of NATO divisions in Europe could not stop the whole Soviet Army, or any substantial part of it, without using nuclear weapons. That, however, can hardly be a sufficient reason for using them, because it should be equally obvious that if we did use them in a "limited" war, the Soviets would do likewise. In terms of our ability to stem the tide of the Soviet Army, we would be as badly off as we were before. Moreover, all the difficulties of policing a limited war in which nuclear weapons were used reciprocally would arise in peculiarly acute form in densely populated and militarily sensitive Europe. We have to ask ourselves what chance we would have of keeping a nuclear war in Europe limited for more than a few hours.

What gives a modest number of NATO divisions the chance of coping with the Soviet Army is not their capacity to use nuclear weapons, which the Soviet Army also enjoys, but the fact that a massive intervention of Soviet ground forces is unlikely except with a Soviet decision to wage total war. As we have already indicated, so long as the United States seems to be committed to retaliate massively to such intervention, the Soviets would have to anticipate our reaction by a strategic bombardment of the United States. A limited-war capability in Europe should be considered as having very little to do with that kind of war. It should be concerned rather with border probings and with periodic testings of our readiness to meet force with force, as well as with genuine accidents in the form of unpremeditated local flare-ups. NATO troops in Europe that are openly dedicated to limited-war strategies and functions are likely to have a stabilizing influence precisely because they will tend to discourage the proclivity for probing and testing which is so characteristic of Soviet military diplomacy.

The Question of Missile Bases in Europe

During 1958 the United States government felt it had developed in the THOR a workable intermediate-range ballistic missile (IRBM) to which the JUPITER was a close competitor. Both of these, incidentally, were liquid-fuel weapons, requiring the loading of fuel and liquid oxygen just prior to each firing. These weapons had been offered to, and accepted by, the NATO heads of government during their meeting in Paris in December 1957.

A number of motives were involved. First, no doubt, was the desire to demonstrate that the United States was not badly outdistanced by the Soviet advances in missile technology, dramatically proved by the successes of the first Sputniks. Second, there was the urge to retain or regain the advantage the United States had apparently enjoyed in the use of advanced bases overseas during the era when strategic bombing depended exclusively on manned bombers.

Even after the American nuclear monopoly had begun to wane, the United States SAC, with its operational bases in the United Kingdom, Spain, North Africa, and the western Pacific, had advantages in operations against the Soviet Union which were lacking to the latter nation's air force. Later it became apparent that the advanced American SAC bases were too close to Soviet territory and hence too vulnerable to be used as operating bases. The decision was made to convert them to staging bases and to withdraw most SAC operating bases to the American Zone of the Interior (ZI). As simple refueling installations, the American advanced bases were much less likely to act as death traps to those bombers which used them in their offensive operations, for the aircraft would touch down at them for only short periods. Part of the theory was that other air bases in Europe could also be used for SAC refueling during a campaign, thus multiplying the number of such bases. Meanwhile the Air Force continued to develop air-refueling operations with compatible tankers, with the primary aim of making it unnecessary for bombers to resort to ground refueling until their return journey from targets. Thus no Soviet attack upon the advanced refueling bases could affect the offensive power of SAC's first wartime strike, or rather the effectiveness of each SAC bomber's first wartime sortie.[18]

It is likely that the utility of these advanced bases was overrated, even for refueling purposes, from the time the Soviet Union demonstrated a thermonuclear capability. So long as the Russians had long-range bombers capable of reaching into our ZI at least on one-way missions, which they had even in the TU-4, the advantage to us of possessing a system of advanced bases—or of tankers for aerial refueling—was far overshadowed by the question of who would strike first when war came. If our bombers (and tankers) were destroyed at their operating bases in the ZI, it would avail them little to have refueling bases abroad.

Illusions of ascendancy always die hard, but this one was hastened in its demise by the Russian missile successes, which heralded the impending arrival of a possibly impressive Soviet ICBM capability. ICBMs not only do not need aerial or ground refueling themselves, they can even destroy on

[18] See A. J. Wohlstetter, *loc.cit.*, especially pp. 222f.

the ground the aircraft that do need them, as well as the tankers and the refueling bases. Incidentally, the public agitation early in 1959 concerning the so-called "missile gap" remained persistently focused on secondary issues. We need not and should not have permitted the Russians to outdistance us in this important field, but the question whether we had as many or as good missiles as they was far less vital than the question: was our retaliatory force, whether aircraft or missiles, suitably protected against Soviet missiles?

Anyway the idea of installing IRBMs abroad seemed to promise return of the advantage to us. If we could not expect to have operational ICBMs as early as the Russians, at least we could have operational IRBMs, and we had on the islands of the western Pacific and especially on the territories of our NATO allies the terrain on which to install them. To our allies we could hold out the prestige of having on their own territories and manned by their own armed forces strategic bombardment weapons armed with nuclear warheads. To be sure, United States domestic law still complicated the handing over of nuclear components for warheads, but this problem could be solved through an international arrangement which left the custody of the nuclear warheads nominally in American hands. The arrangement would give at least an ostensible veto to the United States concerning the launching of these weapons, and of course a real veto in the hands of each ally whose armed forces controlled the missiles. Thus, presumably, only by joint positive action between the United States government and the NATO power concerned could a missile be launched offensively, *even on a retaliatory mission.*

When we bear in mind, furthermore, that the missiles themselves were exceedingly vulnerable, that they were proposed to be mounted with little or no protection, that their locations were bound to be well known to the Soviet forces, and that those locations would be within minutes of flying time from Soviet-controlled frontiers not only for missiles but also for Soviet jet aircraft—including small aircraft such as the Russians have by the thousands—it becomes obvious that IRBMs so located, especially if their numbers were moderate, could have no dependable retaliatory value. Under such circumstances, useful radar warning of approaching aircraft would be totally out of the question; in any case there would be no time to prepare and to launch the missiles, even if the requirement for joint approval on the part of two governments could be promptly fulfilled. Getting approval even from a single government might take too much time. On the other hand, to make too easy the business of transmitting authority for launching nuclear-armed missiles is to increase the danger of unauthorized launchings.

What use could the IRBMs then be? The Soviet Union could neither be indifferent to their presence, especially in Germany, nor oblivious to the fact that they had no retaliatory or strike-second capability. Could the Russians be expected to conclude that we, who had gone to all the trouble and expense of mounting them, would also be oblivious of that fact? Actually these missiles were obviously intended to have a strike-first capability according to the old massive-retaliation idea which envisaged vast Soviet armies striking across the frontiers, presumably without any preparatory attack through the air against our nuclear-armed aircraft and missiles. *If* such a thing happened, the missiles would be there to strike their retaliatory or retarding blows in due course. Presumably, they do serve also as a strike-first or massive-retaliation capability for aggressions occurring elsewhere than in Europe. A strike-first capability is certainly worth something even if it is only that. If backed by invulnerable retaliatory force, it is worth a good deal more. But in each instance one has to consider just what one is getting and what one is paying for it.

No doubt the missiles were to serve still another purpose, one often mentioned as a reason for providing "trip-wire" ground forces of substantial size: the purpose of forcing the Russians to make their aggressions big rather than little. As the official argument usually ran, large bodies of defensive troops would force the Russians to make their aggressions big enough to be unequivocal. Just why it is desirable to force all aggressions into the unequivocal range is not clear, except on the presumption that we have no way of coping with them save by massive retaliation and that it is preferable to have the Soviets clearly start the war than to let them place upon us the onus of having started it.[19]

This urge to mount IRBMs in Europe demonstrates anew how difficult it is for officials to relinquish the massive retaliation idea, however much they may seem to disavow it through the apparent acceptance of limited war ideas and strategies. It is painful to give up the hope that the "all-or-nothing" posture will cow the opponent into utter quies-

[19] General Lauris Norstad, in a speech delivered at the end of January 1957, said: "On the other hand, if our line is being held in reasonable strength, and if the enemy knows this beyond doubt, then any inclination on his part to cross the line makes him face the terrible decision of detonating World War III, with a sure prospect of his own annihilation. The defensive forces deployed on our eastern boundary thus become an essential part of the deterrent." Quoted by Malcolm W. Hoag in "NATO: Deterrent or Shield" and derived from *The NATO Letter*, February 1, 1957, p. 29. One has to add that only if the Soviets start the war in the way suggested by General Norstad is there "a sure prospect of his own annihilation."

cence, even when we have almost daily demonstrations (including, at the beginning of 1959, threats of a renewed Berlin blockade) of the fact that it does nothing of the kind. Also, we hear repeated expression of the idea that *if* the enemy starts the war, he will do it in the one way that enables us to annihilate him. This is only one of the many instances where we have let our fantasies dwell exclusively on "American-preferred Soviet strategies."

If they are mounted on the territories of the continental NATO powers, IRBMs could well make much more difficult the maintenance of limitations on whatever local conflicts break out. With their relative inaccuracy and their consequent need to be armed with thermonuclear warheads, they are hardly weapons for limited war. Moreover, in any kind of hostilities occurring in the area in which they existed, they would certainly be tempting as targets to the Soviet Union. If they were to be installed in far greater numbers than any existing program calls for, and thoroughly and massively shielded in underground shelters proof against all but near-hits with thermonuclear weapons, they might have a retaliatory as well as a strike-first capability. Ideas about giving them protection by moving them about on the highway network of Europe overlook the security problem within those confined areas, the oppressiveness of such a spectacle to the peoples of western Europe, and the fact that in any above-ground positioning these missiles can be destroyed by nuclear weapons exploding at distances of several miles. The enemy, in other words, would have to know only their approximate location, which his intelligence network operating in what is presumably peacetime could easily deliver to him.

There remains the consideration that giving each NATO

nation a more independent power of retaliation tends to off-set the decline in the credibility of American use of SAC for the defense of that nation. From one point of view it reduces the burden on American obligations, which is presumably a good thing. However, one also has to consider the credibility of such a threat from a small power, especially if that power feels it has been given the weapons chiefly in order that it should stand alone. The knowledge that their few missiles—unlike the large American capability—can have only a punitive effect and not a strategic one, and that this punishment can be administered only at the cost of the utter destruction of their own nation will have a powerfully inhibiting effect on most statesmen. It is also true, on the other hand, that small states are sometimes led by very aggressive men. One therefore also has to take into account the dangers in multiplying the number of autonomous decision-makers who have it within their power to start a general thermonuclear war.[20]

The Influence of Limited War on the Probability of Total War

Since the first stirrings of limited-war thinking in the early 'fifties, the proponents of what we now call massive retaliation have raised the objection, among others, that willingness to limit response to any aggression must tend to encourage that aggression. This objection was easier to make while we still enjoyed an obvious nuclear and strategic-bomber superiority than it became later. Nevertheless, there remains an important element of truth in it. The threat of total retaliation would obviously have a more discouraging

[20] At the beginning of 1959, the only American IRBMs actually situated in Europe were in the United Kingdom.

effect on limited aggression *if* we could make the threat in a way that carried conviction.

It is also true that Soviet aggression in some areas could not be effectively countered by a response limited to the locality of the aggression. This proposition may stand regardless of whether or not we use nuclear weapons tactically, because, as we have already suggested, a *mutual* use does not necessarily advantage us. The point is simply that some areas which the Communists might attack are a good deal more accessible to their forces than to our own. There are basically two ways of responding to a problem of this sort, with some variations on the basic themes. One is to apply with determination the threat of massive retaliation to protect those areas; the other is quietly to decide that we cannot protect them by arms.

The danger that limited wars may develop explosively into total wars leads one to consider whether the net effect of readiness to adopt limited war strategies is to increase the probability of total war. This is a question that we can treat only speculatively, but it is extremely important that we do so as best we can. The relevant policy decisions cannot and do not wait.

Most of those who were or remain protagonists of the massive-retaliation doctrine have taken that position not because they preferred big wars to little ones but because they have been convinced that such a policy minimizes the danger of *any* war. It makes sense, they imply, to threaten a possibly suicidal reaction to aggression as long as the chance of aggression is thereby reduced almost to zero. If we accept this argument at face value, we must still be concerned with the degree to which the low probability of war credited to this policy falls short of being zero. The probability of war does not have to be high to impel us to hunt for alternatives to *total* war. We might be willing to accept a much higher probability of wars breaking out if we could confidently expect to keep them limited.

Our problem of choice is easier, however, if we are persuaded that the massive-retaliation policy does not in fact minimize the probability of small wars. We have already considered one major weakness of that policy: its conspicuous lack of credibility. It may indeed be even less credible than it deserves to be. The very act of aggression may trigger emotions in us (including our government leaders) which we ourselves could not have predicted before the event. The Communist attack that started the Korean War had that effect. Sometimes the emotional reaction which we can predict quite well in ourselves is not sufficiently taken into account by the potential aggressors, who may entertain peculiar ideas about us. The decision of the Japanese war lords to attack us at Pearl Harbor was just such an error, for we know that they miscalculated not our ultimate strength, which in fact they projected more accurately than we did, but our resolution to continue the war despite initial defeats.[21]

Such instances of miscalculation suggest one important way in which a massive-retaliation policy may fail to avert war. Another way, considered above, is the case where the potential aggressor disbelieves our general threat and is quite right in doing so; not because our leaders were deliberately bluffing at the time the policy was enunciated but rather because they failed at the time to think it through sufficiently to predict their own or their successors' response under crisis, or perhaps because they did not weigh sufficiently the speed

[21] See Roberta Wohlstetter, *Signals and Decisions at Pearl Harbor*, a RAND Corporation study, to be published.

and direction of changes in the world situation resulting from current developments in arms technology.

One must anticipate on the part of many students of history and of contemporary affairs an attitude of disbelief in such "irresponsibility," particularly where matters of diplomacy and strategy are concerned. There are those, of course, who find it temperamentally congenial to exaggerate incompetence in high places. Their chiding remarks divert attention from the fact that most serious students, on the contrary, implicitly attribute to leaders of government, past and present, an abiding rationality and a dedication to logical, penetrating, farsighted thinking. They do so even when they are describing what should be evidence to the contrary, for they usually seem to regard the relevant events as exceptional. As an example one need only point to the "revisionist" school of American historians, who have dominated American historiography for over a generation and who persist in attributing the outbreak of the American Civil War to a special and presumably exceptional degree of irrationality, emotionalism, and perversity on both sides.

Many colossal and persisting errors of judgment, on the contrary, become explicable only when we realize, against an almost instinctual craving to assure ourselves of the opposite, that high officials in all governments usually struggle under a normal load of human limitations in ability and propensity to think through difficult problems. Even the most able and dedicated find ready-made maxims a great convenience, and they certainly are not often inclined to be dispassionate about the baffling strategic and diplomatic problems with which they are seized or the "solutions" they bring to them. Over the long term a policy of deterrence threatens to founder on the fact that too few people are sufficiently

NEW PROBLEMS AND NEW APPROACHES

rational or sufficiently wise, with respect to either diplomacy or strategy, to make it work.

To return to our problem: the threat of massive retaliation becomes more credible when it is applied *ad hoc* for the purposes of a specific situation. This is the characteristic that gives an ultimatum its force and, usually, its credibility; but an ultimatum is by definition applied only after a crisis has already developed. The object, ideally, is to adopt a firm position before an open crisis has developed, but not so long before as to obscure the pertinence of the threat. The requirements, obviously, are for good intelligence, alertness on the part of the decision-makers, and, especially in this nuclear world, a mighty resolve.

It is customary to blame most policy failures on weaknesses in intelligence, but actually the deficiencies are generally to be found in the alertness and resolution of the leaders. The difference between real and fake determination is difficult to conceal. No one is deceived, for example, about the nerve behind a threat, however blatant and pointed, which is accompanied by public assurances to all the world that the opponent will not dare move in the face of it and that there is therefore no danger of war. If these things be true, the threat is innocuous. The threatener seems to be concerned mostly with assuring himself that he is not living dangerously.

Yet no one wants to applaud resolution in pursuit of an unwise policy. Military people are fond of the maxim, "any decision is better than none," which is a rather exaggerated commendation for decisiveness even in strategy, let alone diplomacy.[22] And as Malcolm Hoag has observed, in con-

[22] If Admiral Halsey had not been so decisive at Leyte Gulf, if he had delayed by ten hours his decision to throw himself against Ozawa to the

nection with a possible diplomatic impasse involving a threat of total war: "That there would be mutual gain in both backing down is by no means a sufficient condition for realizing such gain."

Now we turn to that advocacy of greater caution implied in the arguments for limited war. We have seen that the proponent of limited war denies the allegation of his massive-retaliation opponent that the latter's policy minimizes the probability of *any* war. He adds that, in any case, minimization is not enough. Considering what total war would be like in a thermonuclear age, especially in view of the chances that we would strike second rather than first, any probability for total war which is appreciably above zero is too much. He therefore seeks to limit those wars which he considers the most likely to break out anyway and which he feels his strategy has a decidedly better chance of preventing.

He could point out also that as long as there is a danger, sufficiently recognized on both sides, that limited wars could erupt into total wars, he is not to any important degree encouraging aggression by offering to limit war. On the contrary, as long as his policy makes for a greater readiness on the part of the United States to intervene in local aggressions, the recognition of the ultimate dangers should give more pause to the potential aggressor. This point, however, is generally overlooked, perhaps because the usual advocate of limited war is too often sure that wars can be kept limited with relative ease.

---

north, he would have been in exactly the right place on the following morning to destroy the main Japanese force. In any case, it would have been the *right decision* to stay there. Shakespeare, incidentally, presents a contrast between Othello, the soldier, who is decisive enough, and Hamlet, the scholar, who is not; but there is after all little choice between them in who makes the worse mess of things.

It is in this attitude that our greatest danger unquestionably lies. The certainty that total war has now been "abolished," as Professor P. M. S. Blackett puts it, by the existence of thermonuclear weapons is totally unwarranted.[23] This attitude invites the worst of both worlds, because it increases readiness to intervene against minor aggression at the same time that it encourages a manner of doing so which is most likely to cause the conflict to erupt into total war.

We have to remind ourselves again of the great military advantage of striking first in a total war, or at least of not having our retaliatory craft caught motionless and exposed when the enemy strikes. Air Force officers are quite right in being preoccupied with this point. In peacetime they will continue to make all the preparations which they deem necessary, and which a sympathetic civil leadership will permit, to increase the speed and sensitivity of the trigger-action which sends the retaliatory force on its way. Increasing speed and sensitivity of response is one way to enhance the safety of that force; it is the most obvious way, as well as the one most congenial to military doctrine.

What will be the suitable provocation for the triggering of this force? The phrase suggests different things to different people, but its minimum meaning for many intelligent as well as politically important people is for some time going to include more than simply direct attack upon ourselves. The special character of Europe has been noted. Though it is possible to conceive of alternatives to massive retaliation as the primary means of defending Europe, the alternatives re-

[23] P. M. S. Blackett, *Atomic Weapons and East-West Relations*, Cambridge University Press, London, 1956, p. 5. Sir John Slessor also takes the position that "major all-out war has abolished itself with the advent of nuclear weapons" in "A New Look at Strategy for the West," *Orbus*, II (Fall 1958), p. 320.

main for the most part abstract and ill-defined ideas. At any rate, we are geared to an almost automatic response in the event of a Soviet attack upon western Europe, and there has thus far been no important move to unwind this taut spring. Our posture reflects the conclusion that it is not altogether necessary for the value of a threat that its execution should represent reasonable action.

Any outbreak of hostilities which involves or threatens to involve members of the communist world against members of the non-communist world will have the feel of a crisis situation. It will intensify anxieties about being "caught on the ground" and increase sensitivity to alarms, false and otherwise. Even in a limited war, nuclear bombs may start to fall. General anxiety will be sharpened into fear, which will stimulate the urge to get the strategic air force under way. How resistant to that fear is the President, the one man who can give the appropriate orders? SAC may be given orders to get under way, simply as a precautionary measure, subject to recall. The other side, watching as intently as ourselves, may then spring to action.

However, it is not only the "accidental" outbreak of war that we have to fear. Presumably we have made our decision against preventive war. How about the Russians? If the Soviet leaders should ever decide that by a surprise attack they could confidently count on destroying our strategic retaliatory force, whose very purpose it is constantly to threaten their existence, would it not be their duty as good Bolsheviks to launch that attack?[24] And far from preventing them from

[24] The allusion is to Nathan Leites's thesis concerning the moral imperatives that impel a Bolshevik to exploit to the fullest whatever opportunities come his way. See his *A Study of Bolshevism*, The Free Press, Glencoe, Ill., 1953, pp. 30-34, 442-449, 505-512; also his *The Operational Code of the Politburo*, McGraw-Hill, New York, 1950, especially chs. 16 and 17.

forming such an opinion, *the existence of nuclear weapons is the chief stimulus to their entertaining the idea.*

To repeat: things can be done by us which will make our forces much less vulnerable to enemy attack, and therefore less tempting to the Soviets as targets and less cause to us for anxiety. Perhaps in the normal course of events, with the development of supplementary retaliatory forces that are designed to be relatively safe (e.g., ICBMs in underground shelters and submarines armed with missiles), this problem will take care of itself. But we cannot take for granted that the trend will inevitably be towards greater safety, or if it is, that it will move quickly enough and go sufficiently far. Anyway, there is an interim period when we will not have this capability.

It is precisely *because* the chance for total war is finite and real that we must think earnestly about limited war. There would be less insistence upon using nuclear weapons if it were widely felt that their use would enhance an already too-considerable chance for total war. Similarly, there would be less objection to using them if that chance were truly infinitesimal.

There are in fact two mutually incompatible arguments each of which tends, if accepted, to make the limitations of war extremely difficult, if not impossible. First is the argument, still frequently uttered by important decision-makers, that limited wars will inevitably develop into total ones. There is also the contrary argument that total war has now been abolished and that our relevant energies, ideas, and above all resources have now been freed for a fuller adjustment to limited war. The latter idea tends to be the vice of intellectuals, and the former that of "practical men."

Obviously the former idea favors a dangerous degree of sensitivity in the trigger-action for total war. The latter idea is, however, even more dangerous, for on the one hand it encourages a neglect of the basic precautions enjoined by the danger of total war, and on the other a recklessness about the handling of limited wars that will make it more likely they will erupt into unlimited ones.

⤙10⤚

STRATEGY WEARS A DOLLAR SIGN

THERE is a legend that we Americans have always entered our wars unprepared. It may be true, though it is hard to test the proposition in the absence of a standard that commends itself as logical and objective. It was foolish to enter the War of 1812 against the world's greatest naval power with only a handful of frigates, but it would not have been much wiser to do so with two or three times that force. It is the one war of our history we did not win, that is, the one war in which our strategic position at the end was clearly worse than at the beginning and in which our avowed war objectives received no explicit gratification from the opponent. Even so, the advance in our national fortunes was hardly interrupted by the affair.

It would have been difficult to be better prepared for the Civil War without giving the Confederates a share in the advantages and thus nullifying them. The wars against Mexico in 1846-1847 and against Spain in 1898 we won quite handily. Neither did we do at all badly in the two world wars. It is true we never got an American-designed airplane to the front in World War I, but we got plenty of other American commodities there as well as men. And if we failed to do as well as we might have in the Korean War, it can hardly be attributed to our deficiencies in preparedness. All we can say is that our military expenditures in the years before each conflict rarely reflected the high expectation of war which our hindsight leads us to consider appropriate.

From the beginning of our national history until the eve of World War II, we paid very little in peacetime for our security, but that is simply because we were not obliged to pay more. With what we spent, however ridiculously low some of the figures now look, we were able to buy well-nigh absolute security from foreign aggression against our continental shores. It did require considerable effort to win the two wars against great powers which we fought in the twentieth century, but who can say what kind or how much pre-hostilities preparedness would have made the task much easier? The warships we were building at the time of Pearl Harbor might have been started somewhat earlier, but let us take credit for the fact that we did have a colossal fleet on the building ways! By the time the new ships and all the other new forces began to make themselves felt in the Pacific, the Japanese had hurt our pride and caused us casualties but had actually done us as a nation relatively little harm.

As a result of this history we have developed certain national habits, most of them reflecting an ingrained optimism in our approaches to problems of national security. The size of the American peacetime military budget today suggests that these habits are not unshakable, that they do tend to adjust to changing circumstances; yet it is hard to visualize how drastically the relevant circumstances have changed. Today we are spending far more on security than we have ever spent before in peacetime, but we are fated to remain far less secure. Moreover, insecurity today means something much more terrible and much more nearly absolute than it meant before 1945 even to those countries that thought they knew insecurity.

We do not have and probably never will have enough

money to buy all the things we could effectively use for our defense. The choices we have to make would be difficult and painful even if our military budget were twice what it is today. The fact that we are dealing with a lesser sum only makes the choices harder and more painful.

How can we know these statements are true? Reflection will suggest that they inevitably follow from some of the propositions we have attempted to establish in previous chapters of this book, especially the following ones: (a) because of the scale and speed of destruction possible with nuclear weapons, a general war of the future will be fought and decided exclusively with forces in being; (b) the problem of defense against strategic bombardment presents seemingly insuperable difficulties, and the resources that could legitimately be absorbed in it are limitless; (c) the probability of general war for any given time period is essentially unmeasurable, but is surely more than trivial; and (d) limited wars, which appear even more probable, appear to require independent capabilities.

The fact that a general war will be fought and swiftly decided with forces in being at the outset indicates that most the important strategic decisions concerning that war must be made in the preceding period of peace. This is a sufficiently frightening thought when we consider the poor record for predictions of impending wars, including those embodied in war plans, and even more frightening when we consider how novel and strange are the technological conditions we are dealing with today. But frightening or not, that is the way it has to be. We know, at any rate, that while wisdom may fail in other respects as well, a possible yielding to parsimony presents additional perils.

Limited Budgets and Unlimited Weapons Choices

Strategy in peacetime is expressed largely in choices among weapons systems, which of course are not bought ready-made off the shelf but developed selectively by a process which itself involves heavy costs and many pitfalls. In making choices among weapons systems and related systems, like radar-warning networks, the military budget is always the major and omnipresent constraint. Thus in a book on strategy we are inevitably concerned with (a) how the size of the national defense budget is determined, and (b) what sorts of considerations determine choices within the limits set by the budget. Although in former times it may have been legitimate to neglect these questions in strategic discourse, in our era it is clearly no longer so.

It is interesting to note that the concepts of strategy have always been remarkably akin to those of economics. Both strategy and economics are concerned with the most efficient use of limited resources to achieve certain ends set by society. Most of the so-called principles of war can be stated in the form of propositions which would be familiar to economists, and the effort of doing so would probably result in more precision and insight concerning military problems. Certainly problems of force allocation have to be solved according to some kind of intuitive comprehension of marginal utility theory.[1]

These, however, are considerations which have relatively

---

[1] See my "Strategy as a Science," *World Politics,* I (July 1949), 467-488. Referring also to that article, Dr. Malcolm W. Hoag has developed the relevant ideas very much further, with great analytical skill and elegance. His article, which should be read in connection with this chapter, is entitled: "Some Complexities in Military Planning," *World Politics,* XI, No. 4, July 1959, pp. 553-576.

little to do with money. For the present we are interested in money and its place in national security policy. We want to know how it is provided and how it is spent for military purposes. We want to have some feeling for what kinds of actions and preparations are feasible and what kinds are wholly out of the question. We also want to have some inkling of what is involved in choosing among weapons systems.

The Requirements Approach

Much of the discussion of military needs in Washington, especially during hearings before Congressional Committees, implies the existence of certain fixed requirements for our security which a good security policy meets and a poor one fails to meet. Such fixed requirements are almost invariably arbitrary. Congress has always demanded of the military that they state their requirements in fixed terms, and the military have put themselves to great trouble to oblige. Often an almost religious attitude has developed around certain figures.

Congressmen will ask officers sitting before them questions like: "Have your over-all needs been met?" or, more pointedly, "Do you think this budget guarantees our security?" For their part the military will make statements like this one, uttered by a distinguished senior officer: "National security is a condition which cannot be qualified. We shall either be secure, or we shall be insecure. We cannot have partial security. If we are only half secure, we are not secure at all. We cannot lock the front door and leave the back door ajar."[2] Statements of this sort are usually appended to

[2] This quotation, from a statement by General Jacob L. Devers, is several years old, but it is a dramatic expression of a point of view which still persists, and which will no doubt continue to persist so long as a precise

the presentation of certain magic figures for air wings, ships, or divisions. Perhaps in an era when a modest expenditure could make us quite secure at home, it made some sense to talk about the requirements that would bring such security, though the precision that could be brought to the task was always much exaggerated. Today, however, the requirements approach has lost whatever justification it ever possessed.

There are, to be sure, contingent requirements that are fairly fixed. To man a given number of bomber wings or of warships, for example, requires a reasonably fixed number of men. One can make some adjustments up or down, but beyond certain proportions of manpower to machines, efficiency falls off. We know also that a radar warning line makes little sense unless it is fairly complete, that is, has no large gaps in it, and that a line of given length (determined largely by geography) requires a relatively fixed number of stations in it. But whether it pays to build a particular line, as for example the Distant Early Warning or DEW line, in view of its considerable construction and maintenance costs, its limitations of performance, the existence of other radar lines, and above all the innumerable other demands for defense expenditures, is something that is not at all easy to determine.

Moreover, a radar line is quite distinctive and exceptional in its requirement for a fixed number of installations. By contrast, the fact that we need a force of long-range bombers does not tell us how many or what kind of bombers we ought to have in that force, or what ought to be their performance

---

answer, however arbitrary, conveys more psychological assurance than an imprecise one. For a fuller discussion of the requirements approach, see my *National Security Policy and Economic Stability*, Memorandum No. 33, Yale Institute of International Studies, January 2, 1950.

characteristics. These are only the beginning of the kinds of questions we have to ask and in some way answer concerning that bomber force. As long-range missiles develop, the whole conception of maintaining a bomber force along with the missile force will come under constant review: the problem of proportioning one to the other will be added to existing problems of like nature.

Because our security needs are essentially limitless while our resources are definitely limited, the categories of items which go to make up our national military establishment inevitably compete intensely with one another for funds. Moreover, this competition has to proceed in the marked absence of any clear, generally accepted guideposts for determining the apportionment of funds.

Two Kinds of Dollar Consciousness

One sometimes hears criticisms to the effect that the current administration, whichever one happens to be in power, is too concerned with dollars in making decisions on weapons systems and on other matters pertaining to national security. Such criticisms can refer to one or both of two different issues. If applied to one of these issues the criticism is simply nonsense; if applied to the other it could be warranted, but it may not be easy to determine whether or not it is so. It could be warranted if the assertion is intended to mean that the administration is not spending enough *over-all* on the military services. However, if the criticism is intended to imply that there is too much concern with dollars in the apportionment of resources, and often it seems to have that character, then it is nonsense. The absence of a deep and constant concern with dollars in making choices between weapons systems would argue the grossest kind of incompetence.

Let us take up first the question of the appropriate dimensions of the over-all military budget, usually asked in terms like: How much is enough? or, How much can we afford? Then we shall take up the problem of making choices of weapons systems within the over-all budget that has been set by the government. These two categories of questions are not, of course, conceptually independent of each other, but in practice the establishment of the budget ceiling is sufficiently detached from an objective consideration of military needs to warrant our proceeding in this manner.

How Much Can We Afford for Defense?

Are we spending enough? Or too much? And how do we properly measure these things? If it is true that we cannot hope to buy absolute security and that the best we can hope to do is lessen our insecurity, then the limit on our expenditures has to be determined by considerations other than the fear of running into redundancy in our over-all military power.

We could obviously spend a good deal of money and yet increase our security only marginally, but at a time when we have scarcely begun to do anything serious in the field of passive defense, whether for the civil population or even for our retaliatory force, and seem to be lagging in the missile race, it is clear that there are good uses for more defense funds. We are still very much in the area where additional appropriations could bring us important and perhaps critical increases in our security.

The question of how much is enough is naturally influenced, if not determined, by considerations of how much we can afford. The Eisenhower Administration has repeatedly expressed anxieties about overspending by the national government. These anxieties have been publicly focused on defense expenditures and have resulted in the imposition of fairly tight and arbitrary budget ceilings. From $53 billion in the last year of the Korean War, the defense budget fell to $42 billion in fiscal years 1955 and 1956. In the summer of 1957 the Defense Department adopted drastic curtailment measures in order to force down military outlays to a level of $38 billion for fiscal year 1958. The shock of the Soviet satellites, however, caused some relaxation during 1958, especially in research and development (R & D) expenditures. The reduction following 1953 was much greater than could be reasonably attributed to a liquidation of the Korean War, and in view of rising prices it involved a greater real contraction than the dollar values indicate.

President Eisenhower's anxiety about military spending was certainly not a matter of political expediency. As Chief of Staff of the United States Army in the years following World War II, he repeatedly urged his military brethren—in his lectures before the war colleges, for example—to have an abiding concern for what "the economy can stand." This was at a time when President Truman was attempting to impose a ceiling of some $15 billion (later $13 billion) on the defense budget, an aim with which his Army Chief of Staff entirely sympathized. The latter's successor as Chief of Staff, General Omar N. Bradley, for years preached a similar gospel of strength, not through arms but through economic well-being. Such an attitude is not as rare among soldiers as the layman might think. A general does not always think exclusively as a general might be expected to, one reason being that he is a man with a distinctive personal history as well as being a general.

It should be said that General Bradley, in articles written

after his retirement, expressed regret that he had so often "viewed with alarm" the military strains upon the economy. His reformed thoughts were that he really had no competence to judge when the economy was being unduly strained, and anyway he had referred to questions which were not his primary business as a soldier.

It is obviously true that national military security over the long term requires a healthy economy, for the economy must carry the burden. Anything that slows its growth in capacity to produce or that weakens its resilience detracts from the defense burden which it can carry in the future. But what do we mean by a healthy economy?

Under American conditions, with their relative freedom from balance-of-payments problems, we might identify a healthy and a growing economy by the following general characteristics: (a) a reasonable proportion of the annual gross national product (GNP) is being reinvested in new production capital, replacing outworn and outmoded machinery for improving efficiency as well as expanding the scale of production; (b) the growing population is enjoying at least a stable and preferably a visibly rising standard of living, which of course is measured by per capita consumption; (c) the general price level is relatively stable (which nowadays usually means inching upwards, but not galloping); and (d) there is no excessive burden of unemployment. Some would add that there should be as few government controls on the economy as possible, and certainly far fewer than those we admit in wartime. What is most wrong with controls, besides their being a nuisance and requiring some cost to maintain, is that they tend to conceal and protect distortions in the demand and supply structure which might otherwise be corrected by price adjustments.

What about the national debt, which so many congress-men and senators have exercised themselves about so tire-lessly and which they have sought to control by arbitrary limits written into law? We need only quote a paragraph by one of the nation's most respected economists:

Imagine a rich country, with an annual national income over 400 billion dollars a year, in debt to foreign countries to the tune of 275 billion dollars, paying eight billion dollars a year interest to its external creditors. A debt of this size would be no calamity. The interest burden would be well within the nation's capacity to pay, and there would be no reason for the country to cripple itself in time of need by an arbitrary self-imposed debt limit. But at least there would be some real burden, and it would be prudent for those who manage the nation's economic affairs to give thought to its external debt. The United States has no such debt; indeed we are a net creditor of the rest of the world. Senator Byrd's ordinance of self-denial applies to an internal debt. The people of the United States are both debtor and creditor. The eight billion dollars a year in interest is not a diversion of our production to foreigners. It is paid by us as taxpayers to us as bondholders (either directly or to banks, insurance companies, pension funds, and other institutions that invest our savings in government bonds). Since the debt is, so to speak, within the family, its size can and should be the servant of public policy, not the master. Congress can in any case control the size of the debt by budget-ing for surpluses or deficits as the occasion demands; the debt limit is quite superfluous, except for inhibiting the Treasury's ability to deal with seasonal variation in its disbursements and revenues. The debt limit represents a misdirected collective resolu-tion to be good; its unchallenged appeal can only be based on semantic confusion. Under the debt limit, Uncle Sam fights with one hand tied behind his back, a handicap imposed neither by any necessity of nature nor any wile of his enemy, but by himself.[3]

[3] James Tobin, "Dollars, Defense, and Doctrines," *Yale Review*, XLVII (Spring 1958), pp. 321-334.

For a country like the United States military spending would have a serious adverse effect on the economy only if it seriously cut into investment for the civilian economy or caused an inflation rapid enough to have self-intensifying effects. It would in addition be a marked *political* (rather than economic) liability if the standard of living were to decline or even remain level. The kind of mobilization we had in World War II, when some 40 per cent of GNP was going into the military effort, had marked effects in all these characteristics. But when we are talking about spending something under 15 per cent of GNP on over-all security needs, we can rule out, except through gross mishandling of the pertinent problems, any markedly adverse effects on the usual rate of business reinvestment for the civilian economy. On the contrary, at such levels it is quite possible for it to have a stimulating effect, as it did in the Korean War.

The problem of rising defense expenditures has to do mostly with effects on personal consumption and on inflation, and both concern basically the problem of taxation. When people pay taxes they see themselves relinquishing a certain amount of anticipated consumption. This is painful to them even when their scale of consumption is nevertheless continuing to rise; it becomes excruciating when the taxes are large enough to depress the scale of consumption below previous levels, unless the excitement of a war and the promise of alleviation in the near future beguiles a people from their real or fancied deprivations. It is clear that taxation affects people's behavior as well as their attitudes, and one theory emphasizes the depressing effects of taxation on people's incentives to produce. Because governments, especially democratic ones, feel they have to be very tender with people's feelings about money incomes and consumption levels, they are loath to raise taxes. Generally those in power find themselves competing with their political opponents in promising ultimate reductions in tax rates.

Herein lies the rub. An increase in government spending that is not covered by a rise in taxation rates is likely to mean deficit financing, which, if the margin of deficit is wide enough, tends to foster price inflation. Significant price inflation may bring about the contraction in levels of personal consumption needed to make more resources available for military purposes, but if it is steep enough it makes people even angrier and more bewildered than a sharp tax increase, and it also results in great inequity and waste. A fast rise in prices also makes people want to buy things in anticipation of further rises, which further aggravates the inflation by increasing demand.

In the United States the GNP has been increasing at a rate which if considered over eight- or ten-year periods looks fairly rapid, averaging perhaps 3½ per cent per year at constant prices. Unfortunately, however, this rise is not at all steady. Since the Korean War the economy has shown a really marked advance only in 1955, when the GNP rose by 8 per cent, but in the three following years the average annual rise, in constant prices, was only about 1 per cent. Naturally, the reasons to which these retardations in growth are attributed vary with the speaker's political philosophy or economic school of thought. They may in the net be costly, because losses in production are often not made up. One theory holds that a relatively steady rate of growth greater than that averaged over the past few years is surely achievable, provided the government follows policies which avoid being deflationary.

It is pleasant to fantasy rising rates of military expenditure being amply covered by a steadily rising government income which is roughly proportional to the rise in national income. This could be achieved without raising tax rates and without retarding improvements in other services of government. Unfortunately, as things actually work out, a year of budget surplus brings pressure to reduce taxes, and a shift downward in the level of business activity makes the next year one of deficit. Then the pressure is on again to reduce national government expenditures, of which those for military purposes now comprise the major portion. Also, an administration preoccupied by absolute figures and anxious about their size finds it difficult to remind itself that ours is an expanding economy.

The considerable decline in defense expenditures over the years 1953-1958, inclusive, probably had something important to do with causing the relative stagnation of the economy. Certainly this decline did not reflect the 10 to 11 per cent rise in GNP that nevertheless took place. At the end of that time Soviet missile successes forced a speeding up of missile research and enlarged spending for SAC bases, but offsetting these increases was a retardation of the modernization of planes and further curtailment of the forces available for limited war—in other words, a continuing diminution in important segments of our military strength.

However, even if the defense budget were permitted over time to go up in some degree of correspondence to the real or even the potential rise in GNP, that might not be enough. We must ask whether there is anything sacred in a proportion of about 10 per cent of the GNP, which in recent years has marked expenditures on all national security programs, including expenditures on atomic energy, strategic stockpiling, and foreign military aid programs for mutual security.

Specifically, since we want to keep inflationary pressures under control, we have to ask whether the tax rates on business and individuals could be appreciably increased without harm to the economy.

There are few professional economists in the country who do not feel they could be. In theory, a rise in individual tax rates can have a discouraging effect on personal productivity by lessening the rewards of working. By the same token, however, they may stimulate productivity by making people less able to afford the luxury of not working. It has so far proved impossible in practice to demonstrate whether the discouraging or the incentive effect predominates, for the great majority of people, at the taxation levels the United States has known over the past several years, or even at the much higher levels which the United Kingdom has known.

We know from experience that the tax structure can be badly designed and that it can stimulate both a good deal of waste in the form of unnecessary expenditures and much corruption in the form of institutionalized, large-scale tax evasion. The tax system we have been living with is also unduly burdensome on business saving and on risk-taking incentive for capital investment. The present tax structure probably retards the growth of our economy below the rate that it might otherwise achieve, and thereby increases the relative burden of military expenditures compared with an ideal tax system. But to say that the tax structure should be reformed is not to say that the tax burden needs to be reduced or even kept to present levels. A rise in the tax burden could be coordinated with a reform in the rate schedule to strengthen the incentive effects of taxes on production and to minimize the discouraging effects. Such a reform would be feasible if handed to technical experts, for the hurdles though considerable are almost entirely political.

The following estimate by some American economists writing in 1958 under the auspices of the Committee for Economic Development speaks for itself:

We see no need to be apprehensive about whether or not the American economy can stand the strain of this [1959] or even a considerably larger budget. The risk that defense spending of from 10 to 15 per cent of the gross national product, or if necessary even more, will ruin the American way of life is slight indeed. It is even less likely that there is some magic number for defense expenditures that, if exceeded, would bring economic disaster; rather, the impairment of growth caused by increasing taxes is a gradually rising one. We have not reached a point at which anxiety over the healthy functioning of the economy demands that defense expenditures be slashed regardless of the dictates of military prudence. We can afford what we have to afford. But we are also convinced that the economic costs of national security can be held down by a system of taxation more conducive to economic growth.[4]

Another study done some years earlier by Dr. Gerhard Colm for the National Planning Association presented the same general conclusions supported by some interesting figures.[5] Dr. Colm first pointed out that while the Korean

[4] *The Problem of National Security: Some Economic and Administrative Aspects,* Statement on National Policy by the Research and Policy Committee of the Committee for Economic Development, New York, July 1958, p. 27. See also Gershon Cooper, "Taxation and Incentive in Mobilization," *Quarterly Journal of Economics* (February 1952), 43-66; Malcolm W. Hoag, "Economic Problems of Alliance," *Journal of Political Economy,* LXV (December 1957), p. 523.

[5] Gerhard Colm, *Can We Afford Additional Programs for National Security?,* Planning Pamphlet No. 84, National Planning Association, New York, October 1953. See also the later N.P.A. paper by G. Colm and Manuel Helzner, intended as an addendum to Pamphlet No. 84, entitled *General Economic Feasibility of National Security Programs,* March 20, 1957. Reprinted in Hearings before the Subcommittee on Fiscal Policy of

War drove the annual rate of security expenditures up by about $32 billion between 1950 and 1953, the GNP increased during the same period by about $57 billion (in figures adjusted to the purchasing power of 1952 dollars). This means that the increase in total production stimulated by the war was almost double the increase in the military program itself. Over-all manufacturing capacity increased by 25 per cent from 1950 to 1953. During the same period there was also a 3 per cent rise in per capita consumption, still measured in constant dollars. The inflation which followed the outbreak of the Korean War resulted simply from the *expectation* of a rise in military spending, since most of it preceded the actual increase in the spending.

Thus the Korean War, however unhappy for many people, did not strain the national economy. The point has to be stressed because one of the chief reasons given for the massive-retaliation policy announced in January 1954 was that we could not afford more Koreas, or even the kind of preparations involved in making ready for more Koreas.[6] Other arguments can be made for massive-retaliation policies, but the argument that we cannot afford the dollar costs of alternative policies is simply not true. Considering that the Korean War drove our security expenditures up to only about 14 per cent of our GNP, as compared with the 40 per cent of the

the Joint Economic Committee, 85th Cong., 1st sess., U.S. Govt. Printing Office, Washington, D.C., pp. 356-364.

[6] It must be recalled, for the sake of political objectivity, that the massive retaliation idea was by no means an invention of the Republican Party. High-ranking members of the previous administration expressed similar views on repeated occasions during the Korean War, and one of them who felt especially strongly on the subject also put his views into a book. See Thomas K. Finletter, *Power and Policy*, Harcourt, Brace, New York, 1954.

longer-lasting World War II, it is incredible that the argument should ever have been made at all.

Dr. Colm projected into what was then the future three postulated security budgets, all significantly larger than the budget actually being planned, and analyzed the effects of them. His Program A assumed a budget which, instead of falling after 1953, as was planned, would remain steady at $52 billion into 1956. Program B assumed a rise to $62 billion in 1956, which was some 50 per cent greater than was actually planned, and Program C assumed a rise to $75 billion in 1956, or about $33 billion higher than was actually planned for that year.

Only Program C, according to his findings, was of sufficient magnitude as probably to require the imposition of some controls for the allocation of raw materials. Programs A and B would permit per capita consumption to rise substantially, and even Program C, with its security budget of about 15 per cent of estimated GNP, would permit a continuing high rate of business investment and at least some slight increase in per capita consumption.

There was indeed the following proviso: "Economic possibilities are determined not only by available resources and other objective facts but also by the attitudes of peoples. These, in turn, are influenced by the people's understanding of the kind of world we live in, their aspirations, their sense of responsibility, their trust in leadership, and other tangible factors."

One need not be too impressed with Colm's specific figures, the precision of which is somewhat misleading. The assumptions which are the "inputs" of a study of this kind may be individually reasonable and yet add up to a fair amount of uncertainty. However, as symbols reflecting general magnitudes, his figures would probably be accepted by most economists. The CED memorandum quoted earlier was in substantial agreement with his views. Both studies tell us that the United States, if it had to, could spend on national security more by a wide margin than it is currently spending, without harm to the health or vigor of the national economy, provided only that the tax structure as well as the over-all tax burden were adjusted to the need in a courageous and yet reasonable manner.

To know that it can be done, however, is not to conclude that it should be done. No one can doubt that $45 billion to cover all defense purposes is a great deal of money to be spending each year as the decade of the 'fifties approaches its close. One thinks of all sorts of useful and wonderful things that could be done with that money. On the other hand, there is still about 90 per cent of our enormous and growing GNP left to buy most of those things. The usual cliché stresses how many school buildings can be bought for a tithe of what we are spending on defense. The answer is that we can have those too, if we want them enough. We could raise our security expenditures by 30 to 50 per cent and still provide the best educational system in the world, which we do not have now only because we do not value it enough. Something would have to be sacrificed, but there is an enormous cushion of luxury goods and services to allow for the margin.

We noted earlier that large additional sums for security would probably have substantial rather than merely marginal effects in reducing our insecurity. One might consider this a good reason for spending more, but it could conceivably also be a good reason for not doing so. If there is no end to our insecurity, there does have to be an end to our military expenditures. Why not, then, end them early rather than late? The answer to this is that certain major needs remain towards which much can be done within the ranges of figures discussed in the foregoing paragraphs. We probably could not buy a high-confidence active defense against manned bombers *and* missiles even if we greatly increased our entire national security expenditures, and that is a good enough reason for not attempting to do so. If, however, we were willing to raise our military budget from 10 per cent to perhaps 13 or 14 per cent of our growing GNP, we could provide an impressive amount of useful passive defense over a few years, both for our retaliatory force and for civil defense, and also a strong force specialized for non-nuclear limited war.

Citizens of a democracy must be tolerant of the fact that political parties are intensely dedicated to the winning of elections, and that it is bad electoral form to scare people about anything but the political opposition. It is difficult in a democracy to raise taxes, and ours are already pretty high. Nevertheless, it is in matters of military expenditure and foreign relations that the American people are most given to following the cues of the national administration. These are the areas in which almost any president has his greatest potential for leadership. People are usually aware how ignorant they are in these fields, and if there is one thing they devoutly wish it is a reasonably safe future for themselves and their children.

The Opponent's Intentions versus his Capabilities

There is a final doubt to contend with. Where the recommendation is for increasing a budget which is already so high, may we not be grossly exaggerating the proclivity of the Soviet rival to make war upon us? This brings up the old question: should we adjust our military posture to the opponent's intentions or to his capabilities? Put in this way, the question implies that Soviet intentions are not necessarily warlike. Actually, the same view is implied in the above observations. Any increase in the military budget which would still leave it under 15 per cent of the GNP must be based on the implicit assumption that the Soviet leaders are not intent upon going to war with the United States.

Foreign intentions provide us cues for our defense efforts only when they are clear-cut and either conspicuously friendly or plainly warlike. The Soviet attitude towards us seems less than warlike, but it clearly inclines more to the hostile than to the benign. We also have to acknowledge in ourselves a high degree of distrust and irritation towards them, qualities which are certainly manifested in our policy. On the evidence of mutual attitudes, it seems that war, if not imminent, is also not impossible at any time. Certainly it has not been made impossible by technological conditions; quite the contrary is the case. The margin of possible error is usually greater in reading Soviet intentions than in reading their military capabilities; in any case, their intentions may change quickly and critically. We also know from history that where there is enough tension, war can break out without its being truly willed by either side.

Far outweighing these considerations, however, is the degree to which our security measures are out of joint with Soviet capabilities as we see them developing, and the extent of the disasters that could follow from our vulnerabilities. The intentions-versus-capabilities question implies that one is in a sufficiently secure position to be able to ponder it.

We are not likely to be in such a position in the decade of the 'sixties. The development of Soviet missile capabilities calls for a countereffort on our part which involves more than merely matching them in missiles. It calls for large defensive measures as well. We are not justified in ignoring the challenge by the fact that the Soviet leaders may appear to be similarly ignoring the growth in our offensive potentialities. They did not do so, incidentally, in the manned bomber era, during which they spent considerably more than we did on active defenses, especially fighters. In any case, we cannot let our foresight be limited by the fact that they may presently appear to be limiting theirs.

It is true and important that increases in our defense budget will probably have certain effects upon Soviet behavior, particularly with respect to their own defense budget. But this is a matter for careful analysis. Certain things we do militarily may have their value nullified by the fact that the Soviets are provoked to do likewise. Other actions have a value which is not easily negated by Soviet emulation. Passive defenses, especially, tend to fall into the latter category.

We are in an area of very great uncertainty. The temptation is great to avoid expenditures the omission of which will in all likelihood turn out not to be disastrous. There is no way of measuring the risk of general war, or the degree by which we diminish the risk by putting more effort into our defense. But if uncertainty denies us a clear warning, it also denies us reassurance. Basically, we know the following: that we can afford to do much more for our security without giving up more than a certain rate of growth in our very high standard of living; that a great deal remains to be done; that if it is done the horrors which a general war would bring would be much alleviated; and that the chances of general war occurring would be to some real even if un-measurable extent diminished by our doing it.

Weapons Choices in an Always-Limited Budget

For any individual, the requirement for thrift and the virtue of practicing it vary with his income. If the wealthy man practices thrift it is for amusement, or out of compulsion, or perhaps to avoid losing contact with other people. His basic needs are so easily met that he can afford to *feel* rich. The situation with respect to the national security defense budget is quite the opposite. If we succeed in getting the budget appreciably expanded we can obviously do more things with it, but we can never get the feeling of being rich relative to our needs. Since it is the shortage of resources, measured by dollars, which obliges us to make hard choices, the dollar becomes the instrument by which we measure the wisdom of our choice.

The dollar measures command of resources. Within limits set by the technological environment current at any one time—usually referred to, for any specific activity, as "the state of the art"—we can have anything we want, given only enough time and dollars. Given enough dollars we can even cut down on time, through "crash programs." By spending dollars appropriately we can also accelerate advances in the state of the art. With dollars we can buy talent for defense purposes, winning it away from other pursuits by higher salaries, and given time we can also with dollars expand the total available talent by encouraging and assisting gifted young people to acquire the requisite training.

From one point of view we are already too accustomed to measuring in dollars the value of almost everything. However, our thoughts about price do not usually go beyond market value. Few among us will spontaneously translate the dollar value of something we buy into what the economist calls "opportunity costs," meaning the cost of that commodity or service measured in terms of the best alternative commodity or service which could have been bought or produced with the same money but which we now have to forego. The average person may protest that he uses the "opportunity cost" concept in his own family budget. It is most unlikely, however, that he does so altogether consciously and rigorously. He finds it much more convenient to let habit and hearsay guide him even in some of his major choices, leaving the suitability of his habits to be tested in a random way in the experience of living. In choosing between weapons systems, on the other hand, the opportunity-cost idea is pursued not only consciously but also conscientiously, which is to say with considerable rigor.

The opportunity cost of a weapons system is the best alternative weapons system that could have been bought for the same money. Where two weapons systems can accomplish more or less the same purpose, they become directly comparable in efficiency on the basis of their money costs. There is almost always more than one way of doing something; at least, if only one way exists there are usually several other ways that are conceivable.

Let us consider, for example, the problem of choosing between two kinds of strategic bombers. Each represents in its design an advanced "state of the art," but each also represents a different concept. In one, which we shall call Bomber A, the designers have sought to maximize range. They have therefore settled for a subsonic top speed in a plane of fairly large size. The designers of Bomber B, on the contrary, have been more impressed with the need for a high dash speed during that part of the sortie which involves penetration of enemy territory, and have built a smaller, shorter-ranged plane capable of a Mach 2 dash for a portion of its flight. Let us assume also that the price of the smaller plane is about two-thirds that of the larger.

Perhaps we can take both types into our inventory, but even then we should have to compare them to determine which we should get in the larger numbers. Let us then pick a certain number of specific targets in enemy territory, perhaps three hundred, and specify the destruction of these targets as the job to be accomplished. Since we know that both types can accomplish this job with complete success if properly supported and handled, our question then becomes: which type can do it for the least money?

We do not ask at this stage which type can do it more reliably, because within limits we can buy reliability with dollars, usually by providing extra units. Some performance characteristics, to be sure, will not permit themselves to be thus translated into dollars—for example, one type of plane can arrive over target somewhat sooner than the other type, and it is not easy to price the value of this advantage— but we shall postpone consideration of that and similar factors until later.

Let us assume that Bomber A has a cruising range of 6,000 miles, while Bomber B is capable of only 4,000 miles. This means that Bomber A has to be refueled only on its post-strike return journey, while Bomber B probably has to be refueled once in each direction. This at once tells us something about the number of "compatible" tankers that one has to buy for each type ("compatible" referring to the performance characteristics which enable it to operate smoothly with a particular type of bomber). Up to this point Bomber B has appeared the cheaper plane, at least in terms of initial purchase price, but its greater requirement in tankers actually makes it the more expensive having regard for the whole system. In comparing dollar costs, however, it is pointless to compare merely procurement prices for the two kinds of planes; one has to compare the complete systems, that is to say, the weapons, the vehicles, and the basing, protection, maintenance, and operating costs, and one must consider these costs for each system over a suitably long period of peacetime maintenance, say five years. These considerations involve us also in questions of manpower. We are in fact pricing, over some duration of time, the whole military structure required for each type of bomber.

Now we have the problem of comparing through a process of "operations analysis," how the two types fare in combat, especially the survival expectancy of each type of plane during penetration. In other words, we have to find out how much the greater speed (and perhaps higher altitude) of Bomber B is worth as protection. If the enemy depends mostly on interceptors, the bomber's high speed and altitude may help a great deal; if he is depending mostly on guided missiles, they may help relatively little. Thus a great deal depends on how much we know about his present and projected defenses, including the performance characteristics of his major weapons.

If our Bomber A is relying mostly on a low altitude approach to target, which its longer range may just make possible (we are probably thinking in terms of special high-efficiency fuels for wartime sorties), it may actually have a better survival expectation than its faster competitor. Also, we know that penetration capability is enhanced by increasing the numbers of bombers penetrating (again, a matter of money) or by sending decoys in lieu of extra bombers to help confuse the enemy's radar and saturate his defenses. Perhaps we find that the faster plane would outrun the decoys, which again might tend to give it a lower penetration score than one would otherwise expect. But decoys are expensive too, in acquisition costs, basing, and maintenance, and involve additional operating problems. The faster plane may be less accurate in its bombing than the other, which again would involve a requirement for more aircraft and thus more money.

We have given just barely enough to indicate the nature of a typical though relatively simple problem in what has come to be known as "systems analysis." The central idea is that no weapon can be considered independently of the other weapons and commodities that are used with it, that all endure through some period of time and require men to service them and to be trained in their use, that all these items involve costs, and that therefore relative costs of different *systems*, as considered against some common standard of function, are basic to the problem of choice between systems. Systems analysis, which brings what is modern to present-day strategic analysis, is mostly a post-World War II development.[7]

The kind of problem we have just reviewed takes on new and greater difficulties when we try to compare the relative

[7] Systems analysis for military purposes was intensively developed at The RAND Corporation (RAND standing for "Research and Development"), a nonprofit organization founded in 1948 with the principal aim of undertaking research on contract for the U.S. Air Force, which remains its chief client. Other comparable organizations now include Johns Hopkins University's Operations Research Office (ORO), which has similar relations with the U.S. Army; the Navy's Operations Evaluation Group, administered by the Massachusetts Institute of Technology; and the Institute of Defense Analysis, which works for the Joint Chiefs of Staff and the Secretary of Defense.

merits of a given type of manned bomber and a given type of ICBM. It is easy enough to compare them in terms of effects at target if we assume an absence of enemy opposition. The missile is less accurate and probably less reliable than the bomber, and it carries a smaller weapon in its warhead. Knowing this, one can compute for specific targets the ratio of missiles to aircraft necessary for their destruction. One specifies the targets because accuracy and bomb size are more important for some targets than for others, and the sampling must reflect a reasonable strategy.

However, we are considering not peacetime target-shooting but war, and we therefore have to assume all kinds of enemy opposition, as well as the possibility of our having to retaliate to an enemy surprise strike against us. We have to consider whether the aircraft or the missile is easier to protect before its sortie. The missile will almost certainly have the lesser problem in penetrating enemy defenses, but how important this factor is depends on the magnitude of the problem for the airplane, which especially in low-altitude attack may also have a pretty good chance of survival. There is, of course, a big difference in arrival time at target. We thus begin to find many considerations which are not easily reducible to comparisons in dollar terms.

One of the ways for testing different assumptions concerning war conditions is the war game, an old idea with some interesting new developments. The term "war game" should not suggest to the reader's mind a large-scale military exercise in the field. It is in fact played in ordinary offices or similar rooms, sometimes by as few as two players, or even one, and sometimes by fairly large opposing teams with umpires. A game may take a few hours, or several months. The equipment may be elaborate enough to include an electronic computer, or it may simply comprise a map and a statement of rules. The idea is to construct through verbal descriptions, perhaps using also symbols on a map or chart, an assumed situation at the beginning of a war or campaign, and then to follow it through a series of moves by both sides in which each is exerting his utmost to win. Each side is governed by similar technological and operational rules expressed in "planning factors," which are generally careful estimates of what can be done with given units of strength under varying conditions.

The war game is, even at its most elaborate, an austere abstraction from the real thing. It is a way of eliminating one kind of bias, that is, it is a means of giving the enemy his full due, and also a way of constraining weak human beings to think through systematically a number of consecutive acts or stages in a conflict. By repeating a game several times under different assumptions, one may also develop new insights into the factors which might prove critical.

Systems analysis and war gaming are marvelous ways of bringing informed, scientifically-trained minds intensively to bear on baffling problems. But lest we become too optimistic about our ability to probe the mysteries of the future, or about the degree to which scientific thinking is applied to policy, let us look briefly at some of the imperfections and limitations of these methods. In the first place, neither a war game nor a systems analysis can be any better than its planning factors or assumptions, which are normally worked out with great care and with the use of all kinds of special knowledge, but which are nevertheless estimates untested in war. Any systems analysis or war game will use not one but many such factors, compounding the chances that the model will show significant departures from reality.

The element of chance is recognized and provided for by some appropriate method, but the turns of the dice which often govern the war game may not give us a good clue to that one turn which will govern the real thing. Many considerations which we know to be extremely important in real life often cannot be introduced into an analysis because we lack a means for measurement. These involve especially psychological and other imponderable factors; the closest we usually come to allowing for these factors is insertion of an estimated correction for "wartime degradation" of personnel performance. While our costing estimates are, like our operations planning factors, crucial to our decisions, they are also similarly subject to error. Aircraft or missiles under development have a way of turning out to be very much more expensive than preliminary estimates indicate, but unfortunately not by any constant factor.[8]

We noted also in our examples of systems analysis that some aspects of comparative performance do not translate easily into comparative costs. In our example, one bomber might arrive over target some two or three hours earlier than the other, a missile many hours earlier than either. How important are these differences? One bomber may provide a more comfortable ride for its crew members than the other, and perhaps also a somewhat safer one. The more disparate the items compared become, the larger the number of important considerations which are perforce left to the "mature military judgment" of the senior officer or officers for whom the study has been prepared, that is, to their intuition, which may be a collectively good intuition or the reverse. This conclusion, of course, assumes that the relevant study was well thought out and well executed by its scientific authors as far

[8] For additional commentary on war gaming, see above, pp. 246f.

as it went, and that the military client or clients were duly impressed by it, all of which may or may not be true.

We should also notice that the goals set up as objectives to guide the analyses are usually represented as given. The stipulation in our example was that 300 specified targets be destroyed by either bomber tested, at the earliest time possible following the outbreak of hostilities. We must be clear that it is necessary to state requirements in an arbitrary way in order to test one equipment against another. But these stipulations nevertheless reflect what is closer to the heart of strategy than choices between equipments. The question is, how much are those stipulations subjected to analysis in other studies?

The truth, unfortunately, is that the profound issues in strategy, those likely to affect most deeply the fates of nations and even of mankind, are precisely those which do not lend themselves to scientific analysis, usually because they are so laden with value judgments. They therefore tend to escape any kind of searching thought altogether. They are the issues on which official judgments usually reflect simply traditional service thinking. One case in point, mentioned in the previous chapter, is the almost casual manner in which decisions have been made concerning the use of nuclear weapons in limited wars.

Finally, policy-making is a multi-storied structure, and the higher we get in it the more we tend to be removed from the area of careful, dispassionate analysis. Let us assume for a moment that the analyses relevant to one year's budget reflect the most magnificent scientific rigor and probity, and also that the military clients have responded with great wisdom and modesty in making decisions about weapons and strategies. These are considerable assumptions, but not altogether fanciful ones. Now we make the heroic assumption that the entire military establishment has been unified in its attitudes about the security needs of the country, and that it represents its conclusions in the form of a proposed budget which is tightly organized and beautifully reasoned throughout. Unnecessary items, which is to say weapons systems that make no sense either for the new kind of total war or for limited war, have been thoroughly squeezed out. If we want to relate this pleasant fantasy to the present needs of the country, we have to allow, however, for one major defect in the budget: that it calls for an increase of, say, 15 per cent for the ensuing year with the warning that the pattern will have to be upward for several years thereafter.

Now we have to face "realities," which is to say great political pressures that few in high political office are strongly motivated to oppose. The citizens of the country have been promised tax cuts for years, by both major parties, and they have been assured repeatedly that our defenses are in good order. Word therefore goes out that the line must absolutely be held on the defense budget for the next year. Thus we must abandon items of considerable importance to our security—and also a good part of our illusions about the degree to which scientific method has guaranteed the wisdom and foresight of our security policies. It has indeed helped in making some choices, especially where inter-service and political issues were not greatly involved or where doctrinal biases were not offended. In an imperfect world, that could be much to be grateful for.

‹11›

RECAPITULATION AND CONCLUSIONS

In the foregoing chapters we traced the evolution of some basic ideas on the use of air power in war. We also considered the utility of these ideas in a world shaken by the tremendous revolutionary impact of nuclear weapons, now combined with various novel vehicles of delivery including intercontinental ballistic missiles. We probed the complexities of the present strategic situation, for which our historical experience with war offers so little guidance. In this concluding chapter we shall review the fundamental ideas, or "principles" if one prefers, which have emerged in the course of the book.

This is a more modest goal than that of some other authors, who have not hesitated to urge specific changes in the structure, equipment, and organization of our armed forces. Decisions of the kind they recommend or criticize are not simple to make, but on the contrary involve hard choices between costly alternatives within the constraints of an always-limited budget. These alternatives have to be judged in terms of their accommodation to both political (in the widest sense of the term) and technological realities. The intelligent preparation of each decision must require, somewhere along the line, the application of a great deal of special knowledge and hard work; and the results, which are usually highly classified, are not likely to mean much to the non-specialist.

In this book we have been saying things which—insofar as they escape being commonplace—ought to interest a wider audience besides technical specialists. However, we are interested in the specialists too. Insofar as our basic ideas appear to be in harmony with reason and with our accepted system of values, we can only hope that plans and arrangements made for our national defense will in fact conform to them. If this point seems truistic, let us remember that in strategic planning, as in some other pursuits, there can be many a slip between the acceptance of an idea in principle and the implementation of it through appropriately selected plans and actions.

Perhaps the most elementary, the most truistic, and yet the most important point one can make is that the kind of sudden and overwhelming calamity that one is talking about today in any reference to an all-out or total war would be an utterly different and immeasurably worse phenomenon from war as we have known it in the past. Also, and equally important, the chances of its occurring are finite and perhaps even substantial, the more so as we ignore them. One almost blushes to have to make such seemingly trite statements; but we are daily bombarded with indications, in the words and acts of high officials among others, that the points have simply not sunk home.

It is our major dilemma in thinking about war and peace today that we do so within an intellectual and emotional framework largely molded in the past. Our images, slogans, ideas, and attitudes, on the subject of war, some of which are buttressed by the most powerful cultural sanctions, are transmitted to us from times when war was characteristically, with a few historical exceptions, a limited-liability operation. This is not to say that our attitudes toward war have been static. They have changed markedly since 1914, and especially since the coming of nuclear weapons. Nevertheless, we have more reason today than ever before to appreciate the wisdom of Comte's remark: *"C'est l'ancien qui nous empêche de connaître le nouveau.*" (It is the old that prevents us from recognizing the new.)

If we are to speak seriously and objectively of the needs and purposes of our national strategy, there must be no important areas of discourse where we do not permit ourselves to recognize reality. In spite of the seriousness of the prospect of total war, it is correct and necessary to point out that even a total war which began with the enemy's surprise strategic assault upon us need not result, *if* we take the proper precautions beforehand, in the political extinction of the nation. The appropriate precautions, meaning among other things a reasonable civil defense program, might result in preserving not only many lives (perhaps a majority of the prewar population) but also, ultimately, a good chance for the survivors to recover reasonable standards of living. But we should know that that is all we can promise, and that it is at best a very grim prospect. It certainly allows no room for braggadocio in referring to future international conflicts.

The next specific point we have to recall from foregoing chapters is that the people of the United States have obviously made a decision, with little overt debate but quite remarkable unanimity, against any form of preventive war. The lack of active consideration of the matter confirms only the preordained nature of the decision, which accords profoundly with our national psychology and system of values. Our elected political leaders seem to conform entirely to that decision, as one would expect where any conviction is held so unquestioningly and so nearly universally. The decision has entailed acceptance of a great hazard. Conceivably, though most improbably, it may be reversed in the future. But until it is reversed it is a fact of life that is absolutely basic to all our military planning.

Our Commitment to the Strategy of Deterrence

The reason for restating these rather obvious facts is to point up the depth and degree to which we are henceforward committed to the strategy of deterrence. For, in giving up the "solution" of preventive war, we have accepted a situation where, in the event of total war, *we no longer have assurance of getting in the first blow.* It is not out of the question that we will hit first, but it is clearly wrong to count on it, or even to expect that the probability of our doing so is high. One conclusion that stands out from the foregoing chapters is that if it is unwise or immoral to plan a preventive war in order to guarantee ourselves the first blow, it is something approaching idiocy to invite total war on any other basis.

For this reason among others there is a special "it-must-not-fail" urgency about deterrence. Yet there is little in the experience of our own or any other nation to tell us what kind of behavior, military as well as diplomatic, is truly consistent with a purposeful strategy of deterrence. We cannot retreat into security through abandonment of interests and allies abroad. After all, the enemy's major complaint against us is that we must have for our defense the means of gravely injuring him, and this fact would not be greatly affected by such a retreat. But neither is it appropriate for us to act as though nothing has happened since the summer of 1945 to modify seriously the uses of war and of threats of war in diplomacy.

The fact is that deterrence can fail. The great advantage of striking first, at least under existing conditions, must be viewed as an extremely strong and persistent incentive to each side to attack the other. As long as this incentive exists, the danger of total war arising out of a crisis situation—or even from a premeditated attack by the Soviet Union—cannot be considered trivial or remote.

Thus it seems inescapable that the first and most basic principle of action for the United States in the thermonuclear age is the following: a great nation which has forsworn preventive war *must* devote much of its military energies to cutting down drastically the advantage that the enemy can derive from hitting first by surprise attack. This entails doing a number of things, but it means above all guaranteeing through various forms of protection the survival of the retaliatory force under attack.

The last statement naturally assumes that various things *can* be done, that these will make a large and even a critical difference, and that their cost is well within reason. The criterion of costs being "within reason" invokes a subjective judgment, but the requirement to reduce the vulnerability of the retaliatory force deserves such priority that if necessary certain other kinds of military expenditure should be sacrificed to it; secondly, there is no question that this country can afford, if it must, a much larger military budget than it has become accustomed to at this writing. These points have been made and amplified in earlier chapters, and the arguments need not be repeated here.

We have also considered in earlier chapters the *feasibility* of reducing critically the vulnerability of our retaliatory force. We noted that studies made of the subject have established that a critical change can be accomplished from a potentially high vulnerability to a very much lower one at a relatively modest cost (i.e., something like 10 per cent of what we are already spending on equipping and maintaining our bomber forces). The first requirement is that we adopt a reasonable and objective attitude about "hardening" and its utility, one which rejects as irrelevant the usual references to "Maginot Line complex." Dispersion in itself is not a substitute for hardening; neither, certainly, is the accumulation of more unprotected aircraft and missiles. And although warning, whether strategic or tactical, is decidedly worth buying insofar as it can be bought, we should never depend upon it as a justification for neglecting passive defenses. That will be especially true for the missile age now dawning.

All this applies to land bases only. The aircraft carrier cannot be suitably hardened against nuclear weapons, and the Polaris-type submarine is intrinsically a well-concealed and protected missile base—though obviously it is not without flaws in its armor. The development of a submarine fleet capable of launching missiles like Polaris and its successors will with time provide a retaliatory force of low vulnerability though probably also of limited capabilities. This development, however, does nothing to solve the vulnerability problem of the land-based missiles and aircraft. In view of what we know about relevant costs and also about the hazards involved, the conclusion seems inescapable that a bomber should be bought together with a strong shelter, because it is hardly worth buying without one. Much the same is true of missiles, though the idea of shelter protection for missiles seems to be much more acceptable than the idea of shelters for aircraft, probably because a missile cannot take to the air subject to recall. How strong the shelters should be is a matter for the specialist, but we have to bear in mind that we are talking primarily about protection from thermonuclear weapons aimed with the accuracy that long-range guided missiles are expected to reach by the middle or late 'sixties.

In the not so distant future, mobility may have to replace

hardening as the main prop of security to the retaliatory force. That will be very likely if the accuracies which some predict for the long-range missiles of the future are realized. All sorts of ways are conceivable for making retaliatory missiles mobile. There is, for example, the American railway system with it enormous length of trackage, much of it little used. There is also the inland waterway system. On the high seas, not all missile launchers have to take the form of submarines or large aircraft carriers. The USAF also has its *Bold Orion* project, designed to investigate the possibilities of using bombers as missile-launching platforms.[1]

The second basic principle of action for the United States is to provide a real and substantial capability for coping with limited and local aggression by local application of force. This is to avoid our finding ourselves some day in a dilemma where we much either accept defeat on a local issue of great importance, or else resort to a kind of force which may be intrinsically inappropriate and which may critically increase the risk of total war.

In view of the danger that limited war can erupt into total war, especially under the great incentive-to-strike-first circumstances now prevailing, we also have to accept the idea that the methods of limiting the use of force cannot be dictated by us according to our conceptions of our own convenience. Among the compromises with our presumed convenience which we have to be prepared to consider is the possible abjuration of nuclear weapons in limited war. Obviously we have to be prepared also to fight with them, but that is very different from not being prepared to fight without them. There will be time enough to readjust our con-

[1] See General Pierre M. Gallois, "Mobility in Global War," *Interavia*, XIV (March 1959), pp. 240-244.

ception of what is permissible in limited war when incentives to strategic attack have been markedly reduced.

The third principle follows simply from taking *seriously* the fact that the danger of total war is real and finite. Provision must be made for the saving of life on a vast scale. There is room for earnest debate on how big a program is necessary and on what kinds of shelters are worth their cost, but little room for the assumption that *no* shelters are needed. At minimum there is need for a considerable program of fallout shelters outside cities. The present neglect of a shelter program of any dimensions bears no perceptible relation to the military risks we seem daily willing to take.

The Problem of Stability

The three points made in the foregoing paragraphs are so elemental in their importance that one hesitates to place any other proposition on a level with them. However, the inexorable progress of weapons towards ever more immediate and even automatic response and towards ever more overwhelming power underlines the importance of still another idea, the need to limit or control the unsettling effects of our deterrent posture.

Deterrence after all depends on a subjective feeling which we are trying to create in the opponent's mind, a feeling compounded of respect and fear, and we have to ask ourselves whether it is not possible to overshoot the mark. It is possible to make him fear us too much, especially if what we make him fear is our over-readiness to react, whether or not he translates it into clear evidence of our aggressive intent. The effective operation of deterrence over the long term requires that the other party be willing to live with our possession of the capability upon which it rests.

The issue is an old one. It is implicit in the phrase "sabre rattling." As Admiral A. T. Mahan observed: "Force is never more operative than when it is known to exist but is not brandished." Conspicuous aggressivenes in the handling of armaments does not always pacify the opponent. We know from history that nations have sometimes taken measures for their security which produced negative results, that is, which precipitated an unwanted and perhaps disastrous war. It is clear that the progress of weapons has made the problem of provocation far more immediate and acute than ever before, and that it is going to get more difficult as time goes on.

In general terms, we can hardly be too strong for our security, but we can easily be too forward and menacing in our manipulation of that strength. For example, it may be true that an ICBM deep in our own country menaces the Soviet Union as much as a shorter-range missile pointed at her from just outside her frontiers, but the chances are that the Soviet leaders will be more disturbed by the latter. Unlike the ICBM, the nearby missile seems to denote arrogance as well as strength, and perhaps also a wider dispersal of the authority to fire it. If it is left unprotected, it trumpets the fact that it is intended for a strike-first attack, not retaliation. No one policy of this kind will precipitate a total war, and if there are overriding reasons for that or comparable policies the provocative aspects have to be accepted. On the other hand, over a broad range of policies one sometimes senses an attitude which seems to be somewhat lacking in awareness that deterrence is supposed to last a very long time.

These considerations would have no merit if we knew that the probability of total war was in any case infinitesimal, or if on the contrary we had reason to regard it as being, within a relatively limited time period, almost inevitable.

It is because we have no basis for placing the probability in either the very low or the very high category that we have to take earnest account of the fact that our behavior with the new armaments may critically affect it.

It must not, however, be deduced from these remarks that we are henceforward compelled to be timid in our foreign policy. The opponent too has reasons for being careful which parallel ours, and the almost paranoiac fears which have often been voiced in this country of an "atomic blackmail" before which we would be bound to retreat because of our presumed greater sense of responsibility or caution have at this writing shown very few signs of being realized. It is likely, on the other hand, that we have got too accustomed to an attitude which has become increasingly discordant with the facts—the attitude that our government, trusting in the continuity of its superior strength, is really prepared to use our nuclear total-war capability aggressively over a wide array of issues. This is the kind of "bluff" which results from a failure of self-examination, and the inevitable exposure of it will make necessary occasional readjustments which are all the more painful for being belated.

It is trite to say that our foreign policy has to be in harmony with our military policy, and vice versa. In itself the statement offers little or no operational guidance. It is as preposterous to assume that there is some mathematical equivalence or correspondence between military power and negotiatory strength on any international issue as to assume that the latter is unrelated to the former. The slogan used to explain our rearmament program in 1952—that we must be able "to negotiate from strength"—supposed that there was some marvelously effective mode of negotiation which we thoroughly understood and which we were quite ready to use for clearly-conceived goals but which was currently denied us because of marginal inadequacies in our military strength. This supposition was in no wise correct and, in addition, the power advantage moved over the succeeding years in the opposite direction from what our slogan seemed to suggest—for reasons, incidentally, for which we can hold ourselves only partly accountable. The complex relationships between military power and foreign policy have by no means been adequately explored, and what we have learned or could learn from history on the subject needs to be reappraised in the light of the totally new circumstances produced by the new armaments.

Obsolescence of the Old Imperatives

If the suggestions above appear to conform to elementary logic, experience has nevertheless indicated how difficult it is to follow them. One reason is that they appear to run counter to most of the standard axioms inherited from an earlier day concerning the attitudes as well as the methods by which we should fight. We all remember the old categorical imperatives requiring one to seize the initiative and to fight aggressively and offensively.

These imperatives have now been reinforced by growing awareness of the advantage in total nuclear war of striking first. The temptation has been great, therefore, to escape from the unfortunate fact—mostly by ignoring it—that we not only are not likely to strike first but also that we cannot depend on timely warning of enemy attack to get our retaliatory force under way. It is one thing to want to have better intelligence and better warning, but quite another to arrange one's defenses as though these wants will surely be satisfied. One conception is that we will strike our blow at the moment the enemy begins, clumsily of course, to move against us, but before he has actually struck. The tendency to assume that what it is desirable to do will in fact be done can easily result in a policy which enormously downgrades passive defenses. The feeling is not so much that money spent on shelters will be wasted, but rather that shelters will corrupt initiative. There is also about the "pre-emptive" or anticipatory strike the attitude of "We must, therefore we can." This is a bold attitude to take and it gives us a staunch feeling, but it is an amateurish way of looking at the odds.

Ideas exalting military aggressiveness derive from an age when it was the same force which took the offensive or stayed on the defensive. If an offensive failed, an impromptu redeployment usually achieved a defensive posture. The accent was therefore appropriately on boldness. Even when boldness proved improvident and costly, it rarely sacrificed the life of the nation. Today, failure to meet the requirements of the deterrent posture can clearly have that result.

One trouble with the idea of the pre-emptive strike is that it is not novel enough. We can resolve to react more promptly than the Soviets do to a shrewd sense of impending eruption, but on the basis of military tradition we should expect them to entertain the same ambition concerning us. The odds that at outbreak of war we would win a contest for the pre-emptive advantage might in fact be good, but they could hardly be good enough. The one thing we can be sure of is that such a contest between the two major parties would make it nearly impossible to avoid total war.

The Strategy of Total War

We have given relatively little space to the matter of how to fight a general war if it should come. The reasons for that are clear. For one thing, the strategy of a total war is like an earthquake in that all the forces which determine its occurrence and its character have been building up over time, as have almost all the factors which determine how it runs its course. The strategy of deterrence, however distinctive its mission, embraces the preparations for the total war that may come.

The strategy of modern total war is in some respects simpler than that of World War II, in other respects much more difficult. It is simpler in that there can now be no question that strategic bombardment power—in which we include missiles and by which we mean defensive as well as offensive measures—absolutely dominates the war. To this extent Douhet has come into his own. The dominance of strategic air power predetermines and simplifies the choice of target systems. Because strategic bombardment is so tremendously destructive, the opponent's strategic bombardment power, insofar as it can be reached and destroyed, is certainly the first and most important target system. There is in fact no other target system worth comparable consideration. The "war potential" of the economy of either side can have practically nothing to do with the outcome of the war, because that outcome will be decided before such potential is mobilized and absorbed into the military system. In any case, industrial production is likely to be quickly halted on both sides as a by-product of the first exchange of blows, and certainly the side which wins the air battle can prevent the recovery of its opponent's production. The only circumstance which could invalidate these conclusions is a civil defense program of a scope which has not begun to be thought of.

About military forces, land and naval, which are not involved in the strategic bombardment contest, there is the dual question: (1) *can* they operate effectively in the face of intensive strategic air bombardment, and (2), if they can, are they operating towards any meaningful end in view of the overriding effects of the nuclear strategic exchange? For any contest involving the United States and the Soviet Union the answers to both questions, especially the latter one, would appear to be in the negative. Thus even military targets not connected with strategic bombardment will be almost as irrelevant in deciding the outcome as industrial targets, which is not the same as saying they will be immune. Enemy population as well as industrial production might be targeted on the ground that hitting them would cause communications interruptions and vast general confusion, but they are appropriately targets for exerting pressure, that is, targets to be hit or threatened because they are the ultimate tokens in whatever armistice negotiations may develop.

The strategic air ascendancy which determines the outcome is itself decided by the questions, (a) Who strikes first? (b) With what degree of surprise? (c) Against what preparations made by the other side to insure that its retaliatory force will survive and return the fire? It is barely conceivable that the way in which these and related issues are resolved will mean that no real ascendancy is established with the first exchange of blows. If so, what follows will be not a "broken-backed war" but an extraordinarily destructive yet quick contest to determine who retains exclusive capability for yet further nuclear destruction. Both sides have an overriding interest in establishing negotiations for an armistice as soon as the air battle issue is determined in its main outlines, which means almost at once. If they fail to see that interest, or if they cannot act upon it because of failure of communications, what follows is not strategy but grandiose, wanton destruction.

This is where the difficulty and complexity come in. The unsolved problem of modern total war is that of how to stop it, quickly, once it is decided. It is tantamount to negotiating complete disarmament with a 24-hour deadline, or less. It embraces also the problem of monitoring compliance. It is obvious that none of these things can be done correctly and with dispatch unless the requisite study and planning have been done in advance (preferably on both sides) and the military leaders have been thoroughly briefed on requirements for ending a war. This sounds like a counsel of perfection, and perhaps it is. If so, it only means that a future total war, if it comes, will be enormously more destructive than it needs to be to fulfil anyone's military purposes.

The Strategy of Limited War

We know that the forms that limited war will take in the future will depend not only on the usual questions of where, when, and with whom, but also on the still unresolved and monumentally important question whether nuclear weapons will be used and, if so, how many and what kind. The conception which would dispose of our limited-aggression problems by sending a contingent of SAC aircraft to the spot to do some appropriate bombing must assume the use of nuclear weapons of considerable size. At the other extreme is the intercession which limits itself either to very small nuclear weapons or to none at all. In the latter case we have to assume, on the basis of Korean and World War II experience, that air forces, like naval forces, will play an ancillary role to ground forces. This idea is often rejected or resisted, but it seems indisputable on the evidence.

Whether or not air power, despite being cast in an ancillary role, should attempt to pursue an independent strategy conforming to its own conception of the needs of the forces it is supporting is a big question which ought to be left to specialists. It involves the old and much-debated question of close support versus interdiction, about which there has been much doctrinaire argument. The Korean experience and the campaigns of World War II suggest that the issue is affected most by the circumstances of the occasion—by the degree of activity of the land front, by the kinds of communications available to the opponent, by the size and efficiency of one's own air forces and the kinds of weapons available to them, by the character of enemy air resistance, and so forth.[2]

Much depends on the amount of research and development effort devoted to the tactical use of air power in a non-nuclear environment. At present that amount is trivial, but if we spent on it one-twentieth part of what we are currently spending on ICBM research the results might be impressive.

The Unpredictability of the Outcome

"Consider the vast influence of accident in war," Thucydides reports the Athenian ambassadors as saying, "before you are engaged in it. . . . It is a common mistake in going to war to begin at the wrong end, to act first, and wait for disaster to discuss the matter." These words, written more than 2,300 years ago, might have saved much grief in the world if taken to heart by those who were

[2] An excellent discussion of the air operations of the Korean War is found in the book by Commanders M. W. Cagle and F. Manson, *The Sea War in Korea*, U.S. Naval Institute, Annapolis, 1957. See especially ch. 8, "The Struggle to Strangle." For an Air Force view, see also James T. Stewart, *Airpower: The Decisive Force in Korea*, Van Nostrand, New York, 1957.

tempted to believe otherwise. In wars throughout history, events have generally proved the pre-hostilities calculations of both sides, victor as well as loser, to have been seriously wrong. "Wars" as a modern writer puts it, "are the grave-yards of the predictions concerning them."

Each generation of military planners is certain that it will not make the same kinds of mistakes as its forebears, not least because it feels it has profited from their example. Our own generation is convinced it has an additional and quite special reason for being sure of itself: it is more scientific than its predecessors. Today the American armed forces are eagerly exploiting science and scientific techniques not only to avail themselves of new military tools of increasingly bizarre characteristics, the enthusiasm for which is itself a departure from former ways, but also to predict and analyze the tactics and strategy of future wars. It seems also to be a fact that in this respect the armed forces of the United States are considerably in advance of those of other nations, including our enemies. If so, it is an advantage of very large proportions.

The universe of data out of which reasonable military decisions have to be made is a vast, chaotic mass of technological, economic, and political facts and predictions. To bring order out of the chaos demands the use of scientific method in systematically exploring and comparing alternative courses of action. When the method is true to its own scientific tenets, it is bound to be more reliable by far than the traditional alternative method, which is to solicit a consensus of essentially intuitive judgments among experienced commanders. The new method does not throw out the best of the old, for it attempts to incorporate in an orderly fashion whatever is good in strong intuition, and the military commanders still consider and accept or reject its findings.

However, our experience thus far with scientific preparation for military decision-making warns us to appreciate how imperfect is even the best we can do. Those of us who do this work are beset by all kinds of limitations, including limitations in talent and in available knowledge. Where the object is to predict the future, for the sake of appropriate action, we simply cannot wait until all the relevant facts are in. Besides, we can make progress only as we cut off and treat in isolation a small portion of the total universe of data and of problems that confront us, and every research project is to that extent "out of context." In addition, we are dealing always with large admixtures of pure chance. These are sometimes difficult to take into full account without seeming to stultify our results, and that human beings are naturally loath to do. The same is true of the large range of variables which deal with enemy intentions and capabilities. Finally, we are immersed in bias, our own and that of our clients or readers. With our audience, in spite of our strong efforts to be objective, we cannot avoid being influenced by what we know it likes to hear. Feelings of loyalty and friendship are involved, as well as a normal liking for applause.

The other reason for being cautious of our predictions is one that has been emphasized throughout this book: the utterly unprecedented rate of change that has marked the weapons revolution since the coming of the first atomic bomb. It has carried us far beyond any historical experience with war, and has moved much too fast to be fully comprehended even by the most agile and fully-informed minds among us. Only someone very foolish could believe he had mastered the unknowns and uncertainties which becloud our picture of future war. The rapid changes which have already taken place in men's thoughts about the nature of nuclear conflict should prepare us for the realization that we have been, and therefore may yet be, entirely wrong on fundamentals in our official policies. The grave differences and disagreements which continue to prevail among our acknowledged experts are an additional warning of the same kind.

We know from even the most casual study of military history how fallible man is in matters concerning war and how difficult it has been for him, mostly because of the discontinuity of wars, to adjust to new weapons. Yet compared to the changes we have to consider now, those of the past, when measured from one war to the next, were almost trivial. And almost always in the past there was time even after hostilities began for the significance of the technological changes to be learned and appreciated. Such time will not again be available in any unrestricted war of the future.

Despite all this uncertainty, however, decisions have to be made. A military establishment has to be provided and equipped, and it must develop and refine plans for its possible commitment to action. We therefore proceed to do these things, with a good deal of bustle and also some real efficiency. We have been forced to revise our thinking about weapons; but unfortunately there is not a comparable urgency about rethinking the basic postulates upon which we have erected our current military structure, which in fact represents in large measure an ongoing commitment to judgments and decisions of the past. In this book we have tried to do some of that kind of rethinking.

What we have done must convince us that Thucydides was right, that peace is better than war not only in being more agreeable but also in being very much more predictable. A plan and policy which offers a good promise of deterring war is therefore by orders of magnitude better in every way than one which depreciates the objective of deterrence in order to improve somewhat the chances of winning. Of future total wars we can say that winning is likely to be less ghastly than losing, but whether it be by much or by little we cannot know. As far as limited wars are concerned, they can have little more than the function of keeping the world from getting worse. There is little chance that the basic inherent strength of either the Soviet Union or Communist China can be drained off through wars that are kept limited in any meaningful sense of the term.

A large part of the world in which we live seems headed towards an almost unavoidable disaster, that of uncontrolled population growth, with its familiar vicious circle of poverty making for the almost unrestrained procreation which keeps people desperately poor. Another great part seems to have escaped that danger entirely by increasing its productivity much faster than it increases its population, and by demonstrating its capacity to restrain population growth. It is the latter area, however, the one in which we Americans are lucky enough to live, which is subject to the greatest danger of destruction from nuclear bombs. The two parts of the world share in common the fact that the chief menace facing each of them is man-made. Do they also share in common a bemused helplessness before the fate which each of them seems to be facing?